A
FEATHER
NOT A
GAVEL

Working Towards
Aboriginal Justice

Hon. A.C. Hamilton
Q.C. LL.D.

GREAT PLAINS
PUBLICATIONS

Great Plains Publications
3 - 161 Stafford Street
Winnipeg, MB R3M 2X9
www.greatplains.mb.ca

Great Plains Publications gratefully acknowledges the financial support
provided for its publishing program by the Government of Canada through the
Book Publishing Industry Development Program (BPIDP); the Canada Council
for the Arts; the Manitoba Department of Culture, Heritage and Citizenship;
and the Manitoba Arts Council.

THE CANADA COUNCIL   LE CONSEIL DES ARTS
FOR THE ARTS   DU CANADA
SINCE 1957   DEPUIS 1957

Canadian   Patrimoine
Heritage   canadien

Design & Typography by Gallant Design Ltd.
Printed in Canada by Friesens

CANADIAN CATALOGUING IN PUBLICATION DATA

Main entry under title:

Hamilton, Alvin, 1912 –
A feather, not a gavel

ISBN 1-894283-23-6

1.   Indians of North America (Canada (Legal status, laws, etc.   I. Title

KE7709.H35 2001   342.71'0872   C2001-910163-5
KF8205.H35 2001

Table of Contents

Foreword

By Justice Murray Sinclair

When I was a law student, I was painfully conscious of the fact that Aboriginal people — my people — were over-represented in the justice system which I was striving to join. While that fact had been one of the reasons I went to law school — to see if I could 'do something' about it — the more I studied law, the more I felt overwhelmed by two thoughts. One was that the issue was far too large to ever do anything about. That thought pushed me toward the conclusion that becoming part of the legal system inevitably meant I would become part of the problem and not part of the solution. The second thought — resulting from the manner in which we were taught about the glorious history of the common law — was that the problem of over-incarceration must be with Aboriginal people and not with anything the justice system was doing.

It wasn't until many years later, as my legal career developed, and I had an opportunity to meet with many of the elders and wisdom keepers of the Aboriginal communities within which I worked as a lawyer, that I began to see my way past the second of those two thoughts. I found that what I had observed in law school was the end result of a long process of legalized racial oppression and political deprivation. During that time, I discovered that in the 19th century, Canada had enacted laws depriving Aboriginal people of the right to contract, to sell property, to engage in business, to establish successful farms, to vote, to go to court, to raise their children, to practise their spiritual beliefs, to manage their own affairs, and to select their governments in accordance with their traditions. Canada had authorized its agents of authority, including the police, to arrest Aboriginal people without warrant simply for being outside the boundaries of their communities without written permission. Aboriginal children had been removed from their homes and raised in oppressive and often racist residential school environments in which they were told it was "bad to be an Indian" and would sometimes be punished for merely speaking their own languages.

After several generations of such an experience, I concluded, it would be surprising if any population of people did not experience ongoing conflict within, and with, the society which had established such practices. That realization allowed me to stop blaming the Aboriginal victims of that history. It also allowed me to see that, to a certain extent, non-Aboriginal people were also captives of that same history.

However, identifying reasons why Aboriginal people were being over-incarcerated, and pointing the finger of blame elsewhere, was only temporarily comforting. The real question was and remains — what can be done about it?'

While engaged in the Aboriginal Justice Inquiry of Manitoba (1988-91) with my friend and colleague, The Honourable Al Hamilton (then the Associate Chief Justice of the Family Division of Manitoba Court of Queen's Bench), we had an opportunity to search for some answers. Those answers were set out in the Aboriginal Justice Inquiry Report released in September 1991.

In this year of the tenth anniversary of the release of that report, Justice Hamilton's contribution to the discussion in this volume is important for reasons that are different than those that existed then. While our report highlighted the problems that Aboriginal people faced within the justice system, the reaction to the report particularly on the part of government was to ignore what we said and recommended. Ignoring our report and those of several other commissions however, did not make the problems go away. Instead, a new and different confrontation has descended upon us.

The inadequacy of past approaches is now not only an Aboriginal view, it is also becoming a systemic one. The new confrontation we are facing is marked not so much by outside agitation as by inside pressure for change. The 'in-your-face banging on the outside to get in' Aboriginal demonstrations of past generations are less the problem (although we will continue to see some of that), than is the need for the justice system to begin to confront the way that it does things. It began with a recognition by governments concerned with balancing government budgets that the over-use of incarceration could quickly overwhelm government's ability and willingness to spend. However, it has also inevitably led to a discussion of whether there are perhaps better ways of doing things.

The emphasis on a more careful use of incarceration and a direction to consider alternatives, were the cornerstones of the Federal government's 1996 amendments to the sentencing provisions of the Criminal Code. The subsequent call by the Supreme Court of Canada for judges to consider the restorative justice approach of Aboriginal communities when sentencing Aboriginal accused is forcing lawyers and judges to question established practices.

Civil and family courts are also being called upon to confront the fact that if they are going to be effective in fashioning solutions to competing Aboriginal and non-Aboriginal interests, they will have to re-examine the way that they have been doing things. Old solutions and old ways of providing solutions are (slowly) being shown to be inadequate. That sense of inadequacy has led to comments by the judiciary for governments to find political solutions before courts are forced to try to deal with enormously complex matters using techniques developed in a different era for different types of problems. Yet even political solutions may prove evasive. Courts may in fact have no choice but to deal with those issues, and face the need to change past approaches. If so, the trick is going to be managing the change. The discussion in this volume will I am certain contribute in a meaningful way to that change.

On a personal note, participating with Justice Hamilton (as he will always be known to me), in the AJI was an enlightening experience for many reasons. Not only did I have a chance to meet with an enormous number of intelligent, passionate and thoughtful people who had constructive ideas about the solutions they saw, but I also had a chance to work with a man who was at once a friend and a mentor.

I was a rookie member of the Provincial Bench in April 1988, when asked to participate with the Inquiry; hardly, it is fair to say, able to conduct the type of proceeding needed to develop the credibility that the final report needed. From the outset however, Justice Hamilton knew how things ought to be done, and what we needed to do to achieve the objectives set for us. He knew how to handle the difficult presenter, and what it took to keep things on track during our public hearings, particularly in urban areas.

More importantly, when it came time to write our final report, he knew of the importance of addressing, and how to address, the myriad issues within the existing system that stood in the way of finding justice for Aboriginal accused and victims. He helped me to see that the issue was not too large to solve.

What I gained most from my experience with him however, was the realization that being within the justice system — particularly as a judge — was not contributing to the problem at all — that I indeed could be part of the solution.

For that I will forever be grateful.

This book is dedicated to my advisor, grammar teacher and supportive wife Lorna, to our children and grandchildren, and to all my Aboriginal friends.

Acknowledgments

Continually urging me to write and revise, former AJI researcher Laurie Messer kept me going in the early and confusing days, while AJI office manager Maryanne Boulton kept me straight on some Aboriginal issues and kept my computer functioning. Together they urged me on when I had my doubts.

During the spring and summer of 1999, the University of Manitoba Faculty of Law Research Institute supported my research assistant Lorena Fontaine, now a graduate lawyer, who put me in touch with Aboriginal leaders and found obscure information I required. Her initial writing on youth provided a most thoughtful insight.

Judge Elbridge Coochise of Arizona and formerly Chief Judge of the Northwest Intertribal Court in Edmonds, Washington, gave freely of his extensive knowledge and experience with Tribal Courts in the United States.

The Honourable Eric Robinson, Minister of Aboriginal and Northern Affairs and The Honourable Tim Sale, Minister responsible for the Children and Youth Secretariat of the Manitoba NDP government, through their financial support, made the empirical study at Stony Mountain Penitentiary possible.

Glen Cochrane, the co-ordinator of the City of Winnipeg Gang Unit and Wayne Helgason, the Executive Director of the Social Planning Council of Winnipeg, put the wheels in motion and Professor Doug Skoog of the University of Winnipeg and Sharon Perreault of the MaMaWi Centre developed the research methodology and supervised the interviewers.

Without the guidance provided by Murray Sinclair, now Mr. Justice Sinclair of the Manitoba Court of Queen's Bench, during the Aboriginal Justice Inquiry, I wouldn't have been able to write this book.

Preface

This book deals mainly with issues confronting Aboriginal people, the services that are and are not provided to them by the present justice system, and a proposed parallel Aboriginal system. It nevertheless started as memoirs for my children and grandchildren so they would have some idea of the world as it was when I was growing up — something I had missed with respect to my own parents. The book now blends the two topics and shows how they are related.

As I began to write my memoirs, two realities slowly crept into my consciousness, and diverted me from my intended task. The first was the significant part Aboriginal people and their issues have played in my life in recent years. The second was how little I knew about them when I was growing up, and how little my non-Aboriginal friends and acquaintances still know about them and about the challenges they face.

The focus of my writing changed as I turned my attention to Aboriginal peoples and their problems with the law. My style of writing also had to change, so I took a writing course. At the beginning of the course, the instructor asked why I was taking it and it was a surprise, even to me, when I replied, "So my writing won't sound like a written judgement." I recognized that a formal analysis of facts and the pronouncement of a decision, as I had done as a judge, wouldn't suit a discussion of the broad issues upon which I had decided to embark. In spite of my change in focus, I have nevertheless retained some discussion of my formative years, as I am sure they have had a bearing on my later attitudes and approach to the law.

This book is not intended to be an academic analysis or treatise. On the contrary, I have intentionally made it as non-technical as possible. If it appears to change in tone from time to time, that too is intentional. Part of the reason is that my target audience keeps changing, depending on the topic under review. Many of my comments are directed to my non-Aboriginal contemporaries, in the hope of providing information they may not have. Others are directed at governments that establish and administer the courts. My thoughts on how an Aboriginal court might function are for Aboriginal people to consider as they reform their institutions and regain control over their lives.

My ultimate hope is to see everyone work together to achieve two rather simple goals: reduce the number of Aboriginal people entangled in the legal system and reduce the number of Aboriginal people in jail. The task I have set for myself is to indicate how that can be done.

The title 'A Feather, Not a Gavel' is intended to define the dichotomy that exists between the Aboriginal and non-Aboriginal approaches to resolving human conflict. Where criminal conduct is involved, one is a healing approach, while the other is punitive. The two are diametrically opposed to one another and the question is whether they can be reconciled.

The gavel, although not actually used in our courts, is a symbol of authority — harsh, concise and unyielding. The image is that the system it represents will be strict with people who disobey a judge or break the law of the land. It represents a severe system of justice and exudes a warning to those who come to court.

The feather represents honesty, truthfulness and a kinder approach. An eagle feather comes from the giant bird that flies closest to the Great Spirit and is believed to help an individual gather the courage to perform a worthwhile deed under difficult conditions. Students of Canadian history will remember that Elijah Harper, one of the great Aboriginal leaders of our time, held an eagle feather when he stood his ground in the Manitoba legislature and, as the lone dissenter, voted "NO" to the Meech Lake Accord because it failed to recognize the Aboriginal place in Canada.

The significance of the title will become evident as my story unfolds. The conclusion I would like readers to reach is that the search for justice is more likely to be realized with the healing help of the feather, rather than by applying the authority of the gavel.

PART I

Exploring
the Past

1

Educating the Author

M y sometimes rambling recital of personal experiences, with no immediate connection to the title of the book, will hopefully serve three purposes. The first is to indicate some of the influences that led to the formation of the ideas I will express. The second is to indicate the painfully slow process by which I came to appreciate the experience of Aboriginal people, and the third is to provide some rationale for my critique of Canada's justice system.

In court, lawyers will often introduce every relevant fact and every possible argument, not knowing which may impress the judge. They leave it to the judge to reject the irrelevant in the hope that something of substance will remain to influence the outcome of the trial in their favour. If I err on the side of excess, I do so with the same hope in mind, rather than leaving a reader wondering about the basis for my commentary.

Because of other writing I have done, mostly judgements and reports, I am well aware that not everyone will agree with my comments or suggestions. Some may be openly hostile to the observations I will make and to the changes I will propose. I must therefore explain myself in as much detail as possible so I will not be misunderstood. I must also attempt to anticipate and answer some of the negative reactions my writing is bound to provoke.

I was raised in the Fort Rouge district of Winnipeg, Manitoba. Winnipeg is an interesting corner of the globe and still reflects its pioneering history. It is small, but large enough not to be overwhelmed by the metropoli of the east, and fresh enough to spawn new and challenging ideas. It has been home to Cree, Ojibway and Dakota tribes, trappers, buffalo hunters and the more recent homesteaders. It has welcomed migrants from around the world and remains a diverse society.

My father was the only judge of the Winnipeg Juvenile Court from 1925 to 1946. His dinner-table recitation of his cases and the young offenders who came before him, must have whetted my interest in the law. His was a continuous search for solutions that would benefit young people and a struggle to apply them within the strictures of the law.

He was Irish to the core, his father having been born in Northern Ireland and my mother never called him anything but "Dooley" or "Dool." Although a devout Methodist and, after Union, a member of the United Church, he refused to have anything to do with the Orange Order, believing it to be too partisan and he had as many Catholic as Protestant friends. We lived a block from St. Ignatius Church and the majority on our block were Roman Catholic. Some kids attended the church school and others the public ones, but all were welcome to use the church hockey rink, as long as we did our share of shovelling-off the snow.

Our street was middle class. The houses were mostly narrow two and a half stories. Ours was comfortable in the summer and freezing in the winter. The insulation at the time seemed to be a few sheets of newspaper stuffed into the walls. I didn't realize till years later, that in the winter, Winnipeg is the coldest city of its size on earth. As kids, we wore moccasins or skates from November till the end of March.

Members of our family shared the only radiator in the kitchen. In the morning, my father was downstairs first and made the toast and porridge. My eldest sister huddled by the heat until she left for work and when I came downstairs I was assigned the spot until I left for school. My mother prepared her brown toast, orange marmalade and coffee and, I assume, took over the favoured spot when I left. The upstairs sitting room had a coal and wood-burning fireplace, which was lit every evening. Hanging velvet curtains pulled across the doors to the hall and to my parents' bedroom, helped to keep the sitting room warm.

The summers were long and glorious. We rode our bicycles everywhere, whether it was to the cement works at Fort Whyte, the gravel pits at Bird's Hill to swim, or to St. Norbert to kill river rats. My pal Fishy's father was the bursar of the university so we would often bike there to play in the hay lofts and swing out over the Red River on cables dangling from an abandoned ice house.

Groceries from Eaton's were delivered in shiny dark blue and fire-engine red wagons drawn by prancing black horses. The iceman had a horse-drawn sleigh in winter and a wagon in summer. He cut a block of ice from larger slabs and carried it into the homes on his back, held by his sturdy tongs and my mother rinsed off the sawdust before he put it in the icebox. As this was going on, we kids helped ourselves to the cooling chips of ice left in the wagon. Little did we realize that the ice was made from the murky waters of the Red River. In retrospect, I wonder why we needed ice in the winter.

We weren't allowed to ride our bikes after dark so in the evenings we walked to a show at the Uptown, Tivoli or Crescent theatres, a rugby game at Osborne Stadium, roller-skating at the Winnipeg Roller Rink or in the basement of the Auditorium. If we had to go farther, we took the Main or Mountain streetcars. On the return trip their names were changed to Stafford and Corydon. The Corydon streetcar only went as far west as Wilton Street where it turned around beside Waugh's grocery store. The prairie beyond was our impromptu golf course and the "forest" beyond that was an unending source of adventure.

Like others in the '30s, my parents were frugal. I can still remember my father lying on the sitting room floor, using pen and ink to fill in the faded reds and blues in our Axminster rug, but he was generous to a fault. My mother had to give him a limited amount of cash so he wouldn't give too much away to the down-and-out as he walked to work across the Osborne bridge.

In the summers, hobos came to the homes in the neighbourhood looking for food. My mother always fed them a good meal but they had to eat it on the back porch. She was a bit nervous, accentuated no doubt by the occasional irate phone call from a parent upset by one of my father's decisions, or it may have been because of when the father of a jailed delinquent cornered my dad in the back yard and but for a calming discussion, was ready to flatten him. I stood watching and shivering.

My parents saved for a few luxuries and were able to burn their mortgage in the '50s. I should mention that the salary of a provincially appointed judge was not great, and none of my father's small pension was passed on to my mother when he died.

One of our luxuries was a cottage at Matlock on Lake Winnipeg. The other was a car. We were among the fortunate minority on our street who had a car, although ours spent the winter "up on blocks" in our garage until the back lane became passable to other than horse-drawn sleighs. During the war, my dad received extra gas coupons, as he had to hold court in Carman, Brandon and Portage la Prairie from time to time.

It's strange how seemingly unimportant experiences are recalled in later years that play a part in developing a person's attitude. From the time I was six or so I was a member of a gang. I never attended any meeting, if there were any, but the members, who I guess ranged in age from six to sixteen, greeted one another with our secret sign and call of recognition. The "gang" didn't do anything except hang out around Alsip's pony shed and loft, but if someone from a few streets away gave any of our members a hard time, you could count on someone coming to the rescue.

Because I was small for my age until I was sixteen, I had to learn how to run from the tougher guys and from the bicycle cops who were always after us for playing hockey or ball on the street or for swiping crab apples. Games of Canny-Can, our version of cricket, also seemed to draw their ire. We were never sure how serious the police were but we weren't about to find out. Few of us were ever caught and I never was. I could scale a six-foot fence in a flash and learned that a garage roof was a great place to hide.

The gang, the P.A. Rods, had real standing in the neighbourhood, partly because the leader was an outstanding baseball and hockey player, was tough, and had a dozen or so brothers and sisters to call on if necessary. More importantly, everyone liked Chick O'Connell. While the activities of gangs today may be less passive, I can appreciate the need of a vulnerable individual to have friendship and support. I should add that this gang protection never seemed to stop my stronger pals from regularly beating me up. Thinking back, maybe it helps to get beaten up from time to time. It certainly increases your determination to survive.

I considered the law to be serious business, as I didn't want to be brought up before my dad in court. My reason to obey the law, I must admit, was motivated more by what might happen to me at home, than any belief in the letter of the law. One incident showed the result of my caution, and the damage to my popularity. When we were about fourteen, four of us were biking along Harrow Street and when we came to Grosvenor, I stopped at the stop sign, expecting to catch up in a minute. The others went merrily through the intersection and were stopped by the police, and they had to appear before my dad. They were not pleased and acted as if it was my fault they got caught, and it didn't help to know that their parents were saying — "why didn't you stop like the judge's son?"

Saturday was a special day for me as a youngster. My dad usually took the car to work and sometimes took me with him. He parked behind the court, the Vaughan Street Detention Home, in the area once reserved for hangings. Saturday was a relatively light by-law day when he dealt with kids, like my pals, who had been caught going through stop signs, riding double or riding on the sidewalk. I would sit on the counter talking to Miss Kerr and Miss Craik, members of his loyal staff, or wait in his office till court was over.

Although I think of my father as the kindest person, he did have to at least sound severe from time to time. He did everything possible to avoid sending any juvenile to jail, whether it was to the Home for Boys at Portage la Prairie, the Home for Girls in West St. Paul, the Home of the Good Shepherd, Knowles School for Boys or the Hugh John McDonald Hostel. In the '30s he worked with service clubs, community clubs, churches and employers to provide work and recreation for the youth and arranged with the railways to deliver old box cars and wood stoves to corner lots which the City flooded into skating and hockey rinks. A large number of boys clubs that later became competitive hockey and baseball teams, were established by citizens in the community.

When I was seven or eight, I was the "mascot" to the Older Boys Conference, a three day gathering of members of the boy's clubs at the University of Manitoba who came to swim, play baseball, and talk about their lives and problems. Most were tough kids and great athletes and one later starred with the Toronto Maple Leafs. Another became a well-known hockey coach and others became respected police officers and businessmen. Those I met in later years had good memories of their youth.

Juvenile delinquents of the day were certainly no angels. I remember a chilling phone call coming to our home late one evening in the '30s or '40s. Two juveniles had escaped from the cells in the Vaughan Street Detention Home. During their escape, they killed the Superintendent, Mr. Jenner, who lived in a suite on the first floor. My father rushed down to find out what had happened and to console the widow. The Attorney General of the day, William J. Major, later Mr. Justice Major, was very upset and I recall my father having to go to the legislative building to meet with him. I know none of the details, but believe that no subsequent Superintendent ever lived in the jail.

Child Welfare was part of the work of the Juvenile Court and early women lawyers Isobel Hunt, Nellie McNicol (Saunders) and Mildred

McMurray represented the City of Winnipeg, the Winnipeg Children's Aid Society and the province. Orphanages were often the only refuge for neglected or abused children. The processing of child welfare cases has had a chequered history and still has massive problems. While I am certain those pioneer women lawyers did much valuable work, my recollection is that the big issue of the day was which municipality would have to bear the cost of looking after a child.

Another of my father's efforts to avoid sending kids to jail was to talk to the parents in his office, urge them to keep an eye on their children and to exercise discipline within the home. One of his beliefs, I am hesitant to report, was "spare the rod and spoil the child." Apart from what that did to my more tender parts from time to time, he carried that belief into his work with delinquents. The approach was apparently acceptable to the Attorney General and the public, as I recall no outcry and can find no criticism in the newspaper clippings I have examined. His final effort to avoid sending youth to jail was to apply a punishment they would not forget.

Saturday morning was the time scheduled for the strapping of offenders on their bare bottoms and it fell to Julius Shumilewski, the only male Probation Officer, to apply that part of the court's order. The procedure took place on the south side of the top floor of the Juvenile Court/Detention Home building. You could hear cries of real or anticipated pain from the narrow barred windows under the eaves. I don't know if the by-law offenders were meant to hear, but I certainly did. I'm certain that my presence in the parking lot while delinquents were being reminded of the error of their ways was not by chance. The small windows and bars are still there today to remind me of at least one of my father's efforts to improve young lives. It's funny how for years I kept running into men who had grown up in the north end of the city who had appeared before my dad. They spoke of him with affection but I never asked whether they had been subjected to this ultimate method of persuasion.

I don't question my father's approach to punishment, even though I know it would not be tolerated today. It worked at the time and I am sure saved many youth from the damaging experiences that would otherwise have awaited them in jail. While the use of the strap, and then the paddle, ended in the penitentiary in the '60s or '70s, the judge I succeeded on the Court of Queen's Bench, Mr. Justice Frank Bastin, was also a believer in a sharp but short penalty. Years later I was impressed to hear an elderly Aboriginal woman at God's Lake

Narrows express the same belief. While complaining about the delays in the court system she said, "You have to discipline children right away. If you wait, they'll forget what they did wrong."

Strange as it may seem, some of the clients I later defended also preferred a short and severe sentence. During the '60s I defended two fellows who stole a case of beer from a farmer's truck in Virden and beat him up when he arrived on the scene. The case came on before Judge Cy Buckingham. Both were convicted of robbery with violence and were sentenced to two years in jail and to be paddled. I launched an appeal, but due to the differing wishes of the accused, I referred one to another lawyer in Winnipeg. One offender wanted to have the paddling removed from the sentence, no matter how long he had to stay in jail. The other wanted to get the paddle if the length of the sentence could be reduced.

The case came on before the Court of Appeal in Winnipeg, Chief Justice Cal Miller presiding. He had practiced law in Portage la Prairie and was known for his pleasant demeanour and common sense. The Chief Justice ruled that the paddle be removed, but the length of the sentence was upheld. He did so by ruling that the beating and theft of the beer were not related. The robbery with violence charge was changed to separate charges of theft and assault causing bodily harm. The Criminal Code of the day did not call for the paddle for either of those offences.

Looking back on my childhood, my knowledge of the way others lived was extremely limited. I knew no Aboriginal kids, or kids whose parents came from mainland Europe. The earliest recollection I have of people with different sounding names was when my dad started taking me to the weekly boxing cards at the Stock Exchange Hotel on Logan Avenue. Kids, mainly from the north end and the core area of the city, were matched against one another, the only criteria being weight. I came to learn that boxing was a way of gaining recognition without risking an attack from a bigger kid.

My own boxing career began later, at Sunday School of all places. Bob Vance was an unusual Sunday School teacher, another of my father's ilk, who quietly mixed bible stories with character development and sports. It was Mr. Hill, our militaristic cub and scout leader, who put the fear of God into us in the process of teaching us first aid, knots and other questionable skills.

Although I attended what I assume were good schools — Grosvenor, Robert H. Smith and Kelvin — as far as I can recall, there was little in my education that dealt with Aboriginal history or the part Aboriginal people had played in the development of Canada. I certainly never received any education about Aboriginal people. We learned the rhyme: "In 1492 Columbus sailed the ocean blue" when learning important dates in history, but that, and the names of his three ships, was the extent of my understanding of that event or its impact on the Americas.

Indians were referred to when we learned of Henry Kelsey crossing the western plains. No doubt Aboriginal people were with him and no doubt directed other renowned explorers such as Radisson, Groselliers and La Vérendrye, but the Aboriginal presence was hardly mentioned and their skills and lifestyle were never brought to our attention. We heard of fur-trade wars between the Hudson's Bay Company and the North West Company from Montreal, but the Aboriginal involvement was vague. I don't recall being taught that traders took advantage of the Indians as they made fortunes marketing their products in the salons of London and Paris. The movies of the day linked Aboriginal people with firewater that was pressed upon them. Indians were portrayed as a bloodthirsty lot, preying on settlers and fighting against the American army. The only less violent depiction in the movies was of the faithful scout, Tonto, who did the bidding of the fictional Lone Ranger.

Canada's history seemed to revolve around the arrival of John Cabot, the settling of Tadousac and Hochelaga and the battle for the Plains of Abraham. Political history dealt with the Treaty of Paris, Upper and Lower Canada, the Family Compact and the Fathers of Confederation. I certainly never learned anything about Aboriginal history, sovereignty, Aboriginal reserves or Canada's Treaties with our indigenous people.

I knew nothing about the process of trapping, or how and where Aboriginal families lived or how their children were educated. Until recent years I never heard of the role of Aboriginal people in the shipment of goods from the south to Hudson's Bay. I was not aware of the changes in lifestyle resulting from the end of commercial trapping and fishing, nor was I aware of the tribal gatherings and the trading that went on between tribes. The adjustments required of Aboriginal people by changing economic realities never crossed my mind.

Like most people of my era, I probably saw pictures of bronzed Aboriginal people standing on a rocky shore watching the landing of black-robed people. The pictorial exposition should have roused my curiosity, but without explanation, I missed the significance of the presence of the Aboriginal people. The next pieces of what might fall into the category of Aboriginal history were pictures showing near-naked Aboriginal people riding bareback with lance in hand as they chased buffalo. I recall no discussion of the importance of the buffalo to their survival. As far as my education was concerned, Aboriginal people seemed always to have been on the periphery of the Canadian reality.

My assumption was probably that of the explorers coming from abroad — that the Americas consisted of vast untamed lands that had never been explored and were certainly not already occupied by millions of people. The questions of invasion from abroad, and a prior claim to ownership, certainly never arose. This recital is merely intended to suggest that, when I was growing up, Canadians knew little about Aboriginal history, rights, and the legitimacy of their claims. I hope that by now the school curricula have remedied the omission.

This book will deal with Aboriginal people and how I gradually came to learn about them, how I came to know them as individuals, and to understand something of their history within Canada. My learning process has extended over 30 years and although I know that my knowledge is incomplete, I hope that my stories and comments will help others to better understand Aboriginal people and their issues.

My earliest recollection of Aboriginal people is when whole families came to our cottage selling freshly caught and filleted pickerel and smoked goldeye. I didn't realize how early they had to get up until one of the fishermen took my father and me out in his fishing boat while he pulled in and re-set his nets. I think it was still dark as we drove onto the sandy beachside road. Although the massive wood boat had two sets of oars I am sure my effort to help only slowed our passage through the waves. There were no outboard motors on our part of Lake Winnipeg in those days and nets had to be strung on poles on the beach to dry. Our host had a small fishing shack on the road that lead to the mouth of the Red River. Years later, as we rode or pushed our bikes along the same sandy trail, I remember an elderly lady sitting outside the shack and smoking her pipe, apparently awaiting her son's return.

I can't recall having any contact with Aboriginal people in the city. If there were any Aboriginal kids in school, they weren't identified as different from the rest of us. When I worked at Purity Flour in

St. Boniface during the summer holidays and over Christmas, there was a mixed work force of husky individuals who worked in the chop house, unloaded boxcars filled with grain, or loaded flour and rolled oats for shipment overseas, but I never heard anyone referred to by their racial background. As the last summer of my time there drew to a close, another stage in my maturity and my learning about others was about to begin.

As soon as I turned 18 in 1944, I joined the Infantry. The Air Force was no longer accepting new pilots and all the Navy wanted was recruits to train as cooks. Our basic training was at Fort Garry where the army had taken over the University of Manitoba students' residence during the war. I found the constant running, often with full pack, to be strenuous. If I hadn't worked in the flour mill the summer before I enlisted, I don't think I could have survived, but by the end of advanced training at Shilo, I could easily outrun the new recruits and carry the heavier Bren gun during exercises.

By the time I finished my advanced training at Shilo it appeared that the war in Europe was winding down and was going to be won. As they wouldn't send us overseas at that time unless we were nineteen, I was kept as an instructor in Shilo and was on loan to the Air Force for a time to provide small arms training to airmen returning from Europe, in preparation for the war in the Pacific.

The experience of greatest value to me was having to get along with a platoon full of men from every imaginable background. Some were right off the farm while others were toughs from the north end of Winnipeg. One was a preacher's son, another the son of a newspaper executive. He was unable to take the guff and was discharged early on. We marched and ran, studied map reading, learned to handle rifles, grenades, anti-tank fiats, did rifle drill and field manoeuvres together. We grumbled about the almost inedible food in the mess hall and went to the "Sally Ann" after supper to get something we could eat. We went to Brandon on Saturday night and consumed more beer than we could handle.

The army experience was a maturing one. It indicated how an almost impossible task could be achieved. It certainly showed the importance of discipline and the need to respect the authority of those in command, whether it was the admired Lieutenant or the (at times) much hated Sergeant. He had fought in Europe and was intent on teaching us the skills we would need to survive. The training turned on the principle — kill or be killed.

Many Indians and Métis distinguished themselves in the forces throughout the war and became the de facto leaders of their units. They were treated by other soldiers as their friends. A tragedy of the post-war era was that Aboriginal veterans were refused the money, land or education grants received by other veterans. Forty years later I learned that when they objected to the inequality of their treatment, they were told: "Indian Affairs will look after you." That didn't happen and the unfairness has not been corrected to this day. I was more fortunate.

When I entered Law School in 1947, we attended classes in the morning and articled in law offices in the afternoon. We had two full time professors, Colonel G.P.R. (Pete) Tallin, the Dean, and Colonel Harvey Streight, the Registrar. The other lecturers were practicing lawyers and judges. With their combination of wit, experience, and an ability to communicate, they made the law come alive for us. Principles of law were reinforced by interesting case scenarios or by a carefully devised joke or story. We were required to memorize basic principles of British justice and, at exam time, to give the full names of cases, the report series, volume and page number where they could be found. It was military training all over again but the students readily accepted the routine.

The ribald humour of Sam Freedman, Jimmy Wilson and H.G.H. Smith, kept us in stitches, retained our attention, and implanted principles of law in a manner we would remember. Chief Justice Williams and Mr. Justice Izzy Nitikman maintained their stern demeanour but pounded their lessons home. The odd lecturer was inclined to put us to sleep so a seatmate and I played 'hangman' as they talked, and absorbed enough to pass. "Pop" Sutton was in a class of his own. He taught Wills and Trusts in such a quiet and professorial manner that I was later surprised, when I had to deal with contested wills, how many fine points of law I had absorbed.

For those of us that took a liking to criminal law and its magnificent principles of justice, Deputy Attorney General John Allen was our favourite lecturer. He embellished his discussion with shouts and exclamations of joy as he pretended to unearth some obscure yet pertinent principle of law. At exam time, he came as close as he could to telling us what was going to be on the exam paper. What he was actually doing was forcing us to memorize the significant laws and principles he wanted us to remember. The 98 percent I had in fourth year Criminal Law was a mark I cherished, even if he had told us what we had better learn.

I articled in the prestigious downtown law office of Parker, Parker, Hunter and Hamlin. When getting started, my father gave me two pieces of advice. One was, "If someone asks your opinion on what the law is on a certain point, look it up. If another person asks you the same question the next day, look it up." The second piece of advice was "when drafting a legal document, draft it and redraft it until you are perfectly satisfied with the final form." To show me what he meant, we spent several evenings drafting and redrafting a separation agreement I was preparing at the office. I only submitted the document to the lawyer for whom I was doing the work, when both my father and I were satisfied it covered all relevant issues and was clear and concise.

After a year, I tired of searching titles and getting no court experience, so I moved to Wyrzykowski, Morrisey and Borowski at 663 Main Street. Mr. Rigby, our elderly clerk, lived at the Salvation Army Hostel just around the corner on Logan Avenue. He was an English remittance man and C.T. (Mr. Wyrzykowski) looked after him and doled out his earnings in portions too small to enable him to get into too much trouble. C.T. was a respected court man, Mr. Morrisey a legal researcher, and Mr. Borowski a careful and competent solicitor. My only problem was that I couldn't speak or understand Polish.

Our offices were in that part of the north end of Winnipeg populated by transients, pensioners and other unemployed people. Many lived in squalor in a single room above a store or business, with no facilities. I spent a great deal of time trying to locate missing family members. I had to go through the neighbourhood asking questions and often found the person with only a cot to sleep on and a wooden crate for a table.

During this period I became familiar with the Rupert Avenue Police Court run by Magistrate Maris Garton and Prosecutor Charlie Tupper. You didn't dare leave the room after court began or you could miss your case being called and find your client returned to the cells. One of the procedures much in use in those days was the "floater." If a vagrant, or someone who had committed a minor offence, pleaded guilty, the sentence would likely be "30 dollars or 30 days" but the warrant would be held for twenty-four hours to give the person time to leave town. If they didn't leave they would be arrested again and sent to jail. The problem was that the fastest way to get out of town was to hop a freight train, but the railway police were vigilant and many regulars were back in court the next day.

Sub-standard rooms remain on Main Street, but the occupants have changed. They have become home to many struggling Aboriginal people, many of whom are transients or recent arrivals coming to the city looking for employment and a better way of life. Many are disappointed and have unfortunately turned to substance abuse of one form or another to hide their sorrow. I will later describe their search for employment and the problems of moving to the city.

My familiarity with the area was renewed four years later when I was part of the firm of Goerwell and Hamilton, a name not many will recall. Sten Goerwell had been in the merchant navy during the war. He was a recovering alcoholic and was building an interesting and varied criminal defence practice.

One of my responsibilities, as his junior, was to get people who were in custody, out on bail. The practice of the day was to have family members bring proof of ownership and pledge their property as security by signing a bail bond. If the person showed up for trial, the bond expired. I don't recall any of our clients being released "on their own recognizance." As many of the alleged criminals had no families, and no one who could assist them, we had to look elsewhere for bondsmen. I was given the names of people who, for a fee, would find a bondsman who would pledge his property. I later came to believe that the practice might not have been legal but I had no such knowledge or concern at the time.

Mary (that was the only part of her name I was allowed to know) had several properties of her own and a stable of bondsmen. After she considered the background of an offender, and made sure she had a "free" title, she and the bondsman would meet me at the police station on Rupert Street, collect a fee for herself, a fee for the bondsman, and sign the bail documents. Another contact I made was with a former "runner" for one of the more notorious criminal lawyers of the twenties. The lawyer had passed away but his runner was still looking for business. Another bondsman, Billy Bain, warned me not to trust the runner. He said he would demand money up front to cover his expenses and would never be seen again. My first encounter with the runner in the Albert Hotel beer parlour, confirmed the tactic. He asked for money up front, I didn't pay, and he never did come up with a bondsman.

Calls from Mr. Goerwell usually came late in the evening, telling me the name of the person in custody and where to go to contact a bondsman. This would often take me to one of the seedy hotels on north Main. The night clerks invariably denied any knowledge of the individual until they grilled me to make sure I was connected with Mr. Goerwell and not the police. If I persuaded them I was no threat to their operation (whatever that may have been) the person I was seeking magically appeared. Such was the under-life of north Main in the '50s.

Main Street is now showing signs of change. The Aboriginal Centre of Winnipeg occupies the former CPR station and contains four floors of Aboriginal offices and a rotunda for ceremonial occasions. The Thunderbird House, designed by the internationally acclaimed Aboriginal architect, Douglas Cardinal, now stands on another corner of Main and Higgins. It too provides a spiritual gathering place and contains a variety of Aboriginal offices.

I eventually established my own law practice in Winnipeg but cases were few and far between. To avoid having to keep borrowing from my father every month, we moved to small prairie towns where I could at least eke out a living, until the attraction of the courtroom took me to Brandon, a judicial centre. After doing court work for another firm for a couple of years I established my own firm in Brandon in 1960 and spent most of my time doing civil litigation and defending people charged with criminal offences. I represented Aboriginal and other offenders on charges ranging from assault and theft to rape and murder, and appeared regularly in all levels of court. Appeals were occasionally taken to the Court of Appeal in Winnipeg, and I had the unusual experience for a rural lawyer at that time of arguing two cases in the Supreme Court of Canada, one successfully.

My wife and I employed Aboriginal ladies from the Sioux Valley Indian Reserve to help with housework and our four young children. We enjoyed their quiet efficiency and pleasant humour and became acquainted with their parents and grandparents. One of my secretaries, came from that community as well and I regret that I did not have or take the time to learn more about their culture.

Aboriginal clients lived in Brandon or on one of the seven or eight reserves in western Manitoba and I was beginning to learn something of their personalities and their approach to life. In most respects they were like other people in trouble with the law, but there were differences as well. One difference was that they were inclined to approach situations more openly and more directly than other clients. They were honest and open with me and certainly took the comments of others at face value.

One case in Provincial Court indicates how literally one Aboriginal client took a judge's instructions. Two brothers had been charged with assault causing bodily harm to an older Aboriginal gentleman. The police had arrived at the bus depot to find a bloodied man lying in the gutter and to see a couple of figures running into a nearby lane.

The case came on before Judge Fred Coward, known for his serious approach to the law and for his insistence on running an efficient court. He would abide no nonsense from accused or counsel. The trial was set for 10 but started about 11 a.m. The first witness was a police officer and he related what he had observed when he arrived on the scene. He said he couldn't identify the accused at the scene but soon arrested them in the area. The examination of this witness took till 12:30 so the judge adjourned court and said we would continue at 2:00.

A second policeman was called when court resumed and he started to tell what he had seen. The Crown Attorney asked if he recognized the accused. He pointed to my clients and said, "That's William and that's Andrew Sanderson. As soon as his name was mentioned, Andy waved his hand over his head and almost yelled, "That's me." Although nothing was said, heads came up and all eyes were on Andy. The policeman continued and described how he came upon the brothers in the downtown area. Again he mentioned Andy's name and again the hand went up "That's me " By this time the considerable slur with which the announcement was made became painfully apparent.

Judge Coward looked over his glasses at me and droned, "Mr. Hamilton, is there anything wrong with your client?" Not wishing to jump to any conclusion, I replied "Not that I am aware of, your Honour." "Possibly you would like to speak to your client. He wouldn't want to be held in contempt of court".

I leaned back to where the boys were sitting and again told Andy to be quiet. The questioning continued but another mention of his name induced the same explosive interjection. It became apparent that Andy had spent the noon hour in the pub, no doubt strengthening himself for the ordeal to come. The judge was furious. His court was being mocked and the wheels of justice were coming off.

"You get out of here!" the Judge roared, and a constable escorted Andy out the side door of the courtroom.

The questioning of the policeman continued and he was eventually asked if he could identify the boys he had arrested. The Crown asked if I would admit the identity of the accused who was absent from the courtroom. I declined, and suggested he be identified in the usual way.

There had been no Preliminary Inquiry, and as this was before the days of disclosure, I had no idea what the witness was going to say or how strong his identification of my clients might be.

The clerk went into the hall where he could be heard calling "Andrew Sanderson." There seemed to be an unusual delay as we awaited Andy's arrival. After quite some time the clerk came in and whispered to the judge. The judge stormed out of the courtroom, followed by the clerk and the bailiff. The rest of us stayed in our places, as court had not been adjourned. When the judge returned ten minutes later, he announced with some hesitation that Andy was nowhere to be found and the court was unceremoniously adjourned.

It took a while to find out what had happened. Apparently, when the judge told Andy to get out, he left not only the courtroom, but the courthouse as well. He told me he understood the judge to mean that he had been kicked out of court and, in effect, told to go home.

Months went by as we tried to agree on another date to continue the trial. After the trial was over I learned that the victim had to be arrested twice and placed in custody as he was not anxious to testify against the brothers, who were well known to him. He had been released from custody when the trial had to be postponed, but unknown to me, had to be located again and brought to court from the local jail the day he finally testified.

When the trial finally resumed and all the medical evidence was in, the victim was called as a witness. The Crown attorney, with a show of confidence and a glance at me that seemed to say, "This is it," began his examination in chief:

Q. "Do you know the accused William and Andrew Sanderson?"

A. "Yes."

Q. "Please tell the court what happened on the 12th of September 1966."

A. "I can't remember."

Q. "Do you remember seeing the Sanderson brothers the day you were beaten up outside the bus depot?"

A. "No."

I didn't even have to move for dismissal. The Crown gave up. The charge was stayed and that was the end of one of the most memorable trials I ever had. There were no repercussions as, after all, it was the judge who told Andy to leave. He hadn't told him to wait. He hadn't, as was his practice, told the Sheriff's Officer to watch the accused to see that he waited in the witness room.

Although I may not have appreciated it at the time, I was learning a few truths about Aboriginal culture: Aboriginal people tend to be non-judgmental. They do not like to judge another and do not like to give evidence against one another. They do not like to attribute blame and, if it can be avoided, should not be the cause of another going to jail. Certainly, arresting and jailing someone to force them to testify, is not an honourable thing to do. I learned how literally Aboriginal people take a question or a court order. That lesson was to be of benefit when I became a judge.

Near the end of my days as a practicing lawyer I had a real lesson in Aboriginal protocol. One morning I received a call from Chief John Sioux of the Sioux Valley Indian Reserve. He told me that a man had just died as a result of something that happened on another reserve and the police were expected shortly. A resident of the reserve who had been present when the injuries were caused had taken the wounded man to the hospital where he died. The Mounties had placed the man in custody and told him he might be charged with murder. I agreed to go to the reserve and Chief Sioux agreed to come with me.

When we arrived at the reserve where the incident had occurred, Chief Sioux directed me to drive to a particular house. "Wait here," he said. When he came out five minutes later he explained that he had talked to the Chief and three matters had been resolved. Number one, I was given permission to enter the community. Number two, I was given permission to speak to anyone I wished, and finally, the people in the house where the incident occurred were directed to answer my questions and tell me what had happened.

We drove a mile or so to the house in question. Although I saw no sign of telephone lines, the people seemed to know I was coming and readily discussed the events of the previous evening. It was usually difficult to obtain a great deal of information from Aboriginal witnesses so the difference in this case was dramatic. I was shown the room in which an argument and some fighting had taken place. Blood was evident on the floor and on a couch. A broken window still contained shards of glass, and pieces of glass were evident in the room and under the window on the outside of the house. Because the police had suggested a stabbing, we searched in and around the house, but found no bloodied knife.

No one had seen exactly what happened, as the house had been crowded. An argument and some pushing and shoving had occurred but no one saw the man who was under arrest do anything to the deceased that could have caused the fatal wound. No one could say how the window had been broken, but the theory was that the deceased must have put his arm through the window and been cut in the process.

The case was memorable, as it is the only case I can remember where I had a charge of murder dismissed by Judge Coward at a preliminary inquiry. By the time of the preliminary, I knew more of the facts of the case than the RCMP and the Crown Attorney. More important however, whether I realized the significance at the time or not, I had been introduced to Aboriginal tradition and protocol.

I was appointed to the Manitoba Court of Queen's Bench in 1971. The call from John Turner, the Canadian Minister of Justice, came on a blustery December 23rd morning when I was busily trying to get my files up-to-date for the year-end. When the receptionist called to see if I was able to accept a call from the Minister, I nearly fell out of my chair. I rushed over and closed the door and waited. Finally the well-modulated voice intoned — "Mr. Hamilton." "Yes Mr. Minister," I replied, trying not to sound too excited. After all, with rumours I had heard, why else would he be calling! "We are appointing you a judge of the Supreme Court of Manitoba." I replied: "Thank you Mr. Minister. I am honoured," and in my excitement I added, "What a wonderful Christmas present."

Moments later another caller began, "Good Morning, My Lord." It was the same gentle and scholarly Sam Freedman from Law School days, but now a highly respected jurist. I had appeared before him many times when he was a judge of the Queen's Bench and then of the Court of Appeal and now the Chief Justice of Manitoba. The next call was from Queen Bench's Chief Justice George Tritschler, asking if I would come to his office in Winnipeg the next day. I went, and we agreed on the time and place for the swearing-in ceremony.

The swearing-in took place at the Courthouse in Brandon on January 7, 1972 by Lieutenant Governor Jack McKeag. Chief Justice Freedman and Mr. Justice Israel Nitikman, representing Chief Justice Tritschler, participated. I sat on my first case in Brandon the following Monday. At that time all the judges of the Queen's Bench had to live in Winnipeg, so we had to leave our home and friends in Brandon, and start a new life in Winnipeg.

My 21 years as a practicing lawyer made the change a relatively easy one and I enjoyed the following 21 years on the bench. The work, and the variety of cases assigned to me, was enjoyable and challenging. I now had the opportunity to apply some of the great principles of civil and criminal law in a neutral and independent way. I no longer had to assume the partisan position of counsel for a plaintiff or for an accused.

In those days there were only eight judges on the Court of Queen's Bench, and we handled every imaginable type of case including criminal jury trials. Civil disputes, interpretation of wills, statutes and contracts, labour disputes and divorces occupied the rest of our time. Most jury trials dealt with charges of murder or rape. A few dealt with fraud and I had one lengthy trial involving a charge of conspiracy to import drugs for the purpose of trafficking. I had two fascinating civil jury trials as well.

It is often suggested that judges live in an ivory tower and are removed from what is going on in the real world. I never found that to be the case. Each case, whether a civil or criminal one, was an education in itself. Witnesses instruct judges on the intricacies of construction, on surgical procedures, on police procedures and the gathering of evidence, on fingerprint analysis and lawyers keep them up to date on the latest case law. Judges learn about humanity, about social problems and about human suffering.

The cases I heard took me effectively into people's homes and sometimes into their bedrooms. People told of their reactions to situations at work, to the wording of contracts, and to the impact of contracts upon them. I learned about the real-estate business and about problems in corporate boardrooms. We heard of problems people were having with the law. I still consider the information I heard as a judge to have been a pretty broad and ongoing education.

Judges must be careful about their out-of-court activities. They must avoid all political associations and stay clear of community activities that may involve controversy, particularly anything that might end up in court. After moving to Winnipeg, I was invited to join the Board of Rainbow Stage, a summer theatre company. I thought that offered an opportunity for some uncontentious community service. The activity seemed to be free of controversy and in a field that could not impinge upon my work as a judge. I accepted the invitation, but it wasn't long before I regretted the decision.

The first concern I had was when a child custody case involving a senior employee of Rainbow Stage came before me. I didn't know him personally, so I heard the case. The next concern was when I was sitting on a challenge to the policy of Canada Safeway that forbade employees from wearing a beard. The Chairman of the Board of Rainbow Stage was called as a witness for Safeway. I advised the lawyers that I knew him through my attendance at board meetings, but they asked me to continue hearing the case in any event. The third concern was when the union representing the Rainbow Stage employees went on strike. That was the final straw. I resigned from the Board and abandoned the thought of active community service.

It is essential that judges maintain a neutral and independent stance on the cases that come before them. They must consider the evidence of all witnesses and the arguments of the lawyers before applying the relevant principles of law and justice in giving their decision. This is not to say that judges do not misapply the law from time to time. A dissatisfied litigant may appeal a trial decision to the Court of Appeal to see if the law was properly applied to the proven facts. The comments of that court add to the continuing legal education of judges.

Judges also attend seminars designed to keep them up to date on the latest developments in the law. They discuss their court's processing of cases and consider how it may be improved. They update the court rules to adapt them to technological change. They hear from professors and specialists on many of the social problems that regularly surface during trials. These presentations are general and informational in nature, so they will not influence a judge in deciding a specific case. Judges must still make their decisions based on the evidence they hear in court during the presentation of each case and on the arguments and suggestions of the parties' lawyers.

Our judges took turns travelling to six (now nine) circuit points in the province. When we went on circuit we stayed until all applications, divorces, civil and criminal matters on the docket were completed. The judges led a rather isolated existence while on circuit, as care had to be taken not to socialize with lawyers who might be appearing before you in court. That practice was embarrassing on occasion. One time I was having breakfast in a hotel in The Pas when a lawyer asked if he could join me. I said, "Don't you have something on the docket today?" When he agreed that he had, I said, "Sorry, we can't sit together." Most lawyers know better than to ask, but it seems that one of the tasks of judges is to continually educate some lawyers in matters of court-related protocol.

Often jurors would be eating at a separate table in the same restaurant, and lawyers would be seated in booths with their clients. I had to find a table as far as possible away from all of them. You can imagine the concern or suspicion those on one side of a case would have if they saw the judge who was going to sit on their case, even so much as saying hello to a lawyer on the other side. Assumptions might be made that the lawyer had the ear of the judge or, worse still, that the judge might support the position that lawyer would take in court. In small centres, I have had to leave a restaurant where I planned to eat, when I saw only one of the lawyers and his client having lunch. The best solution was sometimes to buy a pizza and eat it in my hotel room or court office.

Many criminal cases I heard, both in the cities and in the north, involved Aboriginal people as accused, victims, and witnesses. One jury case in The Pas extended my education about life on Indian reserves and tested how I should balance the demands of the law and compassion for the offender. The Mathias Colomb reserve in the isolated community of Pukatawagan, I was told, had few modern conveniences. Few homes had electricity and a television set was a rare commodity.

One wintry night a group of friends, most of who had been drinking moose milk, an intoxicating mixture of beans, potatoes and yeast cake, for several hours, gathered to watch television. There was no electricity in the house where they assembled, so several extension cords were joined together and run from another house to the television set. For some reason that was never explained, the power failed from time to time and the television would turn off. One witness at the trial guessed that the extension cords were probably overloaded. Whatever the reason, young Philip Adamson (not his real name) was blamed for each interruption in the program they were trying to watch. In spite of his protestations of innocence, the attacks turned physical and were intensified when the power failures were repeated as the evening wore on. Finally, in frustration at being unable to stop the unfounded accusations, he decided he might quiet things down if he could shoot off a gun. The noise, he was sure, would bring his attackers to their senses.

Philip left the party and ran the kilometre across the frozen river to his grandparents' cabin and borrowed their .22-calibre rifle. He fired two shots inside their house, to make sure the gun was working. He ran back across the ice towards the party, but as he approached the house in his agitated state, a man came out and started towards him. Philip assumed this was one of the bullies who had been harassing him, so he raised the gun to his shoulder and fired. Too late, he discovered that the man he shot was his brother-in-law, who was coming to calm him down. The charge was second degree murder.

Philip willingly gave the RCMP a statement in which he told what had happened. Forensic evidence was nevertheless adduced, matching the bullet with the gun. His alcohol level was .110 when taken, and would have been higher earlier in the evening. He was not totally drunk, but the instigating bully was verging on the unconscious.

The trial in The Pas was before a jury of twelve miners and other northerners. No onlookers from Pukatawagan were present (they would have had to take a train and find a place to stay) and there were no Aboriginal people on the jury. The jury found Philip guilty on a reduced charge of manslaughter, and recommended mercy. No intent to harm or kill his brother-in-law was shown, but he had clearly caused his death. The situation was so pathetic that, in addition to feeling the grief of the family of the deceased, I felt sorry for the offender and his young wife and infant child who relied on him for support. He had an unblemished past and all the witnesses spoke highly of him, and regretted that the party got out of hand.

Although the maximum sentence was life in prison, I decided that justice would be served by the imposition of a minimal sentence. Even though I knew that my suggestion did not have to be followed by those in charge of the jail system, I directed that he serve his time in the Dauphin jail, the closest one to his home. The sentence I imposed was the least I thought I could get away with without having the length of time increased by the Court of Appeal. The sentence was eighteen months, and with good behaviour he would be out much sooner. I never heard of an appeal being taken so I assume the Attorney General's department also felt the pathos and concluded that the punishment was sufficient.

Court work brought me into contact with many Aboriginal people who, as litigants and witnesses, obviously had difficulty with the rules of evidence and the rules of court. I was amazed to find that very often the comments of Aboriginal witnesses made more sense than the rules themselves. In one case, an Aboriginal witness was being questioned, first by the Crown attorney and then by defence counsel. There were many objections by the lawyers when the witness failed to give a direct answer to their questions. I finally said, "Just tell us what you saw and what you did." The witness quietly replied, "I'm trying to, but they (indicating the lawyers) won't let me." I then insisted the witness answer in his own way, even if he had to present some background information no one asked him for. The jury was not contaminated by the hearsay and it was not hard to distinguish between what the witness heard and saw and what he assumed. It was easy for me to tell the jury to concentrate on what the witnesses saw and heard, and to disregard the balance.

Aboriginal people are very honest witnesses, but are nervous in court and almost never volunteer information. It is therefore necessary for counsel and the judge to frame their questions with care. A beautiful example of this is told by Judge Billy Martin, a long time resident of the north, first as a lawyer and later as a seasoned Provincial Court Judge. An Aboriginal lady was testifying in a trial and counsel wanted to test her memory of the events she had witnessed.

The Crown attorney asked: "How much did you have to drink Mary?"

"Two," she replied.

"Two glasses?" the lawyer asked.

"No," was the only reply.

"Two bottles?" The lawyer was bound to get to the truth of the matter.

"No." He still hadn't unearthed the secret.

"Two ounces?" he tried once more.

"No," was still the response.

The imagination of the Crown attorney was spent. He threw up his hands in disgust and sat down. The defence counsel then took his turn and went through all the "two" options he could think of. He too received "No" to each of his suggestions.

The seasoned judge, used to dealing with Aboriginal people, quietly said:

"Mary... two what?"

"Two pails," she demurely replied.

They had been drinking moose milk from honey pails. This proved the adage — ask the right question and you'll get the right answer, particularly of an Aboriginal witness I would add. Trials enabled me to hear of life on Aboriginal reserves and the hardships people faced, but it was not until 1988 that I really began to understand the extent of their problems.

I referred earlier to the magnificent principles of justice we learned in law school that I tried to apply when on the bench. My love for the law, although it is hard to define, probably related to how the principles are supposed to be applied to protect individual rights and assure equal treatment of all litigants, rich or poor, famous or unknown.

Others in the justice system take a similar pride in fulfilling their responsibilities. Police officers love the law in the sense that they appreciate the challenge of seeing that people live their lives in peace and according to the law of the land. They enjoy the challenge of investigating crimes and bringing offenders to justice. The whole *raison d'être* of lawyers is to see that justice is done between competing positions, even if their task in a specific case is to concentrate on their client's needs.

Lawyers are sometimes criticized for their aggressive defence of a particular position. Crown attorneys may be criticized for wanting to prosecute and convict people who have made a human mistake. Defence counsel are often criticized for trying to "get people off" no matter what heinous crime they have committed. As unpleasant as some of these positions may be, even to the lawyers, the legal system needs lawyers working as hard as they can to represent their client's interests. If the criminal law is strong, the person will be convicted. If the law is flawed, or the proof is weak, the accused will be released.

In both situations the lawyers are the defenders of the law and take pride in the part they play in the legal system. While some lawyers who are good at their particular field of law, and have developed a reputation as experts, are well paid, they still have a burning desire to do the very best they can, and many take cases from time to time where they receive no payment at all. For example, there is an association of lawyers which fights to have cases of prisoners who maintain their innocence, reheard.

General practitioners, like those in the medical profession, must have a broad general knowledge and be able to deal with a wide variety of issues every day. They may not be in the news, but they too provide a valuable service to people needing assistance. They too have a love of the law. Some of the best lawyers are law professors, who study the law and the latest cases in their field and try to pass on their knowledge to law students. Other lawyers work for corporations, and provide guidance in company law, taxation and in corporate administration.

Most lawyers I know are more interested in doing a good job for their clients than they are in their own financial gains. They are basically part of a caring profession, caring for the legal concerns of their clients. As long as that service component remains part of their approach to life, they are acting as professionals. The best lawyers and judges have a "love of the law," and an insatiable desire to see that justice is done.

These high ideals are sometimes difficult or impossible to achieve. We know, and I will comment at some length on the fact, that not every person in Canada has access to a lawyer or to appropriate court services. It is difficult for those within the justice system, be they judges, lawyers or others, to step back and critically analyze the performance of their part of the system, and make the changes that are needed to keep it up to date and to deal with new and different situations. It is harder yet for them to accept and to act on reasoned criticism that is directed at them.

It was the next step in my odyssey that brought into focus the extent of the problems with the justice system. It was those problems as well, that severely challenged my belief in our legal system, and the high principles for which it stands. Nothing in my background as a lawyer or a judge, prepared me for what was to lie ahead. My real education about Aboriginal people, and the issues that confront them, was about to begin.

2

Aboriginal Justice Inquiry

J.J. Harper, a well-known Aboriginal leader, was killed on a residential street in Winnipeg on March 9, 1988, during a struggle with a police constable. Earlier that year, the trial of two of four suspects in the 1971 abduction and brutal killing of Helen Betty Osborne, a nineteen year old Cree student from Norway House, was completed in The Pas with the conviction of one. The two incidents raised charges of racism and discrimination from Aboriginal and non-Aboriginal people alike, and calls for a public inquiry into them and into the manner in which the justice system was dealing with Aboriginal people.

Tanner Elton, the Deputy Attorney General, came to my office in the Law Courts within a few days of J.J. Harper's death. He told me the government was thinking of establishing a judicial inquiry to look into the two cases, and to examine other justice issues. He asked if I would be willing to act as the Commissioner, and he assured me the Inquiry would only take six months of my time. I said I would get back to him.

I was certainly interested, but as I started to think about how an Inquiry might deal with general justice issues I was unsure how I would proceed. While there were certain issues I thought should be explored, I had few initial thoughts as to how that might be done. Where would I find Aboriginal people to tell me of their concerns? Would they speak to me? Would I hold hearings and take evidence, or would I just make inquiries and recommendations? How does anyone go about examining a whole system of justice? To put it mildly, I had some misgivings. I discussed the matter with my wife and I told my Chief Justice of the approach that had been made. He was rightly concerned about my work as Associate Chief Justice and no immediate decision was made.

Tanner Elton came to see me again. He asked how I would feel about another Commissioner being appointed as well. I must not have shown a great deal of enthusiasm so he added, "The government is thinking of appointing Murray Sinclair as well." My reaction changed instantly. I didn't know Murray Sinclair personally, but until his recent appointment as a judge and as an Associate Chief Judge of the Provincial Court, he had appeared before me as counsel on several occasions. I had a high regard for his ability as counsel and for his sensitive and balanced approach to cases.

One case on which he had appeared, involved an Aboriginal child who had been raised in a white home by caring foster parents. The Aboriginal parents, represented by Murray Sinclair, now had their lives in order and wanted the child returned to them and to the Aboriginal way of life. After hearing from both sets of 'parents,' and of their shared love and concern for the child, I asked counsel if they would meet and try to devise a solution to the apparent impasse.

After an hour or two of discussions between the parties and their counsel, an agreement was reached that appeared to be in the best interests of the child. The boy would continue to live with the foster parents and attend school in Winnipeg, and the natural parents would be welcome to take the boy out with them whenever they were in Winnipeg. During the summer, the boy would spend time on the reserve, get to know his relatives and learn the traditions and life-style of his parents. Murray Sinclair was, it seemed to me, the architect of the solution.

The possibility of working with Chief Judge Sinclair as Co-Commissioners immediately dispelled my earlier misgivings and I said I would be delighted to work with him. I also said I would accept an appointment to the Inquiry if the Chief Justice approved. I asked Tanner Elton to have the Minister of Justice or the Premier meet with the Chief Justice to discuss my possible appointment. The correct protocol had not been followed earlier — the Chief Justice should have been approached before I was. The Chief Justice was not enthusiastic about me accepting the appointment, but finally told me to do what I wanted. That was hardly a ringing endorsement of an undertaking I thought provided an opportunity to do something of value for the administration of justice, but I agreed to act as a Commissioner.

Our appointments were controversial to say the least, and Judge Sinclair and I were strongly criticized for agreeing to participate. I regret the evident dissatisfaction among the judiciary and the extent of the animosity that was shown. Some judges had a sincere belief that judges should not be involved in inquiries and I could understand their position, even if I did not agree with it. Judges of our courts had been involved in the Northern Flood Inquiry a few years earlier without opposition from other judges.

The reason for the opposition to our undertaking may have been that we were to examine the justice system itself and some may have foreseen the criticisms that would surface. Whatever the reason for the opposition, it was never explained to me. I looked on the Inquiry as an opportunity to take a look at the legal system and to assess and improve its performance.

The Inquiry was established by an Order in Council of the Pawley government on April 13, 1988, a little more than a month after J.J. Harper's death. When the NDP government was defeated and the Conservatives assumed office two months later, the new Filmon government expressed its support for the inquiry. In passing, I might add that I had never had any connection with either government, or the political parties they represented.

The Minister of Justice in the new government asked if we would like to have a third Commissioner, so disagreements could be settled by majority vote. Although Judge Sinclair and I had only worked together for a few months at that time, I was happy to respond, "Don't worry Mr. Minister, we are going to agree," and we did.

The legislature passed 'An Act to Establish and Validate the Public Inquiry into the Administration of Justice and Aboriginal People.' It provided in part:

3(1) The Commissioners shall investigate, report and make recommendations to the Minister of Justice on the relationship between the administration of justice and Aboriginal peoples of Manitoba, guided but not limited to the terms of reference set out in the Schedule.

The Schedule provided:

Purpose of Commission
    The purpose of the Commission is to inquire into, and make findings about, the state of conditions with respect to Aboriginal people in the justice system in Manitoba and produce a final report for the Minister of Justice with conclusions, options and recommendations.
    The commission's deliberations are to include consideration of all aspects of the cases of J.J. Harper and Helen Betty Osborne and

the commission may make any additional recommendations that it deems appropriate with respect to those cases, including a recommendation that there be further consideration of particular matters or further inquiry into any aspect of either case.

Scope of Inquiry

The scope of the commission is to include all components of the justice system, that is, policing, courts and correctional services. The commission is to consider whether and the extent to which Aboriginal and non-Aboriginal persons are treated differently by the justice system and whether there are specific adverse effects, including possible systemic discrimination against Aboriginal people, in the justice system. The commission is to consider the manner in which the justice system now operates and whether there are alternative methods of dealing with Aboriginal persons involved with the law. For example, the commission may review the following issues:

Policing:
 ‣ policing issues in relation to Aboriginal people;
 ‣ deployment of personnel and accessibility of policing services;
 ‣ arrest and charging procedures;
 ‣ cultural sensitization for police officers and affirmative action programs;
 ‣ the conduct and training of wildlife officers relating to Aboriginal people.

Access to and adequacy of legal counsel:
 ‣ eligibility and access to Legal Aid;
 ‣ access in remote communities.

Court Processes:
 ‣ use of bail and custody;
 ‣ prosecutorial discretion and plea bargaining;
 ‣ role of court communicators;
 ‣ effect of time delays from arrest to trial;
 ‣ family proceedings;
 ‣ youth court;
 ‣ child welfare proceedings.

Court Dispositions:
- ▸ comparative types of dispositions among Aboriginal and non-Aboriginal people;
- ▸ use of custodial sentences;
- ▸ availability of sentencing alternatives.

Post sentencing:
- ▸ differential success of Aboriginal and non-Aboriginal groups on probation;
- ▸ availability and use of fine option program;
- ▸ prison experiences, such as temporary absences and parole;
- ▸ use of half-way houses;
- ▸ reintegration to communities and reserves.

Other:
- ▸ awareness and knowledge of justice system by Aboriginal people;
- ▸ communication between justice system personnel and Aboriginal people;
- ▸ employment of Aboriginal people in justice system.

Some, who were later unhappy with the many matters dealt with in our report, were probably unaware of the extent of our responsibility.

The Province provided a suite of offices to accommodate our staff of twelve or so. We made a decision early on that, although the individuals might change from time to time, half the staff would at all times be Aboriginal. Jeannie Daniels was one of our advance people and Eric Robinson, now the Minister of Aboriginal Affairs and Northern Development in the Doer government, was the other. One or other of them went into every community in advance of our visit to explain the purpose of the Inquiry and to encourage people to tell us their experiences. Eric Robinson, who had experience with the media, also made arrangements for the audio and TV recording of all our proceedings and directed our survey of the inmates at the penitentiary.

Tom McMahon, a young lawyer who had to resign from his employment with the provincial government to avoid any possibility of a conflict of interest, became our Executive Director. His experience with government proved to be invaluable as he prepared budgets and made proposals and periodic reports to government on our behalf. Our office managers, Darlene Black, and later Maryanne Boulton, in addition to running the office, kept the accounts in order and worked with Don Fenwick of Touche-Ross, our auditor.

Professor Brad Morse, a University of Ottawa law professor, well-versed in Aboriginal history and operating systems around the world, was our director of research. He did some draft writing for us and worked with Doris Young, Laurie Messer and Eileen Shewchuk, our in-house researchers. Experts in certain fields provided us with draft opinions, which we accepted, revised or rejected. Judge Sinclair did most of the writing on Aboriginal issues, while I concentrated on court and general justice matters. We read and discussed one another's drafts until we were both satisfied with every statement in the report.

The Winnipeg Convention Centre was selected for our opening session. A substantial crowd attended and we heard from Chief Oscar Lathlin, (a Minister of the Crown in today's government), representing the Assembly of Manitoba Chiefs, Ron Richard of the Manitoba Métis Federation, Mary Richard of the Indigenous Women's Collective, MLA Elijah Harper (later a Member of Parliament), his daughter Holly, and the Provincial Minister of Justice, the Honourable James McCrea. They outlined some of the problems of the past and suggested issues they thought we should examine.

As it would have been too expensive to continue in that location, we moved to the Freight House in Winnipeg's North End, which was more accessible to the Aboriginal people from whom we wanted to hear. We invited everyone who wished to express an opinion on Aboriginal-related matters to come and speak to us. Our staff prepared each agenda to accommodate the number of speakers to the time allotted for each day. The Winnipeg hearings were interspersed with out-of-town hearings, visits to jails, trips to northern centres and visits to reserve communities.

Before we began our hearings we met separately with the RCMP, the City of Winnipeg police and representatives of the Bar, to tell them of our mandate, our intended approach, and to solicit their co-operation.

Dale Henry, the Officer Commanding the RCMP division, asked if he might have an officer attend each of our meetings. We agreed, on the condition that if the presence of his representative inhibited anyone in his or her presentation, we could ask the officer to leave. This condition only had to be applied on two occasions. One rural hearing was set to begin at 11:00 a.m. The staff was ready to start but there were only about three people in attendance, one being the local constable. As time went on, Judge Sinclair disappeared to make some inquiries.

It appeared that some hard feelings had developed between the local detachment and the community and people were not prepared to speak in the presence of the police officer, so we asked him to leave, and the hall filled to capacity within fifteen minutes. We heard particulars of the conflict, passed them on to the Officer Commanding, and although we never received any report, were satisfied that efforts were made to improve the police-community relations.

Generally, the presence of the officer was beneficial. If problems with the RCMP surfaced, we found the problem was quickly corrected. If the force disagreed with the criticism of a presenter, we would receive a written explanation within a few days. We were then free to re-examine the issue if we wished. We did not call presenters back, as we took people at face value, and tried to free them of the challenges of cross-examination they might have experienced during a police investigation or in court. We did however check some allegations by asking others to comment on the same incident.

Aboriginal people welcomed the Inquiry. Community feasts were often organized to welcome us, and traditional prayers and pipe ceremonies opened our sessions. Aboriginal people took the hearings very seriously. Presenters told us this was the first time anyone representing government had ever asked them for their opinion on anything, let alone on an issue of such importance. It was certainly the first time they had ever had an opportunity to comment on the workings of every aspect of the justice system.

The Inquiry took me into another world, a world unlike my own, a world where people struggle to survive, where they hope and dream of a better way of life, and where their dreams are repeatedly destroyed.

I had the privilege of visiting Aboriginal communities in every corner of Manitoba where Chiefs and Councillors spoke of dealings with government since the time Treaties were signed. Men, women and youth came forward in large numbers to describe their daily problems, and their problems with the justice system. It was as a Commissioner that I began to explore and then to understand the enormity of the problems facing Canada's first people.

This short review of the Aboriginal Justice Inquiry (AJI) deals with some of my personal experiences and my own reaction to the Inquiry, to the people of the communities we visited, and to the issues it unearthed. Some of the stories are light-hearted as I wish to put a personal face to the people and the situations I encountered. I also try to put a human face to the inquiry itself, even though it dealt with the most serious and basic of issues — justice. The process was an education for me and I hope to pass on to other non-Aboriginal people some of the appreciation I developed for a wonderful yet distinct people, and for their culture.

Judge Sinclair's presence was the secret to the Inquiry's success in obtaining the co-operation of the Aboriginal community and the manner in which people so openly shared their experiences with us. I am convinced that, had I been the only Commissioner, they wouldn't have spoken to me with such candour or welcomed me to their communities with such enthusiasm. Judge Sinclair is well known and highly respected by Aboriginal people throughout the province, and in other parts of the country as well.

My appreciation of Judge Sinclair increased as time went on. He was a master at conducting meetings, encouraging people to speak, and at solving administrative problems we encountered, in a calm and pleasant manner. Not only did I find that we communicated with one another in an easy manner, we reached agreement on serious issues quite easily. As an Ojibway, and as a former officer of the Manitoba Métis Federation, his knowledge of Aboriginal life and issues was extensive. His knowledge of the fine points of criminal law was outstanding.

I knew there were problems with the justice system in the way it dealt with Aboriginal people, and with others as well. I knew there were improvements that could be made, and in accepting the appointment I thought I might be able to make things better for Aboriginal litigants and for the system itself. Little did I know the depth of the problems about which we would hear. My eyes were opened as I started to see the system through the eyes of litigants, accused persons, prisoners, people on parole, witnesses, families and at times whole communities.

I like to think that the Inquiry provided the public at large with a unique opportunity to participate in a learning experience through the regular reporting done by radio, television and the print media. Most Manitobans have never visited a reserve community, and had never had the opportunity to see Aboriginal people expressing their concerns and suggesting workable alternatives.

Among a multitude of others, we received oral and written presentations from the Departments of Justice and Family Services, the

Manitoba Human Rights Commission, the League for Human Rights of B'Nai Brith of Canada, the John Howard and the Elizabeth Fry societies and the Manitoba Action Committee on the Status of Women. We heard from over a hundred organizations that provided Aboriginal services of one sort or another and over eight hundred people spoke to us.

We visited every provincial jail and youth centre and the penitentiary at Stony Mountain. We examined their facilities and programs and discussed them with each Warden or Superintendent. We met with inmates and listened to their concerns and suggestions. While attending an Aboriginal conference in Ottawa, we visited Corrections Canada and the National Parole Board. We met with officials from the federal Departments of Indian Affairs and Justice.

Special sessions were established to hear from the police, the Bar Association, and other organizations. Elders were brought together for a special two-day meeting to hear their opinions and to receive their advice. Another special hearing was with Court Communicators. Chester Cunningham spoke to us about his twenty plus years of counselling and the diversion of native offenders in Alberta and his good working relationship with judges. We heard from clergy, probation officers, alcohol and physical and sexual abuse workers. We heard from Legal Aid Manitoba and from Ma Mawi Wi Chi Itata, the non-mandated Aboriginal child welfare agency.

In preparation for our visits to northern communities, I bought a heavy-duty parka, skidoo pants, bush boots and a short quilted jacket. I had heavy mitts and took a sleeping bag on many trips. Even though the weather was nice when we left Winnipeg, I never knew how long each trip would last, so I went prepared for any eventuality. Looking back, this greenhorn from the city must have been a strange sight and the object of some mirth to the sturdy northerners. My caution was however justified on a few occasions.

'The Spanish Fly' was our main mode of transportation. We tried to economize as much as we could and one of the real economies was to engage a private company to fly us to the northern outposts. The plane was a lumbering Twin Otter, which could land and take off on short runways. It flew 'slow and low' so we always had a good view of the frozen wilderness and the distant communities as they emerged on the horizon. The walls of the plane were unlined, probably because it was usually a cargo, rather than a passenger plane. We laughingly told one another that the plane, with its signs in Spanish, must have once seen service in the drug trade.

Baggage and recording equipment was strapped into the back of the plane and the metal seats, covered with old dried leather, folded down to accommodate us. We always travelled with the advance person who had visited the communities where we were going, the Videon community cable TV cameramen, our Director, and one of the researchers. We intentionally left our trips to the remote northern communities until the lakes were frozen, the mud solidified, and the airstrips serviceable. In one community a scraper had to clear snow from a lake to make a strip on which we could land.

God's Lake Narrows was the first isolated community I had ever visited. We landed on the deserted strip, were assured that our luggage would follow by truck, and quickly began our walk to the hotel on the edge of the lake. The lodge, as it was referred to, was an old exotic looking structure. It boasted a large living/dining room, a sizeable kitchen and a large veranda that faced the lake, and must have been lovely in the warmth of summer.

Bob Lowery, a veteran northern reporter for the *Winnipeg Free Press*, was there. He was an invaluable source of local history and information about the communities, their residents, and their problems. He was particularly helpful to me as I struggled to understand the remote communities, their people, and their problems. This was a new world to me, and Bob seemed to appreciate my situation. It was a pleasure to be present in Winnipeg in 1998 when the Aboriginal community honoured him for his contribution to the public's understanding of their issues over the years.

The Commission entourage stayed overnight at the lodge. The women stayed in the lodge, while Judge Sinclair, Tom McMahon and I shared a room in a construction trailer. The building was freezing when we arrived, but when we finally got the propane heater to work and jumped into bed, we were boiling within an hour. We eventually turned the noisy and smelly stove off, and opted for a cool rising and a cold shave in the morning. When we got to the lodge for breakfast, we were told that the women who had stayed in the lodge were warm until the fireplace went out. They then had no gas or electric heat and were shivering when we arrived.

Most of the lake looked frozen but we had to cross open water to get from the Métis side to the reserve. We were ushered into aluminum motor boats a few at a time. I settled into the front seat when John Boivin, another northern reporter, suggested I turn around and face the back of the boat. I had hardly opened my mouth to reply when he said "trust me." As our drivers crossed the choppy fast-flowing channel, the spray froze to my parka and the biting wind had me pulling up my hood to protect my face.

During the hearing on the reserve we heard of problems with the fly-in court system, the multiplicity of remands, and the slow pace of the legal process. We were told that the dockets were full and that the monthly visit by the court was not long enough to deal with every case. Criticism was levelled at the judges who flew in but rushed back to Thompson before dark. "Why don't they stay overnight at the lodge and keep the court going till it's up to date?" someone asked. "Why are they in such a rush?" said another.

At every stop in our northern journey we heard the same concern about the court system with its white judges, white prosecutors, white legal aid lawyers, white court reporter and white clerks who came and left together. We were continually reminded of their apparent lack of concern for the convenience of the people. Aboriginal people don't go to court unless they have to and no one goes just to see what is going on, apparently a city phenomenon. We were told that when they do go to court they can't understand the process and can't follow what the judge, police and lawyers are talking about.

We were told that Aboriginal tradition requires a wrongdoer to admit his fault, but how this fine principle has the unintended affect of Aboriginal people getting themselves into a lot of trouble when making statements to the police. They have no understanding of the intricacies of the criminal law, and the difference between various charges that might be laid on the same set of facts. With no one to advise them, they often admit to charges that are more serious than the circumstances warrant. They cannot understand why the legal system is so punitive and sends so many people to jail.

The second issue was the delay in Youth Court proceedings. Provincial Courts dealt with adult matters first and then with young offenders. In the meantime the youth and their parents, who had been ordered to attend, often wait all day. If youth matters cannot be dealt with before the court party leaves, they are remanded to next month's sitting. Youth matters therefore suffered the most from the early departure of the court party. The elderly lady I mentioned earlier, complained that the Youth Court was not dealing properly with the youth and their parents. Again, I do not know if this injustice has been corrected.

At the time of our visit, the Provincial Court didn't hear cases in God's River, the location of our next hearing. Its people, often young offenders and their parents, had to fly the twenty or more miles to God's Lake Narrows at a cost of $250 a person, for each court appearance. A mother told us that she and her son had to make that trip by plane five times before a plea of guilty could be entered and a reprimand imposed. Boat or skidoo travel is too dangerous as the lake is large and can be dangerous at times. One man told us his son suffered frostbite when he took him by skidoo. I am told that the Court now sits in God's River, but there are many communities where it does not sit at all.

Another strange situation was related to us in God's River. The community had taken money from its budget and had installed sewer and water lines so the residents could have those services in their homes. All the trunk lines were dug in and the system was ready to go into operation, but the community had run out of money and needed help to connect the system to the individual homes. The Department of Indian Affairs refused to help, so the system sat unused and the initiative of the community turned to disillusionment.

Problems in getting to court were not limited to the north. We heard of problems encountered by people living at the Sioux Valley reserve in southern Manitoba. If they have to attend court that means travelling to Virden or Brandon, each over thirty miles away. Not everyone has a car, and those that have one can't continually be put upon to provide transportation. Most who have to go to court rely on hitchhiking, but it is not always possible to get a ride. If an offender fails to show up, a charge of 'failing to appear' is entered. That doesn't help the individual, as they then have a criminal record, and more seriously, a record of disobeying a court order. In my experience, judges aren't even told that people appearing before them have these sorts of problems getting to court.

When we were leaving one northern community, the pilots had trouble getting the plane to start. They tried everything they could think of, including radioing mechanics in Winnipeg for advice. After an hour or more, while we stood outside in the ever-increasing cold, and trying a variety of methods to get the engines to start, they finally attached the hand crank into the cowling. It was hard to turn but when they had almost given up, the engine gave a cough, then a few sputters, and finally started to run. The second engine, inspired by this success, easily began its accompanying roar. Once both engines had run for awhile we were allowed to board and head for our next port of call. The flight to Grand Rapids across the seemingly endless waters of Lake Winnipeg at an altitude of about 500 feet, was a little nerve wracking. Even though I had confidence in the plane, I did wonder what would happen if the engines failed again.

Grand Rapids is on the west side of Lake Winnipeg where the North Saskatchewan River completes its journey from the Rocky Mountains and empties into the lake through the hydroelectric plant constructed in the 1970s. The plant is a massive structure next to the Indian Reserve and I expected to see a prosperous area with a good level of employment. We were unable to find any Aboriginal people who worked at the plant, although I understand a few do work there.

Instead of benefits, we heard only of hardships suffered by the residents when the plant was built. We were told of the flooding of the area, including the original community, church and all. We were told that logs and other debris still contaminated the water and that the former commercial fishing operations no longer existed. Former livelihoods were destroyed and the community was plagued by minor criminal conduct and was in disarray.

Many former residents had been moved to Easterville on Cedar Lake, and we were told at our meeting there of their flooded land and tangled waters and the failed attempts to establish a new commercial fishing business. We saw unused equipment and boats rotting on the shore. The community, with its old and newly transported residents, was in a state of conflict, as the formerly independent communities did not get along. Their forced unification was not appreciated and was not working.

Other communities told similar stories of the flooding caused by hydroelectric developments. At South Indian Lake, I learned in greater detail how the continual change in water levels affects the beaver houses, and the beaver population. Apparently beavers build their lodges and settle in to raise their kits. If the babies are born and the lake level rises, they drown. Some communities suffered from flooding, others from a drop in water level, but all suffered from the disruption to hunting, trapping, fishing and the despoiling of the waters.

During our visit to Norway House, the Commission staff, Videon cameramen, and some reporters, gathered at the famed Playgreen Inn for supper. As we settled into the metal folding chairs at the long collapsible tables, a waitress asked if we would like something to drink before we made our supper selection, and we each indicated our choice. I was stunned when the drinks arrived. I looked to see what my neighbours were having, then as my gaze went around the table I realized that not one of the Aboriginal people had anything alcoholic to drink, but each of the non-Aboriginal people did.

I was embarrassed to consume the beer I ordered. Since that time I have kept looking, and what I saw in Norway House has been repeated over and over again. Substantial numbers of Aboriginal people have stopped drinking. Many say they drank heavily at one time but are proud to announce the number of years it has been since their last drink. I wonder how many non-Aboriginal people practice that degree of discipline, and how many are making that sort of effort to turn their lives around.

By this time in our journey I had noticed that those coming to our meetings took off their boots at the doorway to the auditorium where meetings were held. Some entered in stocking feet, and others wore moccasins or slippers. The next day I bought some beaded slippers from an Aboriginal lady some distance from Norway House and wore them at the rest of our hearings. I was told that very few in the community still made moccasins as hides now have to be shipped to the city for tanning, and if someone wants to make slippers, they have to buy back the tanned leather. The result is that making moccasins is no longer a viable industry. I wondered why, when government is encouraging and making grants to so many businesses, there is no effort to revive this ancient skill and establish this sort of reserve-based industry.

Our meeting at Red Sucker Lake ran late, so Tom McMahon tried to contact the people who were to meet us at Ste. Theresa Point, to say we were delayed. He couldn't reach the people he wanted, so he left a message at the convent, saying we would arrive at eleven. The modern twin we had on that trip dropped us at the airport at about eleven thirty at night, and took off for Winnipeg. Absolute stillness greeted us when the sound of the aircraft faded into the star-lit night. We looked around for the trucks or skidoos we expected, but none were there. From time to time we could hear the roar of approaching skidoos, only to hear the roar fade into the distance as the skidoo went on to some unknown destination. On each occasion someone would say, "Here they come now." No one came, and we were left in utter silence.

Some of us sat on the lone baggage wagon and everyone dug into their packs and put on extra clothes. I donned my skidoo pants and was pleased to have my heavy parka that night. The ever-resourceful

Judge Sinclair suggested we should do something, so he and I left the others and started to walk along the snow-packed road that lead away from the airport. After what seemed like twenty minutes, we saw a light in the distance and headed for it. It was the Hudson's Bay store, and it was open as the manager and some of his staff were completing the year-end inventory.

After several phone calls, Judge Sinclair spoke to someone who had planned to meet us. It took some time, but eventually a number of half-ton trucks arrived and we were driven across the water-covered ice to Ste. Theresa Point where the men stayed in the priests' residence and the women in the convent. We bedded down, three or four to a room, and had a well-deserved sleep.

In the morning we went to the convent and enjoyed the hearty breakfast the nuns had prepared for us. Laurie Messer, one of the researchers who was travelling with us, told of the problem she had gaining admission to the convent the night before. If it hadn't been for a *Free Press* reporter who had arrived earlier and let her in, she might have spent the night out of doors. The nuns had received Tom's message that we would be in at eleven, but they assumed that meant eleven o'clock the next morning. They cancelled our transportation and were all in bed when Laurie arrived. After all, who in their right mind would arrive at that tranquil spot at eleven at night.

The next evening we headed for Wasagamack. The lake ice was not thick enough to support the half-ton trucks normally used in winter, but was strong enough for skidoos. We were each assigned to a machine and driver. All the skidoos revved up at the same time and took off at full throttle. It was obvious that a race was on, and we southerners were caught up in the enthusiasm of our driver trying to beat everyone else to our destination. I had no idea where we were going or how far it was, so I just held on with my arms around my driver.

As time went on, my back was in agony and my legs were cramped and exhausted. My arms felt like lead and I could only pray that we wouldn't hit a bump that would send me hurtling through the air into a tree or onto the frozen wastes. Suddenly we stopped, and I breathed a sigh of relief thinking we had arrived, but there were no lights and no signs of habitation. The reason for the stop soon became obvious. Fast-moving open water lay directly ahead, and I, along with passengers from other skidoos, was told to walk across a point of land. Our drivers made a detour of some sort and picked us up a few minutes later, and away we went again. I was now huddled down behind my driver, thankful (for the second time) for my bulky apparel. When we finally arrived, my parka was a sheet of ice, my eyebrows refused to move, and I could barely walk.

It was dark when we arrived, and pitch black when we left Wasagamack and headed back to Ste. Theresa Point. This time I faced a real dilemma as my driver was a woman, and although she invited me to put my arms around her, I was concerned about where or how I could do that without embarrassment or reproach. After some experimentation, I finally kept my feet well back on the foot rests and leaned forward. In that position I didn't even have to hold on.

The meeting in Wasagamack was as different as night and day from my light-hearted adventure. During our meeting Chief Nott told us of life in his community. He suggested the houses would be torn down if they were in Winnipeg, as they had been improperly built and had no heating, water, or sewage system. The government had not spent a cent on housing for over two years and was neglecting this most basic of needs. He said the construction of the nursing station had been mishandled and was another drain on the community resources. Indian Affairs refused to fix the leaking school roof, and required the community to spend $56,000 from its limited capital account. The community had no airstrip, and it cost $100 each way for a helicopter to the Island Lake airport during freeze-up and break-up.

As far as self-government was concerned, the Chief said it was impossible to even consider it without economic development, and he had no faith in either level of government to bring that about. He felt his community was under-funded and continually manipulated. He bemoaned the lack of education and recreation for young people. He made the point that Aboriginal people may be treated equally when compared to one another, but not when compared to white people. He spoke of continuing problems of dealing with a new language, a foreign religion and the court system. The Chief's remarks were translated to us from his native Cree. His was a damning assessment of the overall treatment of Aboriginal people, and one we were to hear echoed in every submission throughout the north.

No court services were provided in Wasagamack so people had to go to court in Garden Hill. Another presenter explained that there is no word for "guilty" in their language, and that the closest to it in Cree meant doing of some act, but it had no illegal connotation. It was a common belief that all legal matters should be dealt with by the Chief and Council. Instead, the authority of the Chief was regularly undermined by the police and by the courts. We heard that the RCMP threaten people, and take statements from youth without parents being informed. Presenters said the court system was inappropriate to their needs, as it didn't correct problems in the community; it just sentenced people and took them away. They complained that offenders do not even have an opportunity to explain their actions to the judge.

People, they said, are prosecuted for exercising rights they have had for centuries. Their fishing practices were being interrupted, and boats, nets and other equipment were being seized. A major complaint was that the Aboriginal culture was not respected. They said that children should be taught that laws are there to protect them; instead they see that the law seems destined to control them. With any meaningful jobs going to outsiders, and a 90 percent unemployment rate, their young people become dependent on welfare. These are real and serious problems for the Aboriginal residents and their leaders were asking us to something about them.

It was a glorious January morning when we waited for our plane to pick us up at Brochet, for the trip to Lac Brochet. I should have known it was going to be cold when the pilots left us in Brochet the morning before, and headed for the shelter of the Thompson airport. Early-risers drove us to the landing strip, dropped us off, and headed back to town. As the sound of the trucks faded in the distance, utter silence prevailed. No buildings offered protection from the elements, so we paced and shivered and waited for the plane, and once again I was happy with my bulky garb.

The expected time of arrival came and went and, as I recalled our earlier abandonment at Ste. Theresa Point a month earlier, a sinking feeling began to mount. We finally saw the plane on its final approach and I was inclined to shout for joy. Everyone else was calm, so I subdued my feeling of relief. No "sorry we're late" was forthcoming from the pilots, and I stoically pretended that I too knew this was the way things happen in the northern wilderness. I still couldn't help reminding myself that we were 700 miles from home.

The flight to Lac Brochet took an hour or so and as the roaring engines made conversation impossible, I gazed out the window and gradually became enthralled by what I saw. The snow was clean and endless in its expanse and its domination of the scene was complete. There were no buildings, no roads, no skidoos and no sign that anything had ever moved across the land, yet the spindly trees proclaimed their presence and ability to survive. It was stark and frightening and beautiful, all at the same time. Having seen the lonely communities from which we had come, I marvelled at the people's similarity to the landscape around them. They are alone in a bleak and seemingly unproductive wilderness, but they too cling steadfastly to what they have.

When we landed, there was only one pick-up truck to meet us and we tossed our equipment on board. The camera crew and Jeannie Daniels, the advance person on that trip, rode in the truck as it always took some time to set up the equipment and have presenters ready to begin. Judge Sinclair and I walked to the settlement.

This approach on Judge Sinclair's part was a lesson I was gradually coming to understand. In the halls of justice, judges are carefully pampered. Clerks and Sheriff's Officers see to their comfort and cater to their every whim. I was used to starting court at 10 a.m. sharp, whether the lawyers were in the courtroom or not. I found that if I did that once during a trial, thereafter the lawyers were always in court and ready to proceed at the appointed hour. That, I discovered, is not the way to act in another's community. We were the visitors, and it was the Chief and his people who had been kind enough to extend us an invitation to visit. It was the community members who were the important people during our Inquiry.

On the matter of protocol, it was at a meeting at Sagkeeng (Fort Alexander) that I again appreciated the respect to be given to a Chief. We arrived at the school auditorium where we were to hear from people from the community, and the camera crew and our own staff had the video and audio equipment ready to go. Although there were a fair number in attendance, Judge Sinclair continued visiting and speaking to people. He particularly liked to speak to young people about their interests and activities.

He didn't seem to be making the usual final arrangements to have the meeting begin. He always welcomed those in attendance, explained the purpose of the Inquiry, and our desire to hear the experiences of the people with the justice system. He would explain that this was their opportunity to make comments and suggestions as to how legal services might be improved. He hadn't begun.

I pointed out to him that it was well past the intended starting time and suggested we get under way. He didn't respond. Fifteen minutes later I repeated my comment and this time I learned why we hadn't started. "The Chief isn't here yet," he said. As usual, Judge Sinclair was not critical of my lack of understanding, nor did he explain the comment in any detail. I gradually got the message, not from what he said, but from his example and my developing experience.

At a subsequent meeting when we awaited the arrival of a Chief, I was given more of the rationale. I was told that the Chief was coming to the hearing and knew of the starting time we had proposed. The comment to me on that occasion was, "He knows we're ready. He's obviously tied up and has a good reason for not being here." When the Chief arrived, on both occasions, the hearings began. The reason for the Chiefs' tardy arrival was never mentioned nor did I again question a late start. I should have remembered my first encounter with First Nation protocol when I went to the reserve with Chief John Sioux.

Protocol again raised its head in Brandon. Our hearings were in the Agricultural Extension Centre and we were assigned a large room on the second floor. The room had a low stage and the people setting up the facilities had Judge Sinclair and me seated behind a table on the stage. One of the first presenters who came to the microphone and small table at floor level, who must have had some courtroom experience, objected to us being at a higher level than he was. Without comment, we took a short recess and had our table moved to floor level. On checking my notes in preparation for this writing I found that, long before the Brandon meeting, a presenter had thanked us for sitting at his level, instead of being elevated as in the regular courts.

Back to Lac Brochet. It is normal to find bright blue skies and an absence of cloud on the prairies. In spite of that, I can't recall another sight of such pristine purity as the one that greeted us as we trudged the mile or so from the airstrip. A light frost hung in the air and the lack of wind contributed to the eerie silence. The snow shone. It had been compacted and polished by the wind, and was like concrete.

We expected the preparations for the meeting to be well underway. To our surprise the truck had not been unloaded and people from it were standing around. They had been unable to find the place where the meeting was to be held. Judge Sinclair once again took charge, found the person responsible, and we proceeded to an old building. It wasn't very large, but we were later thankful for that. It had not been prepared for our arrival and was icy cold; however, young men soon started bringing in chairs and a couple of them started a fire in the pot-bellied stove at one end of the room.

By noon, that end of the room was warm and presenters started to arrive. We started with sandwiches and coffee for everyone and by the time we finished there were enough people on hand to start. Presenters were complimentary about certain RCMP members and less enthusiastic about others. Parents complained they had no idea what was happening in court. They and their children speak Cree or Dene, and there is no interpretation by the police when someone is being arrested, or in court. One mother complained that youth are talked into pleading guilty and that if there is not a direct threat, the inference is clear that the youth is expected to make a statement.

Shamattawa was another isolated northern community where there had been a number of killings and other disturbances in the years prior to our arrival. We were pleasantly surprised to learn that the community had changed, and was currently fairly peaceful. Much of the credit was given to the approach of the RCMP sergeant who was in charge of the detachment. He had developed the practice of picking up local youth in his ATV and giving them a ride to wherever they were going. He was also communicating with other community members on police matters, and that novel approach was appreciated. The reduction in crime was dramatic.

As we travelled, our lunches with community members were usually fairly routine. We either had soup and sandwiches or stew and bannock, all of which I enjoyed. It was nevertheless a treat to have a more varied meal and at one location (and it's better that I not divulge the location) we had salad, potatoes, a variety of vegetables, and delicious roast meat. When I asked what the meat was, I was met with an evasive answer. I was left to assume there might be some legal question as to whether the animal was in season or whether it was proper to serve it to us. Some in our group thought it was probably deer, but I thought it better not to ask any more questions.

Another meal of note included succulent dark meat. I asked Judge Sinclair what it was, and following his standard process of letting me educate myself, he said, "Can't you tell?" As I still looked puzzled he said, "Look." I looked on the serving plate and finally realized what had been so delicious. We had devoured the meat but the skeleton of a rabbit, head and all, remained on the platter.

Tadoule Lake, a Dene community west of, and on a parallel with Churchill, was our most northerly stop. Our pilots flew low, hoping to spot a herd of caribou, but none were seen. The land was bleak and barren and there were not even skidoo tracks to tell us when we were nearing civilization. Eskers formed the only break in the endless landscape. I had never heard the term 'esker' before but someone explained they are stone ridges forced up in prehistoric times. They appeared to be twenty or so feet high, although it is hard to judge from the air. If they are mini-mountain chains I could imagine them being pushed up by the pressure of competing subterranean plates when the world began. The Oxford dictionary, I now find, describes them as more mundane post-glacial gravel ridges.

At the landing strip, we were met by a sizeable delegation. The Chief honoured us by taking us from the airport into the settlement in a dogsled pulled by eight small but wiry huskies. The Chief ran all the way, cajoling, whistling at, and occasionally picking up and tossing down a dog entangled in a trace. I was amazed at the stamina of the man. He made two trips to and from town, providing each Commissioner with a private ride.

The band had not always lived at Tadoule Lake. Prior to 1956 it was located near a Hudson Bay trading post at Duck Lake, but with the fall in the price of furs, the company found it unprofitable, and shut it down. Although the band asked for financial assistance so they could remain in their homes, the Department of Indian Affairs refused. Aircraft soon arrived without notice, and every man, woman and child was transported to Churchill. Instead of having private and tranquil homes, they lived in turmoil in substandard, crowded, and hastily constructed shacks.

The sense of community was lost and, in despair, many turned to drink. Brawling, assaults, and murder became the products of the new lifestyle and the community was diminishing and deteriorating beyond belief. Community leaders asked the government to return them to their former home, but again the government refused. Requests and then demands were repeated but to no avail.

In desperation, the remaining Dene started to walk away from Churchill to establish a new community in some distant but unknown place. Only after seeing their resolve, did the government assist them to establish a new reserve at Tadoule Lake. The community remains poor but is far removed from the destructive influences it faced in Churchill. Councillor Thorassie told us, "We are beaten and down, but we are not giving up."

This remarkable story of tenacity and survival speaks to the desire of Aboriginal people to live as they have for thousands of years — to overcome the adversity of climate, slim resources and obstacles created by others. It also speaks volumes about the determination of all Aboriginal people to be proud and self-reliant. The story is significant in that it portrays another Aboriginal belief, that the white man and his world has caused great harm to their people, and that they can do better on their own.

Tadoule Lake rolled out the red carpet for us. It seemed that the people in that remote part of Canada were expressing their joy at finally being asked what their problems were, and how they could better be addressed. They had sensible suggestions as to how the legal system and its services could be improved and how the community itself could look after most of its own problems.

Our hearings at Tadoule were held in the tiny council chambers, a room no larger than a simple office. Probably few people attended council meetings, but on this occasion a room ten times the size would have been appropriate. Onlookers had to take turns waiting outside in the cold and staying in the room for a short period of time. It was only the ingenuity of Cliff Giesbrecht, the CBC cameraman, that gained him a permanent spot in the room that allowed him to get some footage to broadcast. He crouched on top of a filing cabinet in a corner of the room.

Jeannie Daniels, made an interesting discovery. She found she could understand the Dene as they spoke, although she was Navajo and born on their large reservation in Arizona. This ability to communicate gave proof to stories we had heard that the Navajo had once crossed the Bering Straits and had moved slowly south. They had obviously left some of their members behind during their migration.

Supper was a gala feast and celebration. The ladies of the community prepared the moose, caribou and other delicacies. I particularly remember the choice of out-of-the-oven apple and cherry pies. The whole community, Chief and Councillors, Elders, men, women, youth and small children, attended. I was amazed at how well behaved the children were, much better than I was, or our kids were, when out for supper. The community members could not have been more generous in the way they treated us.

Pukatawagan provided an example of a local initiative. There had been a lot of trouble and killings in the community over the years and at one time "Puk" was considered the most violent of all the Aboriginal communities in Manitoba. When Pascal Bighetty became the Chief, he required all guns to be brought to his office. If a member of the band needed a gun to go hunting, or for any other legitimate purpose, he merely had to go to the office to get his gun, but when the task was completed the gun had to be returned to the Chief's office. Serious crime and killings diminished dramatically.

At Berens River, on the east shore of Lake Winnipeg, we were treated to a lesson in Aboriginal lore and tradition. Elder and former Chief Albert Bittern, a frail and elderly gentleman, agreed to meet us in his home. His daughter welcomed us and led her father into the living room and settled him into a comfortable chair. A few reporters were permitted to listen, but they were told they could not take notes and no cameras were allowed. I am sure he wanted us to understand the history of Aboriginal people and their once superior way of life, and to be able to put that into context with some of the destructive changes that have occurred in modern times. As he didn't say we couldn't make use of the information in our studies, I feel no breach of confidence in relaying what I remember. I believe it important for my fellow white citizens to be aware of traditional teachings and to know of the thoughtful expression of concerns by Aboriginal people.

His wide-ranging recital was translated from Cree into English by his daughter who, it was obvious, was familiar with the stories and their significance. Aboriginal people have certain family members who are responsible for remembering the stories told at campfires in hunting days and, in more recent times, in the home. They are the history keepers and it is their responsibility to keep the oral history alive and to pass it on to the next generation. I assumed his daughter had that responsibility.

Chief Bittern explained the traditional place of the Chief in society. He portrayed the Chiefs before the coming of the white man as God-like figures who obtained their wisdom and their strength from the Great Spirit. They would regularly fast and go into the forest to contemplate and to renew their wisdom and moral strength. They would talk to the trees, the birds and the animals, and to the Great Spirit. Indians, he said, believe they share Mother Earth with all living things and have no dominion over any of them.

Chief Bittern explained that the Chief was the spiritual advisor and moral leader of his people and he had to set a good example for them. The powers of the old Chiefs were legendary. He gave the example of a young woman being swept into the lake in a storm, and the Chief being able to walk across the water to the island where she lay, and to carry his future bride to safety. He spoke of the raven, the mischievous "trickster" who can appear in any form, to confound humans. His was a story of life and death and of the continuing importance of his ancestors and of ancient beliefs and traditions. He clearly felt a close attachment to his God and believed in the need to remain connected to the old ways, to ensure the continuing survival of Aboriginal people.

He spoke of the changes that have occurred since the days when the whole family spent the winter on the trap line and moved with the seasons and the animals. The need for the education of the children, reflected in treaty negotiations, began the movement to centralized year-round communities. He bemoaned the present role of Chiefs, and was saddened to see them become politicians, fighting with government and ignoring their traditional responsibilities. In this philosophical vein he worried about the future of Aboriginal people. He hated to think of the destruction of their independence and to see the change in their way of life during his lifetime.

His was a tale of a wondrous history and tradition that displayed a continuing memory of a people, the depth of their religious beliefs, and their pride in the grandeur of their race. It ended on a sad note of reflection on the near destruction of the Aboriginal people as individuals, and of their principles and traditions. Their tenuous future on their native soil was ever on his mind, but in spite of that, he remained optimistic about the ability of his people to survive the present crisis. He said that his ancestors had forecast bad times, but at the same time, the eventual survival and prosperity of his people had also been assured.

His message confirmed what I was later to observe. Aboriginal people are tenacious and hold to their principles, in spite of tremendous opposition. They seem to have a unified will to survive and to do what is fair and right. If a treaty takes 20 years to negotiate, Aboriginal people will persist for that length of time, and will maintain their resolve. Their patience and persistence is not seen in the broader society that is anxious to devise immediate solutions to current problems. Aboriginal people and their Chiefs will wait, not always patiently, until their rightful place in Canada, and their rightful sharing of its resources is recognized. I certainly learned and benefited from the old Chief's experience and knowledge.

Our hearings in Winnipeg brought out the wrath of Aboriginal city residents as they described their personal experiences with police brutality, the courts' indifference and the oppression of bigotry and discrimination they encounter on a daily basis. Many discussed the problems facing people moving to the city. A Métis leader said, "Dreams become nightmares when they come to the city for a better way of life." A former non-Aboriginal director of the Main Street Project that cares for inebriated street people on a short-term basis, made the unpleasant but astute comment, "Where people have had evil done to them, they do evil to others." The concerns were overwhelming. They varied from stories of alienation to ones of sorrow, poverty and abuse.

We heard a great deal about stereotyping. A Winnipeg native told us that he drove a large car. If he was in blue jeans and an old sweater, the police regularly stopped him, questioned why he was driving such a big car, and how he could afford it. He wasn't allowed to go on his way until he proved he owned the car. On the other hand, he said that if he was wearing a suit and tie, and driving the same car, he was never stopped or questioned.

A young Aboriginal man told of being arrested and taken to the police station, for running down a city street. He explained to the police that he was late, and was running to meet his girlfriend, but he was not believed. He asked us to consider whether, if he had been white, he would have been apprehended.

A number of Aboriginal women told of being harassed by police officers. We heard several stories of Aboriginal men being beaten during their arrest, although they offered no resistance. Others, who had observed similar incidents, verified this sort of conduct by the police. There were too many examples from credible people who did not even know one another, to think the complaints were anything but legitimate. They made me wonder what would cause such conduct, and I could find no reason other than outright racism.

The whole justice system, whether it was the police, jailers, parole officials, lawyers, or the courts, was severely criticized. Probably the most severe criticism was the statement of a man who had been through the system more than once. He prefaced his remarks by saying that the justice system and the courts should be respected and not feared but then added, "The system shows more respect for a pit bull terrier."

To say there was bitterness toward the whole system would be a gross understatement. It was not only Aboriginal people who spoke out. One provincial employee, while commenting on the fact that most of the youth in the youth jails had been in some sort of care before going there, said the legal system and law enforcement "is in a pathetic state." One of the calmer but equally severe comments came from a Mennonite minister, who said, "Something is very wrong with the system."

Aboriginal people discussed their poverty and their marginal quality of life and many said they felt like outcasts in Canadian society.

Socio-economic causes of crime were discussed, as was the de-humanizing effect of racism. The same was said of unemployment. Aboriginal people want to work, but the opportunity is regularly and repeatedly denied to them.

As with our northern hearings, women in the cities demanded an attack on the prevalence of sexual abuse. They told us that those who complain are further victimized, if not by the justice system, then by abusers who have not changed their ways. We were told that alcoholism, often a symptom of cultural shock, needs further and continuing attention. Many spoke of seeing kids struggling with drugs, pregnancy, and selling their bodies. With limited resources and inadequate authority to respond, the Aboriginal population stands helplessly by.

The lengthy delay in getting to trial was a common complaint in the cities, as it had been in northern communities. The lesser availability of bail for Aboriginal people was seen as discrimination on the part of judges, and the inappropriate conditions of bail and parole were seen as a lack of understanding of the realities of Aboriginal communities, and as a further example of bias.

We were impressed with the presentation of Ken Filkow, Chairman of the Manitoba Human Rights Commission, and his advice that it is perfectly legal to take surveys of numbers of Aboriginal people in specific areas of employment as long as the purpose is to help establish proactive employment programs. Max Yalden, the Director of the Canadian Human Rights Commission, while discussing prejudice and problems encountered by Aboriginal people said, "Stereotyping is a substitute for thinking." He suggested that Canada over-uses jails, as it hasn't given thought to how else to deal with problems. He said the easy answer too often is to "keep people out of society for awhile."

It was not only Aboriginal people who were critical of the justice system or who thought changes should be made. We set a day aside to hear from lawyers, and others appeared on their own from time to time. We heard from several members of the Attorney General's Department who made a joint presentation, and from Legal Aid Manitoba, and we heard from lawyers throughout the province. Some of their comments and suggestions were:

> Use local magistrates who understand the accused and the community.
> Mediate the less serious criminal charges.

Police should release more people on a promise to appear.

Omit sureties for Aboriginal bail.

Stop transferring accused from one place to another.

Establish remand and custody facilities in the north.

Make sure native people understand court-related matters.
Provide translators.

Summary offences should be dealt with less formally.

Limit the preliminary inquiry to witnesses whose credibility
would be in dispute at trial.

Conduct preliminaries like a civil Examination for Discovery.

Eliminate the delay in providing particulars of a charge.

The Crown should make disclosure to the defence on the first
court appearance.

The RCMP should disclose their case early on.

Educate law students, lawyers and judges about Aboriginal
culture.

Use jails less. They are only for the poor.

General deterrence does not work and should not be a factor in
sentencing.

Have community committees advise judges on sentences.

Dedicate resources to rehabilitating people.

The Crown should not be entitled to stand-aside jurors.

Aboriginal people are underrepresented on jury panels.

Police have too much influence in parole decisions.

Develop some sort of separate Aboriginal justice system.

A lawyer who had practiced in the courts in northern Manitoba for twenty years at the time, gave us the benefit of his insight and described how he saw the legal system providing services to Aboriginal communities. He acknowledged that the residents do not trust the white authorities who fly in on the same aircraft and fly out together at the end of their working day. Some of the problems he encountered as a defence counsel were:

People do not understand the court system.

Communicating with them is difficult.

Court facilities are poor.

There is not enough time to interview clients.

Spousal abuse is a problem.

Even if court orders are obtained they cannot be enforced.

The main problem is poverty and unemployment.
The cost of access to the courts is excessive.
Only criminal courts go to the people.
Too many people are sent to jail.
Lawyers can't interview young offenders as they are flown to Winnipeg.
Apply diversion systems to young offenders.
Sentences for Aboriginal people may not be more severe but the effect may be.
Try having community committees deal with criminal matters.
Use more restitution and work programs.

This lawyer did say it is hard to be objective about the justice system. I am sure that applies to everyone in the system. We like to think our system is pretty good, or that some small adjustments will cure any problems that do exist. It is hard to come to the conclusion that drastic changes are required, whether in the remote north or in the cities. In The Pas, lawyers told us they are able to get early trial dates and have a good working relationship with the Crown, yet one lawyer wondered why a preliminary inquiry is necessary now that disclosure is so common. The Pas is of course served by the Court of Queen's Bench every month and has a resident Provincial Judge.

I have spent some time on the comments of lawyers as I have the impression that some, including government administrators and judges, felt that Judge Sinclair and I just pulled our concerns and suggestions out of a hat. Some obviously considered our recommendations to be unrealistic and many thought we exaggerated the mess the system is in. I don't believe we did. I believe these comments from others working in the system support the concerns expressed by Aboriginal people, and support the conclusions of the AJI report.

What a contrast we saw when Judge Sinclair and I visited reservations in the United States. Our first trip took us to Reno, where we spent two days sitting in on educational courses for Tribal Court personnel. Registrars were learning how to keep court records, how to issue court processes, how to empanel a jury and generally how to run a court system. We heard tribal judges and non-aboriginal legal experts instructing them on the intricacies of the criminal and civil law. There were Aboriginal court employees present from all the western states.

That trip also took us to the University of Washington in Seattle, where Professor Ralph Johnson kindly shared his vast knowledge of the United States Tribal Court systems, their laws, and the extent of their jurisdiction, with us. We then visited the Northwest Intertribal Court System at Edmonds, Washington and discussed the details of its circuit court system with its long-serving Chief Judge, Elbridge Coochise. We learned of how their circuit-type Tribal Court was established and how it operates.

Our second U.S. trip took us to a number of reservations in Arizona where we made further inquiries about their system. While Judge Sinclair examined the administration and operation of the Navajo Court System, and met with some academics, I visited other Tribal Courts and talked to their judges, lawyers and administrators. I visited the Hopi, Gila and Salt River Reservations. Each had its own police, jails and Indian judges. Most had a separate Youth Court, usually referred to as 'Children's Court,' with separate judges. Each court applied the civil and criminal laws passed in its community. I was told of the public relations work required of the judges, to maintain the support of the Tribal Council and community residents.

Judge Sinclair and I met up and visited the Court at Chinle together. We met with Judge Wayne Cadman of a Navajo District Court, and spoke with the three Peacemakers that were attached to his court. We heard how cases were referred to them and usually resolved without any other proceedings being required. We were told that Tribal Courts handle 90% of all the crime in their communities, even though their jurisdiction is limited.

We were so impressed with the efficiency and acceptance of these court systems by Aboriginal communities that we sponsored a meeting of Tribal Court Judges in Winnipeg. We wanted to let people from the Department of Justice and members of the bar and the judiciary, have an opportunity to learn about the American system. Six American judges, Professor Johnson from Washington State and several Tribal lawyers and administrators attended. We were disappointed, and I was personally embarrassed, by the lack of interest and poor turnout. With a few exceptions, most of those we had expected, never came.

It is still a mystery to me why local people and the federal and provincial governments don't see, or don't want to see, the substantial advantages and benefits Aboriginal people in the United States have enjoyed by having their own justice systems for thirty or forty years. Is there an arrogance that prevents Canadians from looking abroad for better ways of doing things? Is there a belief that our system is perfect? I am at a loss to understand the apathy and resistance to change.

The Inquiry lasted for three and a half years. It enabled me to meet Aboriginal people in their own communities, to see the conditions in which they lived, and to observe their problems. The lack of adequate housing, limited health services and the massive unemployment, on and off reserves, was obvious. I was shocked by the manner in which court services were delivered to them, the limitations placed on their basic rights, and most importantly, the lack of local involvement in the justice system. It took quite a while to appreciate that Aboriginal people were trapped in a justice system they did not understand, did not want, and that dealt with them in an inappropriate manner.

Volume two of the Aboriginal Justice Inquiry Report deals with the deaths of Helen Betty Osborne and J.J. Harper. Our counsel for both cases were Perry Schulman Q.C. (now Mr. Justice Schulman) and Randy McNicol Q.C. We conducted formal court-like hearings into these cases when the community hearings were almost completed. In the meantime, our legal counsel and the investigator they engaged, had been lining up witnesses. We took no part in these preparations, other than to ask that the four suspects in the Osborne case be called to testify, if they were willing to speak to us.

Betty Osborne was a nineteen-year-old Cree from Norway House who was boarding and attending Collegiate in The Pas. During the early hours of November 13, 1971, when walking home from visiting with friends, she was dragged into a car containing four men, and was driven out of town. The next day, her mutilated body was found in the bush and the snow near a pump house on the shores of Clearwater Lake, not far from the all-Aboriginal Guy Hill Residential School she had once attended.

It took several months for the police to identify the suspects, Lee Colgan, Wayne Archie Johnston, James Houghton and Norman Manger, and it was sixteen years before Johnston and Houghton were charged with murder. An early error on the part of the RCMP contributed to the delay. On the day after the murder, a taxi driver told the police he had followed a car on the highway near the scene of the murder at about 4:00 a.m. His description was incomplete, but by mid-December, under the hypnosis suggested by members of the investigation team, he correctly identified the numbers on the licence plate. Inquiries at the provincial motor vehicle office left no doubt that the vehicle was the Colgan family car.

The RCMP still did not seize the car. When the question of bringing the car in for examination arose, an officer from the town detachment said he had checked it, so it was not searched. It turned out that he had only glanced into the back seat and that may even have been before the murder. No thorough examination of the car and its contents was made for six or seven months. Mr. Colgan Sr. was well known in The Pas and the police seemed to have assumed that as he was a respected citizen, his vehicle could not possibly have been involved. An earlier search of the car would have unearthed the same bloodstains and the piece of brazier strap that were later discovered, but it might have unearthed other evidence as well. In any event, the police would have been able to identify the suspects earlier in their investigation.

Another police mistake was allowing Manger to slip through their fingers after he had consented to take a polygraph (lie detector test) in Regina. A friend of the suspects got him out of the beer parlour where the police were watching him, and took him to the suspects' lawyer. The lawyer threatened the police with harassment proceedings for persisting in their attempts to talk to his clients. Our report was critical of the lawyer for acting for all four suspects, when the degree of their involvement obviously differed. The lie detector test might have been of no help, but it might have provided some leads. It would at least have established who was in the car and whether Manger was telling the truth about being drunk and unable to remember what happened.

The police investigation was intense for a while, but gradually fell dormant as attempts to interview the suspects were thwarted by their friends and lawyer. Although the file was reviewed from time to time, no real progress was made until Constable Urbanowski was assigned to the case on a full time basis in 1984. He did a meticulous review of the file and statements that had been made at the time. The RCMP advertised and asked anyone with information about the killing to contact them. Several people came forward and told of conversations they had heard years before. One woman told of being at a party when she was fourteen and hearing Johnston brag about having repeatedly stabbed "her," although no name was mentioned. He said it felt great to kill someone. The girl had been immediately threatened and warned not to say anything about what she had heard.

Colgan was arrested following Urbanowski's review. Shortly thereafter his then lawyer, Donald MacIver (the earlier lawyer having died,) approached the Crown and discussions began about Colgan giving evidence in return for immunity from prosecution. An immunity agreement was signed and Colgan provided a statement. If the first lawyer had declined to act for all the suspects in the first place, and if Colgan had had his own lawyer sooner, this decision on Colgan's part might have been made sixteen years earlier.

Lee Colgan testified at the trial and again before us. He told us that Houghton was driving when Betty was dragged into his father's car and that she resisted them, their advances and suggestions. He said that Houghton drove to his parents' cottage and then on to the pump house. Colgan said he remained in the car while Johnston and Betty were outside, that he heard banging noises on the back of the car, but did not get out to investigate. He saw Johnston come back to the car for a screwdriver and said that at some point, Houghton got out of the car but couldn't see what he was doing. Johnson and Houghton finally got back into the car and reported that the girl was dead. Marks in the snow led the police to believe that two people had been involved in dragging the body into the bush. Although the witness that had come forward hadn't heard the name of the person Johnston said he killed, the evidence of Colgan made the connection.

Without Colgan's evidence it is unlikely that charges would ever have been laid, and to obtain his evidence, the Crown had no choice but to agree to his immunity from prosecution. The Crown does that in rare cases where the evidence of one person is essential to convict another of a serious crime. It is impossible to say whether Colgan breached his undertaking to tell the truth. He did testify, and there is no way of proving that he lied. We didn't think he told us everything he knew, but there is no way of proving that either. There would also never have been a trial if it had not been for the persistence and dedication of the RCMP, and I can't remember a case where the police expended so much effort over such a long period of time.

One of my lingering concerns about the case is the system that permitted the empanelling of a totally non-Aboriginal jury. I am not criticizing the judge or the lawyers, as it is the Criminal Code that prescribes the selection procedure. This case was but one example of how easy it is for lawyers to control the composition of juries, or at least to eliminate Aboriginal people from them.

The Sheriff assembles a large panel of potential jurors at the beginning of each criminal assize. The names of those on the panel are written on cards and placed in a box and when a name is drawn, the person goes to the front of the courtroom and faces the accused and counsel. Each lawyer has the right to exclude twelve prospective jurors by exercising 'peremptory challenges,' that is, they may challenge a juror without giving any reason. The prosecuting lawyer at the time of the Osborne trial could only challenge four jurors peremptorily but had the right to achieve the same result by 'standing aside' forty-eight potential jurors the first time their names were called. If a panel is exhausted and the jurors who have been stood aside are called again, they cannot be stood aside a second time.

At the trial, either the Crown prosecutor or one of the defence counsel, rejected all the Aboriginal people who were called forward. The result was a jury composed totally of non-Aboriginal people. When I say Aboriginal people were rejected, it is more accurate to say that people who appeared to be Aboriginal were rejected, as it was only their place of residence and appearance that identified them as Aboriginal.

The Criminal Code has been amended since the Osborne case. Now a Crown Attorney has no right to stand aside any jurors and the Crown and the defence have equal numbers of peremptory challenges, and any number of jurors can still be challenged for cause. The change is a good step but still does not address the problem of the peremptory challenges, which in effect permit people to be excluded because of the colour of their skin. It is an insult to Aboriginal people to assume they will not discharge their responsibilities as jurors according to law. There should be no assumption that any prospective juror "is not indifferent between Her Majesty the Queen and the accused." If counsel are concerned about the independence of a potential juror, they should question the person before they are sworn-in as a juror and challenge them for cause if they wish.

I don't know who challenged whom in this case, but it is not uncommon for defence counsel to try to keep Aboriginal people off a jury if their client is white and the victim is Aboriginal, or for the Crown to do so if the accused is Aboriginal. Each wants to have jurors they think will favour their position. Those tactics should not be sanctioned by the criminal law of Canada. All that counsel or an accused should be entitled to, is a jury of twelve fair-minded people who will listen to the evidence, receive instruction on the law from the judge, and bring in an appropriate verdict. According to provincial law every citizen has the right to sit on a jury and that right should not be lessened because a citizen is Aboriginal.

As I said, I am not critical of the lawyers for playing according to the rules as they are written. The Crown attorneys have an obligation to try to obtain a conviction of someone they believe to be guilty, and defence counsel have a duty to their clients to provide the best possible defence. That does not mean that Parliament cannot amend the Criminal Code if it is not working, or if it is interfering with principles of fundamental justice. Further changes should be made as the present law permits overt discrimination and is an example of systemic discrimination as well.

In my opinion, lawyers — whether they act on behalf of the Crown or for an accused — should have only one ground of challenge, a challenge for cause. If, after questioning, no bias is perceived by the presiding judge, the person should be admitted to the jury. I suggest that a judge should make the decision, rather than having the last two jurors do it. The use of two jurors as 'triers' and deciders of this issue is archaic, and of no practical advantage. When compared to the many serious issues trial judges are called upon to decide during a jury trial, ruling on challenges for cause is not a difficult task. The judge knows the principles of law to be applied and would not have to explain them to each set of lay jurors who now have to decide whether another is likely to be biased.

The Inquiry examined whether people in The Pas withheld valuable information from the police. The four suspects had a pact that none of them would say anything and their close friends apparently knew something and they also kept quiet. A few, like the woman I mentioned, were frightened into silence. Some statements Colgan made to a storekeeper implicated him to a degree, and the merchant should have spoken to the police, but he intentionally refrained from doing so. Colgan also made a confession of being at the scene of the murder to the Sheriff, and that was not immediately passed on to the police. The problem with these statements is that while they might have proved Colgan was in the car, they still would not have proved who committed the murder.

We found that there had *not* been a broad 'conspiracy of silence' among the residents of The Pas. Some people may have heard rumours about who was responsible but they had no proof to offer and, the police had heard the same rumours. Even if the rumours had included the names of those who were in the car, that would still not have helped the police determine who had done the killing.

At the trial, Johnston was convicted of murder and Houghton was found not guilty. In the AJI report we recommended that, even though he had been acquitted of murder, Houghton should still be charged with other offences like abduction, being a party to assault, and possibly as an accessory after the fact to murder. The Crown has now examined that possibility on at least three occasions and has concluded that a conviction would be unlikely, as the only evidence implicating Houghton would be that of the less than credible Colgan.

When Houghton was called as a witness before us, it was abundantly clear that he knew much more than he was telling. He admitted (unintentionally and reluctantly) that his conduct was inconsistent with that of a person who has nothing to hide. He admitted that he would normally make inquiries if he heard people were saying untrue things about him, was aware of rumours involving him in this killing, but made no inquiries. His evidence did not ring true, but it was still not evidence of guilt, and would not have supported a conviction. The only evidence that implicated him was that of Colgan and that evidence was incomplete, as Colgan said he never saw Houghton even touch Helen Betty Osborne.

All I can suggest at this time is that in the future all indictments against accused people include all the offences that naturally arise from the circumstances. It should be left to a judge and jury to decide what the verdict should be. If the options of the jury in this case had been broader than the all-or-nothing choice they had, it is possible that Houghton might have been convicted of a lesser offence. In saying that, I am mindful that it is a difficult choice for a Crown Attorney to make. The Crown hopes for a conviction on the most serious charge and is concerned it may not get that conviction if lesser charges are left to the jury as options. When I was a defence counsel, I certainly preferred to defend a major offence where the jury had a limited choice - guilty or not guilty of murder. My experience of sitting with juries nevertheless made me a firm believer that they almost always bring in the correct verdict, and can be trusted to do just that.

Another part of the case that caused concern was the insensitive manner in which the RCMP treated Aboriginal friends of the deceased. They were dragged down to the detachment office and vigorously questioned. Some had to identify the badly marred body. Others were shown a horrendous photograph of her body. One friend was driven to a lonely country spot and threatened. All this took place although the police had come to the conclusion that an Aboriginal person would not have committed such a violent crime. Some had concluded that the killer was demented. Racism, it appears, played a significant part in the actions of some officers. The only alternative conclusion would be that all their investigations were conducted in an insensitive and improper manner.

The final area on which I will comment is the racism that was rampant in The Pas at the time of the murder. There was little communication between Aboriginal people that lived on the north side of the Saskatchewan River and white people that lived in town. Beer parlours were rowdy places and fights and arguments broke out or were provoked by someone on a regular basis. Aboriginal people had to sit on one side the movie theatre, while the whites sat on the other. There was no communication and little interaction between the two cultures and they had little in common. I used to think there was at least a grudging respect between the two societies, but I doubt even that was accurate.

At the time of our hearings, tension was extreme and I hoped that the investigation of the tragedy would help to clear the air. I was told of subsequent efforts by the Chamber of Commerce and the First Nation to improve communication but my more current information is that while relations may have improved somewhat, feelings of distrust and lack of meaningful dialogue persist. There must have been some improvement, however, as the Aboriginal and non-Aboriginal electors in The Pas chose former Chief Oscar Lathlin as their representative in the Manitoba Legislature.

In spite of any improvements there may have been, it is important to remember that Helen Betty Osborne was stabbed with a screwdriver fifty-two times and was killed because she was Aboriginal, and would not have been if she had been white.

In hearing evidence on the Harper death, as in the Osborne case, we had to be careful not to specifically make findings of guilt or of civil or criminal responsibility. That limitation on the power of Inquiry Commissioners had recently been proclaimed by the Supreme Court of Canada in the *Susan Nelles and The Toronto Hospital for Sick Children Inquiry*. Our language may therefore have appeared to lack the precision of a court decision or judgement, but we reported the facts as we found them.

After spending the evening visiting and drinking with friends, J.J. Harper left the Westwood Inn about 2:00 a.m. and walked toward his home. At 2:38 on March 9, 1988 he died when a bullet from City of Winnipeg Constable Cross' revolver, hit him in the chest. There were no witnesses. Constable Cross told us he had tried to stop Harper to question him and grabbed hold of him and turned him around. He said that Harper resisted and pushed him, that he held on to Harper and both fell to the ground.

Cross denied having his gun drawn when he approached Harper. This statement (I can now say) was suspicious to say the least, and became even more suspect due to the manner in which the police investigated the matter and gave their evidence to the Inquiry. What followed reminded me of *'me thinks thou dost protest too much.'*

Three police cars and six officers had been in the area following a stolen car. When the suspects abandoned the car, Cross chased and caught the juvenile 'Allan,' while other officers chased and caught Pruden, the driver. Cst. Eakin had seen a man walking along the street (who was likely Harper) but paid no attention to him as he was obviously not the car thief. The arrest of Pruden was immediately broadcast, and Cross heard the announcement while he was in his patrol car. It was while Cross was walking or running to join the other officers, and to see Pruden, that he came upon J.J. Harper walking along the sidewalk. Two more officers had joined the others by that time and they all heard the sound of the shot that ended Harper's life.

It was clear that Cross had no right to demand Harper's identification or to stop him from continuing on his way. Cross admitted that he was not intending to apprehend him, and that he had no reasonable grounds to do so. It was impossible to tell exactly what happened after Cst. Cross grabbed Harper, but whatever the details were, the death followed Cross' illegal act. Harper did nothing wrong in the way he responded to the officer's demands, and he was perfectly entitled to keep walking.

Cst. Cross told us that his gun was out of its holster, that he had hold of the butt of the gun with his finger on the trigger, and that Harper had hold of the barrel when the gun accidentally discharged. At that point there were clearly a number of unanswered questions police officers routinely explore, such as why a person who never intended to shoot, would have his finger on the trigger. Because of the way in which the investigation was conducted it was impossible to confirm or to refute significant parts of Cross' statement.

The police investigation, if you can call it that, was sloppy and unprofessional. Instead of an independent investigation to determine what had happened, the police actions and statements were directed to protecting a fellow officer. Things that would have routinely been done following a death in a struggle over a gun were not done. The revolver was improperly handled. An investigating officer took charge of the gun, but put it in his own holster, and then put it on the seat of his car. He took no steps to keep it from being handled by others. No fingerprints were taken from the butt of the revolver, or from its barrel, that might have reinforced or questioned Cross' version of events. The officer who would normally have done the fingerprinting was specifically told not to do it. Blood on clothing was not analyzed, and what may have been powder burns, were not examined.

A statement was not independently taken from Cst. Cross. A lengthy statement was eventually given by him but with the assistance of other officers. There was unconfirmed evidence that a senior officer at the scene had told Cross what to say and what not to say. Cross was treated as faultless, and everything was done to maintain that position. No reference was made to the comment made by Cross to Constables Smyth and Hooper that "he went for my gun and I shot him."

The conduct of some of the officers who were at the scene cast doubt on the investigation. Some improperly consulted with one another before they completed their notes and reports. One completely re-wrote his notebook and gave false evidence at the inquest. He was told to change some things he had in his earlier notes that a senior officer didn't like. He gave us the ridiculous explanation that he couldn't remember the name of the officer. The same absence of mind plagued the memory of other officers, who acted on instructions from above.

Some officers clearly lied. The most obvious lie was that no officer had his gun drawn during the search for Pruden. Two totally independent witnesses, and Allan, who we believed on the point, clearly established that was not the case. One witness, when driving by, had seen an officer with a gun drawn. Another, who had reported the event to the police, but had never been contacted again, came forward during our Inquiry. He was a very credible witness, and said that when he was stopped at a stop sign, he clearly saw an officer looking up and down the street with a revolver in his hand. It seemed that other officers didn't want to leave open the possibility that Cross had his gun drawn when approaching Harper. It is hard to find any other rationale for these false statements. I would not have thought it unreasonable if the officers had their guns drawn, so one has to wonder why they lied.

The police and their union were defensive and uncooperative and resisted our efforts to get to the truth of what happened. They went to court on several occasions to block the Inquiry and the evidence our counsel wished to examine. A wall of silence surrounded the police.

The worst example of the defensive and obstructionist attitude of the police was the hastily done report of the Firearms Board of Inquiry. It concluded that there was no negligence on the part of Constable Cross and that it was an assault of Cross by Harper that started the situation.

The Chief of Police released a statement to the media the day after the death, which misstated several crucial facts. Among other things it said; "a lone police officer was searching the area for the second suspect when (he) observed Harper." The search was over, and there was a lot more than one officer searching for the suspect. The media release also said: "In the opinion of this officer Harper matched the general description of the second male." He did not. The only similarity was that both were Aboriginal. The Chief of Police said he concurred in the Board's findings. No reason was given as to why Cross would stop Harper, when the chase had ended and the car thief had been caught, but of course the Chief of Police might not have known that detail at the time.

In the Harper part of our report we recommended cross-cultural training, increasing the Aboriginal presence on the force and the application of psychological testing to weed out job applicants with racial or other inappropriate attitudes. Chiefs Dale Henry and David Cassels applied stricter expectations on police officers. Relations with the Aboriginal community improved and I hope there has been an improvement in the manner in which Aboriginal witnesses and suspects are treated.

Another of our recommendations was that all statements taken from suspects be video-taped. The movement in that direction has been slow to evolve but I understand that some statements are now being taped, but I still have a concern as I understand that the preliminary conversations between the police and the suspects are not being taped. That will continue to cause suspicion about how a confession is taken. The police, to ensure their own integrity and the integrity of the system, should be taping all their discussions in cases where serious harm or a death is involved.

As in the Osborne case, racism was the dominant factor in J.J. Harper's death. His misfortune was being on the sidewalk when Cross came running by. His second misfortune, in light of what transpired, was being Aboriginal. If he had not been Aboriginal he would not have been stopped, and if he had not insisted on his right not to speak to the officer but to continue on his way, he would not have been grabbed and his death would not have occurred.

The Helen Betty Osborne and John Joseph Harper incidents brought the terrible consequences of racism to public attention. While our report may not have produced solutions, I believe that holding the facts and horrendous results up to public scrutiny was of value. While Canadians do not like to admit it, racism exists in Canada. Its insidious nature is directed at those who appear 'different from us.' A first step in reversing racist attitudes, and their bedfellow stereotyping, is to admit they exist in the form of discrimination. The next and more difficult step is to take positive measures to eliminate them.

The AJI report made over 150 recommendations. Almost none of them have been acted upon. There is either an inability to understand the need for improvements or the same century-long governmental inertia. The result is clear; Aboriginal people continue to suffer at the hands of an inappropriate justice system. The Doer government in Manitoba has established a study to see what recommendations might be implemented and it has laid the groundwork to improve Child Welfare services. The federal Department of Justice remains silent.

3

Sovereignty

W hile playing golf, chatting with an acquaintance over lunch or flying on an aircraft, I am sometimes asked: "What are you doing these days?" If I say that I spend most of my time on Aboriginal matters, I am, more often than not, confronted with what seem to be pent-up emotions. "Why should Aboriginal people have rights other Canadians don't have?" they ask. If I suggest that they have special rights and need the authority of self-government, I am challenged about creating a 'third order of government.'

I will usually say that Aboriginal people require different approaches to deal with their particular problems and needs. "But why are they different, aren't we all Canadians?" the questioner demands. I am soon entangled in explanations that only address part of the question and don't satisfy their concerns. Canadians are generally sympathetic to the plight of their indigenous people but most don't understand the basis for their claims or the reasons for their special needs.

From the standpoint of the questioner, the questions are quite legitimate. To find the answers and to try to discover what is holding most Aboriginal people back, in the efforts they are making to improve their lives and opportunities, it is necessary to examine their history and the manner in which they have been treated over the last few hundred years. To find some of the answers it is necessary to go back in history to examine the rights Aboriginal people once had and to see whether they have been lost or taken from them, and to see what rights remain.

By the time the wave of settlers arrived on the eastern seaboard of what is now the United States of America, the rights of indigenous people were better recognized than during the destructive days of Columbus and Cortez. British law recognized the Aboriginal peoples' right to occupy the land, although the extent of their ownership of it was uncertain. That is understandable, as the extent of the Aboriginal occupancy of the land was not yet known.

The British proceeded on the basis that if settlers occupied portions of land without objection from the Aboriginal people, they were entitled to claim ownership of them. A clear distinction was however drawn with respect to the land obviously occupied by Aboriginal people as their settlements and hunting grounds. The right of the Aboriginal people to use and occupy those lands was unquestioned, and settlers' attempts to purchase them, was a tacit recognition of Aboriginal title.

The Dutch, the English and the French entered into treaties with the Indians. Just the fact that treaties were employed recognized the special place and the special rights of the indigenous people. Governments would not have negotiated treaties, if they had not accepted the fact that they were dealing with an independent sovereign state, and a people that owned the land. A treaty is not just an agreement between two parties, but is a formal document reserved for extraordinary agreements. It is an inter-governmental or inter-nation agreement, signed by two or more nations.

The year 1763 is an important date. The questionable land acquisition practices of early settlers caused the British government and King George III to intervene. The King put a stop to the private purchase of Aboriginal land by issuing the Royal Proclamation of 1763 in which he gave directions to the colonists, and to their Governors, as to the only manner in which Aboriginal lands could be acquired. In effect, that document recognized the continuing right of Aboriginal people to the lands they occupied and it recognized their sovereignty. If there was any doubt about Spanish and other European rights, this document certainly put an end to the doubt.

The Royal Proclamation of 1763 provided in part:

And Whereas it is just and reasonable, and essential to our Interest, and the Security of our Colonies, that the several Nations or Tribes of Indians with whom We are connected, and who live under our Protection, should not be molested or disturbed in the Possession of such Parts of our Dominions and Territories as, not having been ceded to or purchased by Us, are reserved to them, or any of them, as their Hunting Grounds.

And We do hereby strictly forbid, on Pain of our Displeasure, all our loving Subjects from making any Purchases or Settlements whatever, or taking Possession of any of the Lands above reserved, without our especial leave and Licence for the Purpose first obtained.

We do, with the advice of our Privy Council strictly enjoin and require, that no private Person do presume to make any Purchase from the said Indians of any Lands reserved to the said Indians, within those parts of our Colonies where, We have thought proper to allow Settlement; but that, if at any Time any of the said Indians should be inclined to dispose of the said Lands, the same shall be Purchased only for Us, in our Name, at some public Meeting or Assembly of the said Indians...

The Proclamation therefore recognized the existing right of the Aboriginal people to the land, part of which later became Canada, and prescribed the only manner in which title could be transferred from them. It is clear that there was to be no interference with the Aboriginal way of life, their political organization, or their ability to manage their own affairs as they saw fit. The newcomers could only acquire land if the Aboriginal people chose to sell it to the government following negotiations.

The Royal Proclamation's validity has been reinforced in recent times by its recognition as part of Canada's Constitution Act, 1982. It is referred to in Section 25(a) of the Canadian Charter of Rights and Freedoms.

25. Aboriginal Rights and Freedoms not Affected by Charter — The guarantee in this Charter of certain rights and freedoms shall not be construed so as to abrogate or derogate from any Aboriginal treaty or other rights or freedoms that pertain to the Aboriginal peoples of Canada including

    (a) Any rights or freedoms that have been recognized by the Royal Proclamation of October 7, 1763: and

    (b) Any rights or freedoms that now exist by way of land claims agreements or may be so acquired.

Section 35 in Part II of the Constitution deals further with the recognition of the special place of Aboriginal people in Canada. It provides:

35. (1) The existing Aboriginal and treaty rights of the Aboriginal peoples of Canada are hereby recognized and affirmed.

    (2) In this Act, "Aboriginal peoples of Canada" includes the Indian, Inuit and Métis peoples of Canada.

The Royal Proclamation still plays an important part in treaty discussions that are ongoing in various parts of Canada. The demands of government that Aboriginal peoples give up their existing Aboriginal rights to receive new Treaty benefits are seen as contrary to the approach dictated by the Royal Proclamation and are strenuously opposed. Aboriginal people have not forgotten that they have sovereignty and they want it recognized and reflected in new treaties.

The only point on which I would take issue with the decisions of the Supreme Court of Canada at this point, is that Aboriginal people should not have to prove the extent of their territory, their trading practices and their lifestyle. In my view, it should be assumed that Aboriginal people had all the characteristics of an organized society and a first claim on the land. The onus should be upon the subsequently established governments to show that those attributes do not extend to the lands claimed by them, and to prove any limitation they can on the extent of Aboriginal sovereignty.

The question of sovereignty is particularly important when it comes to considering the situation in British Columbia, Labrador and the Maritime Provinces, where there has never been a comprehensive treaty that has removed the ownership rights of Aboriginal people. There are also Aboriginal communities in other provinces that fall into the same category. If a treaty has never been signed with them, Aboriginal peoples retain their sovereignty and the right to occupy and use their lands as they see fit.

Most early treaties were ones of peace and friendship and did not deal with the acquisition of land. The Two-Row Wampum Treaty, concluded between the Iroquois Confederacy and the British was represented by a belt or sash with two parallel rows of coloured beads separated by rows of white beads. It signified that the British were to travel on the river of life in their large ship containing their laws, religious beliefs, customs, traditions and ways of life. Travelling alongside, but separate in their own canoe, were the Iroquois, who carried with them the Great Law of Peace and their traditions, customs, spiritual beliefs and way of life. The treaty confirmed that each nation would enjoy the bounty of the lands and waters, but would continue to govern their own affairs as independent nations. The mutual promise was that neither would interfere in the affairs of the other.

All the Mi'kmaq and Malliseet Treaties of which I am aware deal with peace and friendship or with limited marketing arrangements, as in the 1999 Marshall case. None purport to define the extent of the

Aboriginal lands and none purport to have the Crown purchase any. If that is the case, the Aboriginal title and sovereignty remain in full force and effect. The Maritime provinces have tried to repudiated treaty rights, saying that any rights that may have existed, have been superseded by subsequent legislation that infers that the provinces own all the land.

This position is similar to that criticized by the Supreme Court of Canada in *Delgamuukw v. British Columbia*. There is no law that conveys title to a province or to the federal government, by the mere effluxion of time. While I don't totally agree with the proposition, the law at least says that for a government to say it has extinguished Aboriginal title, it must do so in clear concise legislative language.

The Canadian government of today, in its dispute at Burnt Church, is in contravention of the Supreme Court decision in the two Marshall decisions dealing with the Aboriginal right to harvest lobster. It has refused to re-examine its harvesting regulations to take Aboriginal rights into account and has failed to negotiate with the First Nations.

The negotiation of the numbered treaties in western Canada, which started in the 19th century, dealt with the sovereignty issue, although it is questionable whether Aboriginal people appreciated the fact. Unlike the wars in the United States that resulted in the killing of hundreds of thousands of Aboriginal people and the herding of others onto reservations, Canada followed another route. Its method followed the directives of the Royal Proclamation. Treaties became the means of removing Aboriginal people, and their claims of ownership, from vast stretches of arable land, to make room for the rising flood of homesteaders.

Treaties No's. 1 to 11 (thus the term 'numbered' treaties) were signed at outdoor meetings convened by government agents purporting to speak for the Queen of England. Chiefs from large areas gathered with their advisors and families and negotiated their future as best they could. Government officials translated much of the negotiation. If the Chiefs spoke English at all, they were certainly not schooled in the art of inter-national negotiation. Their people were starving and needed food, and parents wanted their children educated so they could survive in the changing world.

These treaties, by their terms and the manner in which they were negotiated, explicitly recognized the sovereignty of the Indian Tribes. Long before the term 'First Nation' became common, the treaties recognized and respected their Nation status. It is also significant to note that the Numbered treaties did not purport to take away all Aboriginal rights, only their rights to the use and occupation of the tracts of land referred to in them. It is also significant that these treaties were defined as such. They were between two internal Canadian governments: the Aboriginal governments represented by Chiefs, and the National government represented by the Queen.

Treaty Number One begins:

"ARTICLES OF A TREATY, made and concluded this third day of August, in the year of our Lord, one thousand eight hundred and seventy-one, between Her Most Gracious Majesty the Queen of Great Britain and Ireland, By Her Commissioner Weymyss M. Simpson, Esquire, of the one part, and the Chippewa and Swampy Cree Tribes of Indians, inhabitants of the country within the limits hereinafter defined and described by their Chiefs, chosen and named as hereinafter mentioned, of the other part."

We are fortunate to have a record of some of the discussions surrounding the treaty-making process. The Honourable Alexander Morris, the former Lieutenant Governor of Manitoba and one of the government negotiators, kept a record of the discussions. These appear in *The Treaties of Canada with Indians of Manitoba and North-West Territories including the Negotiations on Which They Were Based*, published in 1880.

The book records the recollections of the author, assisted by the recordings of a shorthand reporter, and it describes the discussions with the Aboriginal people in considerable detail. The federal negotiators were Aboriginal Commissioner Simpson, and Messrs. Dawson and Pether. On reaching Red River they were joined by the Hon. A.G. Archibald, the Lieutenant Governor of Manitoba and the North West Territories. They were also joined by Hon. James McKay, a member of the Executive Council of Manitoba and a "half-breed" said to be intimately acquainted with the Aboriginal tribes and possessing much influence over them. Some Aboriginal people thought their reserves would cover half of (the then smaller) Manitoba, and it took some persuasion to get them to sign the Treaties that spoke of much smaller reserves of land.

In his letter to Governor General, the Earl of Dufferin, Morris referred to the objective of the treaties as:

"opening up the Territories for settlement, by obtaining the relinquishment of the *natural title* of the Indians to the lands of the Fertile Belt on fair and just terms."

The federal government, through its negotiators, made a number of commitments, some of which are contained in the written documents and others that were given as inducements to sign. The only commitment the Chiefs made in the treaty was:

"to hereby bind and pledge themselves and their people strictly to observe this treaty, and to maintain perpetual peace between themselves and Her Majesty's white subjects, and not to interfere with the property or in any way molest the persons of Her Majesty's white or other subjects."

According to the Morris record, some of the oral promises and commitments made on behalf of the federal government were:

"Now the whole burden of my message from the Queen is that we wish to help you in the days that are to come, we do not want to take away the means of living that you have now, we do not want to tie you down.

What I have offered does not take away your living, you will have it then as you have now and, what I offer now is put on top of it.

I want the Indians to understand that all that has been offered is a gift, and they still have the same mode of living as before.

The government will not interfere with the Indian's daily life; they will not bind him."

The book also records specific commitments made by Commissioner J.S. Dawson. The following comment relates to another Treaty but I think it reasonable to assume that similar promises were made during the negotiation of all the numbered treaties. He said:

"I will give you lands for farms, and also reserves for your own use."

The most important of the promises, in my opinion, is the one that seemed to guarantee self-government:

"The government will not interfere with the Indian's daily life."

My interpretation of the provision, in other words, is: 'You can run your own affairs in any way you wish.' This interpretation is borne out by the reported comment of Chief Tus-tuk-ee-skuais, stating his understanding of what became Treaty No. 6:

> "I am glad that we have everything which we had before still extended to us."

It is also important to note that the numbered treaties did not take away the sovereignty of Aboriginal people and did not eliminate their separate identity, or their historic rights.

In spite of the unilateral assumption of jurisdiction and ownership by federal and provincial governments of Canada, Aboriginal people are still the outright owners of portions of Canada, and that ownership arguably carries with it the right to run their own affairs as they please. It may follow as well that they already have self-government and need no further authority from the federal or provincial or territorial governments. It is of course another matter to have government accept that proposition. This caveat on Canadian ownership is nevertheless still recognized by the federal government in its recorded policy that proclaims that the treaty-making process should be completed.

One practical problem is that when Canada was being formed, by the establishment of governments here and there, the waters became muddied. In agreeing to establish Canada, the eastern provinces, its first members, asked that the British North America Act of 1867 be passed by Parliament at Westminster. The Canadian authorities, and Parliament in Britain, ignored the continuing rights of the Aboriginal owners and took it upon themselves to divide all legislative powers between the new federal and provincial governments.

If the Statute did what the Royal Proclamation decreed not be done, it ignored Aboriginal sovereignty. It can be argued that it is at least ineffective in purporting to give federal or provincial governments authority over Aboriginal land and Aboriginal people. If the BNA Act was not legal, or does not apply to the rights of Canada's indigenous people, it has left their rights undisturbed or at least remaining as a cloud on the title of Canadian Governments.

If, as stated in *Delgamuukw*, there must be a clear intent of government to extinguish Aboriginal rights, there was certainly no intent to do that in dividing powers in the British North America Act. Governments merely ignored the Aboriginal presence in Canada and as a result ignored their rights. At least, I would argue, they did not extinguish them. I would go even farther and suggest that Canadian governments do not have, and have never had, the right to unilaterally extinguish the Aboriginal right to their traditional land. Government can negotiate a change in ownership, if the Aboriginal people agree, but they cannot take it or abolish the concomitant rights of ownership. That fact seems to me to have been recognized by incorporating the Royal Proclamation in Canada's Constitution.

The statements and promises made during the treaty negotiations were clearly inducements that were made to persuade Aboriginal people to sign and they should be used when interpreting treaties to explain their meaning and intent. If the statements were false, they were fraudulent, and would permit an amendment of the treaties. It is clear that the statements were not honoured, as the Aboriginal people *were* tied down. They did *not* have the same mode of living as before. Government *did* interfere with their daily lives. It *did* bind them and it did *not* give them lands for farms *and* reserves. In view of the actions of the federal government that followed quickly upon the signing of the Treaties, one has to question the sincerity of the negotiations and the promises that were made to induce the Aboriginal people to sign.

The greatest interference with Aboriginal sovereignty has been the Indian Act of 1876. It, and more so its administration, took away the last vestige of Aboriginal independence and authority. It contradicted and overrode the terms of the treaties and the promises upon which they were based. It gave ever-increasing power to Indian Agents to prevent the free movement of Aboriginal people, their ability to farm, and to associate with one another. It forbade the raising of money or the hiring of a lawyer to present grievances.

Instead of enabling Aboriginal people to run their lives as before, the federal government took charge. Its patronizing approach already existed in the form of Upper Canada legislation, the Gradual *Civilization Act of 1857* and the *Gradual Enfranchisement of Indians Act of 1869*. The term 'enfranchisement' has always been confusing to me. It means to disenfranchise people as Aboriginal and to make them a regular citizen, that is to enfranchise them as a Canadian. Both Acts were part of the established assimilation policy and both gave government officials authority over Aboriginal people and took authority away from them. Not surprisingly, no mention of these Acts or policies appears in the Morris journal and there is no reference to them in the numbered treaties.

Few changes in the Indian Act were made until 1951, and then little of substance. That may be because the government was still trying to apply the Act and impose its own paternalistic policy on Aboriginal people, the policy that existed since Canada was born. The federal government still clings to its self-imposed power and authority over Aboriginal people. It is time they re-directed their energies and took another look at their self-imposed fiduciary responsibility.

Another matter to consider when examining the treaties, is that they were made between parties with vastly differing bargaining strengths. One side had the power of government and its advisers behind it. The other side was not represented by lawyers or anyone else, and had limited or no understanding of the negotiation process. One side knew the potential wealth of the resources being bargained for, while the other side knew nothing of their value to settlers, to the future of the country as a whole, or the wealth the lands could produce. It was an uneven process. The question should be asked: Did one party take advantage of the other? There is no doubt in my mind of the answer.

A challenge to the validity of the treaties could call to the fore the *contra preferendum* principle of contract law. The stronger party would have to demonstrate that no advantage was taken of the weaker one. The equitable doctrine of *Rectification of Contract* enables a court to inquire whether a written agreement properly records the intentions of the parties. If there was fraud, concealment or unconscionable behaviour by one party, a court could alter the contract to reflect the actual agreement. In view of the incompleteness of the treaties, a court could add the other promises that were made.

Before it is assumed that I am recommending a challenge be launched, I hasten to add that Aboriginal people to whom I have spoken do not want to overturn the treaties, no matter how little they may provide. If nothing else, they establish a link, first with the Queen of England, and then with the federal government. They don't want to let the federal government off the hook, and do not want government to be able to negate the promises that are contained in the treaties. They do not want what is left of their homeland to disappear. A benefit isolated reserves do provide, in spite of many shortcomings, is a safe haven from the ravages of the non-Aboriginal world. But even if treaties are not going to be challenged, I think it important to recognize that they could be.

Even if a challenge to the validity of the treaties is not advanced, it seems to me that the treaties should be renewed and updated. Treaty renewal agreements could spell out the support and other advantages the federal government now agrees to supply. They could clarify the continuing jurisdiction of First Nations and the extent of self-determination or self-government. It is somewhat pointless to argue about the meaning of treaties when it is clear that more modern agreements are required. A treaty renewal process could be applied to all treaties in Canada and be beneficial to First Nations and to the federal and provincial governments as well.

If there is a treaty renewal process, or if self-government agreements are entered into, they can provide the tools to enable the current needs of Aboriginal people to be addressed. They can clarify uncertainties over land rights, the extent of local authority, and all the other matters the newer treaties have dealt with. It is never too late to correct the errors of the past. It is never too late to again recognize the principle of sovereignty and to define the extent of self-government. Those matters, and more, should be the subject of renewed negotiations between the senior levels of government and Aboriginal people.

Treaty renewal might be a long and difficult process but it may be less difficult than entering into a multitude of self-government agreements. An advantage of treaty renewal is that each of the older treaties covers twenty or more First Nations. Renewals could at least set the parameters of self-determination and make detailed arrangements with First Nations easier to achieve.

The jurisdiction of the federal and provincial governments, as it affects Aboriginal people, also needs clarification. It is unclear which level of government has jurisdiction over, and responsibility for Aboriginal people living off reserves. Uncertainty surrounding this issue causes not only disputes between governments as to which of them should fund this or that program, but it interferes with services that are desperately required. The uncertainty also makes it difficult for Métis and urban Aboriginal organizations to obtain support for services they are trying to establish.

The uncertainty seems to have been resolved for the moment by an unnatural compromise that requires both levels of government to share services equally. That solution is really no solution at all, as it leads to inaction. Programs such as the Ganootamaage diversion program for offenders in Winnipeg took five years to get off the ground, as government financial support and co-operation was required. The federal government would only provide support if the province agreed to provide equal funding. The province refused for years.

It is these sorts of obstacles that limit improvements Aboriginal people would like to make. It is hard to appreciate the extent to which government policies and actions have almost destroyed a culture and a distinct people. It is even harder to understand why the improvements Aboriginal people are trying to make are suffocated by the bickering and lack of co-operation within the federal bureaucracy and between the federal and provincial governments.

While Aboriginal people once lived nomadic lives or lived in family groupings or small villages, the coming of foreign explorers, the buffalo hunt and the fur trade, demanded new and different societal arrangements. The buffalo once provided food and clothing and hides to cover homes in the depth of winter and cooking utensils, needles and thread were made from their various parts. The fur trade provided a market for animal pelts and employment in the transportation of goods to the east and to the north. Hudson Bay, Fort Alexander, Fort Rouge, and other forts, provided the point of contact with the white men and their influences, some good but some destructive.

The location of Aboriginal reserves in the wilderness, near the source of livelihood at the time the treaties were signed, seemed to suit the Aboriginal way of life. They later proved to be uneconomic. Today most reserve land, on the rocky terrain of the north, will not grow food, let alone provide jobs or other economic activity needed to support the people. Fishing, hunting and trapping are no longer viable industries. It may be that mineral development will some day provide the needed wealth and employment, but the financing needed for exploration and development by Aboriginal people, is hard to come by.

I don't see governments exchanging lands to provide opportunities for employment and economic development. First Nations are trying to buy new land and establish businesses on their own, using monies from long-overdue Treaty Land Entitlement payments that make up for the shortage in the provision of lands promised in the hundred year old Treaties. Even these attempts (such as the establishment of casinos) are resisted, rather then being supported by provincial and municipal governments.

In spite of inertia with respect to treaties that already exist, new treaties were completed between 1975 and 1994 in James Bay, Northern and Northeastern Quebec and with the Inuvialuit, Gwich'in, Sahtu

Dene, Métis and later, Nunavut. Also in 1994, the Council of Yukon First Nation Umbrella Agreement was confirmed and final agreements were signed by some of its signatories, the Vuntut Gwitchen, Nacho Nyak Dun, Teslin Tlingit and the Champagne and Aishinik First Nations.

Those treaties were completed pursuant to the federal Comprehensive Claims policy, first established in 1969. Subsequent amendments were made in an attempt to make the policy more acceptable to Aboriginal people. By 1973 the policy was:

> "The Government is now ready to negotiate with authorized representatives of these native peoples on the basis that where their traditional interest in the lands concerned can be established, an agreed form of compensation or benefit will be provided to native peoples in return for their interest."

The phrase 'in return for their interest' was taken to mean that historic Aboriginal rights would end; in other words they would be extinguished. That was not acceptable to Aboriginal people and treaty-making slowed. A revised Comprehensive Claims Policy was announced by the Honourable Bill McKnight, Minister of Indian Affairs and Northern Development, in 1986. The introduction to that policy states:

> "Large parts of Canada continue to be used by Aboriginal groups living in their traditional territories. The basis for any comprehensive land claims policy, therefore, is self-evident. It is the fulfilment of the treaty process through the conclusion of land claims agreements with Aboriginal groups that continue to use and occupy traditional lands and whose Aboriginal title has not been dealt with by treaty or superseded by law.
>
> The federal government's approach in this important matter has been to seek to clarify the land and resource rights of Aboriginal claimants, governments and the private sector, through the negotiation of settlement agreements. Through such negotiations, a range of land and resource-related matters has been addressed, including land ownership, and the right to the use and management of wildlife and renewable resources. Other topics directly or indirectly linked to land and resources have also been dealt with in the context of these negotiations. Claims settlements

have thus provided an opportunity for government and claimants to redefine the most fundamental aspects of their relationship by a process of negotiation."

This was a good explanation of the policy and need for treaty-making to continue, but on the issue of extinguishment, the policy statement still contained unacceptable conditions:

"Above all other issues, the requirement that Aboriginal groups agree to the extinguishment of all Aboriginal rights and title as part of a claims settlement has provoked strong reactions from Aboriginal people. The federal government has examined this feature of the former policy carefully and has concluded that alternatives to extinguishment may be considered provided that certainty in respect of lands and resources is established.

Acceptable options are:

(1) the cession and surrender of Aboriginal title throughout the settlement area in return for the grant to the beneficiaries of defined rights in specified or reserved areas and other defined rights applicable to the entire settlement area; or

(2) the cession and surrender of Aboriginal title in non-reserved areas, while:

 ‣ allowing any Aboriginal title that exists to continue in specified or reserved areas

 ‣ granting to beneficiaries defined rights applicable to the entire settlement area.

It is important to recognize that the Aboriginal rights to be released in the claims process are only those related to the use of and title to land and resources. Other Aboriginal rights, to the extent they are defined through the constitutional process or recognized by the courts, are not affected by the policy."

The treaty-making process was becoming stalled again as Aboriginal people felt the policy still provided for the extinguishment of their rights. In 1993 I was appointed as a fact finder by the Minister of Indian Affairs and Northern Development, The

Honourable Ron Irwin, to obtain the views of all interested parties on the extinguishment requirements contained in the latest policy.

My task was to travel across Canada to meet with Aboriginal people, provincial and territorial government ministers responsible for Indian Affairs or their representatives, with Third Parties and with the general public. Third Parties are those who are not signatories to a treaty but who might be affected by it. They include lumber, fishing, mining and other resource industries, farmers, municipal authorities, tourist and wildlife associations. I held meetings in the capital city of each province and territory, and in a number of First Nation communities. Over seventy meetings were held and another seventy written submissions were received.

Aboriginal people were universally opposed to the extinguishment of their rights, even in exchange for new and more specific ones. It was clear that the latest policy changes had failed to address their fundamental concerns as the 'cede and surrender' provisions still meant the extinguishment of Aboriginal rights. Aboriginal people told me they wanted treaties to recognize that they continue to have historic Aboriginal rights. Once that reality is accepted they are willing to have a Treaty indicate the extent of their rights with respect to certain lands.

During the hearings, most Aboriginal people spoke of broader issues. Many of the concerns centred on the Department of Indian Affairs whose paternalism has stripped them of their authority and the will to do things for themselves. They want to reduce crime, to improve the education of their children, to have better housing, and to have productive work to do. Most importantly, they believe they can solve their own problems if government will just get out of the way and give them the authority to do so.

Third Parties with whom I met also discussed broad issues, whether they supported or objected to the extinguishment policy. Some of the matters discussed were whether there should be any Treaties at all, and whether Aboriginal people have any special place in Canada. The history of indigenous people, sovereignty, the history of Treaties and every other imaginable native issue were all discussed at one time or another. The attitudes of those who made a living from the country's natural resources were similar to one another. They spoke of the need for economic development and the need to protect their right to harvest the forests and the seas. Tourist operators spoke of the need to accommodate Canadian and American hunters, fishermen and sportsmen, and the importance of their business to the economy. Ranchers, who lease large tracts of land from government, did not want new treaties or claims to interfere with the benefits they enjoy.

The debate was at times intense. At other times the discussions were on a reasoned and rational plane. At the public meeting in Quebec City I was impressed by some of the early writings on Aboriginal issues that university professors and historians presented. The public meetings in Halifax and Victoria were valuable, as university and other scholars, and members of the clergy, showed their support for Aboriginal people and discussed how their situation could be improved.

My visit with the Innu in their Village of Sheshatshiu in Labrador indicated how far ranging some of the issues were. The Innu were interested in treaties and certainty but did not want to discuss them until other issues were addressed. In the meantime they had terminated their treaty discussions. They were concerned about the low-level flying of international pilots training at Goose Bay who disturbed their people and the animals. The Chief spoke of the inappropriate and ineffective justice services that were being forced upon them by the Province of Newfoundland and they had blockaded runways to stops judges from coming to their communities. They didn't agree with the proposed mineral developments at Voisey's Bay and had blockaded that area. They felt their inherent and historic rights to the area were not being protected and were unmoved by promises of massive employment and the construction of a smelter.

In St. John's, I met with the corporate representatives of Diamond Resources, which had made the discoveries leading to the Voisey's Bay development. They were upset with the slow pace of treaty negotiations between the federal and provincial governments and the Innu and Labrador Inuit. They felt that if treaties could be signed with those people, there would be the certainty that would enable them to proceed. They said they were prepared to negotiate with the federal or provincial governments, or with the Aboriginal governments, but they had to know which had the authority to give them the permission and licenses they required. This discussion was interesting as it indicated a willingness to negotiate with a First Nation government. Here was a resource industry supporting the treaty process and the certainty it would provide. The request they made of me was to urge the federal and provincial governments to get back to the bargaining table and to get the treaties signed.

My discussions with the Inuit in St. John's were positive. While they held steadfastly to certain basic principles, they showed willingness to compromise. The next day I met provincial people who were involved in the treaty negotiations. Their misunderstanding of the Inuit position was amazing. They thought some matters had been resolved when my meeting with the Inuit had made it clear that those issues had not even been discussed. The lack of communication and misunderstanding was amazing.

I was impressed by the programs the Quebec government had for dealing with the problems of Aboriginal people. It nevertheless expressed the same sentiment as most of the provinces — the extinguishment of Aboriginal rights was a pre-condition to any new treaty. The exceptions were Nova Scotia, British Columbia and the North West Territories, which did not think extinguishment was necessary or appropriate. Those governments favoured self-government for Aboriginal people and the settlement of their continuing rights through treaties.

Several First Nations with whom I met had already signed treaties, but told me of problems they had with the negotiation of their Treaty and with its application. The James Bay Crees (not the term "Cree" used in the West) were still upset at the manner in which their treaty had been completed. With the desire, particularly of the Quebec government, to export power to the United States, deadlines had been imposed and the Crees were presented with a take-it-or-leave-it final document. Community meetings had been held but they often resulted in rifts within families and communities that have become deep and lasting. The Crees have been to the Supreme Court on several occasions about the interpretation or application of the Treaty.

All the modern treaties differ in the way self-government is dealt with, as each was negotiated separately. The Yukon Umbrella Agreement took twenty years to negotiate and there are still ten individual agreements to complete. Some in that group were refusing to enter into a final Treaty if it contained any 'extinguishment' or 'cede and surrender' clause.

The situation in British Columbia is unique, as although there are Indian reserves, only a few were the result of discussion with Aboriginal people. The 'Douglas Treaties' were entered into in the 1650s and recorded the purchase of Indian settlements and enclosed fields in the southern part of Vancouver Island. It is of interest to note that each of those 14 or so treaties provides that the Tribes "are at liberty to hunt over the unoccupied lands, and to carry on our (sic) fisheries as formerly." Treaty 11 of 1899 also includes part of north-eastern B.C.

All the other reserves in British Columbia were unilaterally established by government, and not by the negotiation process required by the Royal Proclamation. It is the residents of those communities that are now seeking properly negotiated treaties to resolve the extent of the land they own and to confirm their other rights.

TNAC, the Treaty Negotiation Advisory Committee, represents Third Party interests in British Columbia, keeps an eye on treaty negotiations and advises the government of their point of view. I met with TNAC in Vancouver on two occasions. Although there was some support for Aboriginal people and their efforts to improve themselves, most objected to any extension of the rights of Aboriginal people and were opposed to government entering into any new treaties. In the alternative, a few of the committee members said that if there were going to be treaties, they should contain self-government provisions so everyone would know the extent of First Nation authority.

Meetings with Aboriginal people and members of the public in other parts of British Columbia were productive. One of the best public meetings was at Terrace, where there was an almost equal balance of Nisga'a, Municipal and local people present. It was the first meeting where each side listened to the other quietly and with respect. They discussed what turned out to be common concerns about what would happen if and when a treaty was completed. They discussed their common interest in employment and resource protection. Some early testiness had indicated anticipated antagonism, but as the meeting progressed, it gradually disappeared. After the meeting adjourned, people stayed around and those who at first seemed to be on opposite sides of the debate over treaties, were engaged in friendly discussions and were speaking of future meetings.

It was clear that there hadn't been much dialogue between the First Nation and the public. I am aware that First Nations resist having the public directly involved in treaty discussions and are even reluctant to negotiate with a provincial government, believing discussions should be only with Ottawa. In spite of that basic position, the need to involve the province, with its extensive interests and authority, seems to have been reluctantly accepted. I like to think that face-to-face meetings between First Nation spokespersons and the general public would help to allay the many misgivings and misunderstandings about treaties and self-government. More communication might well benefit the long-range aspirations of Aboriginal people.

Resource industry representatives generally see new treaties as a threat, although Aboriginal leaders have tried to suggest they would not be. I think it possible, as slim as the possibility may be, that more personal and direct discussions between Aboriginal people and third parties would be beneficial. The resource industries need to hear directly from Aboriginal people and to learn more about how a treaty would work and how it would or would not affect them. Discussions might even indicate how Aboriginal tribes and resource industries could arrive at agreements on how the aspirations of each could be accommodated. If the co-operation of industry could be obtained, that would substantially alter the dynamics in British Columbia. The process would of course also require a positive, rather than antagonistic, participation on the part of third parties. If the attempt doesn't work, the present arms length process would have to apply.

I was dismayed as I watched television and listened to the heated debates about the approval of the Nisga'a Treaty. The one-sided tirades of some speakers sounded selfish and mean-spirited, as if they wanted Aboriginal people to stop being Aboriginal and to give up their few remaining rights. They sounded as if they wanted Aboriginal people to stop their efforts to improve their lives and their striving for a better place in Canada. The demands for a referendum were disgraceful. A referendum would certainly have destroyed the Treaty if the opposition to it was based on selfishness and hatred.

I wonder if those opposing the treaties have considered the alternative. If the Aboriginal peoples' quest for treaties and self-government is rejected, what will happen? I would be concerned that the previous situation would return, with arguments and roadblocks to try to stop the destruction of the forests and to retain historic rights. Fighting, in and out of court, about the right to fish and hunt would likely resume and intensify.

It didn't appear that the opponents were aware, or wanted to mention, that treaties provide an opportunity to resolve these and many other issues. Treaties are designed to balance competing needs and aspirations and of course, provide an opportunity to reverse inequities of the past.

The second part of my responsibility to the Minister, after the fact finding was done, was to advise on how 'certainty' could be obtained in new treaties without requiring the surrender of Aboriginal rights. I pointed out that not only government and third parties want certainty, but Aboriginal people want it as well. Everyone wants treaties to be certain in their effect and need them to be clear and concise.

I suggested a different approach be taken to the manner in which treaties are drawn. Treaties that have been completed in recent years have concentrated on what the First Nation may and may not do. The self-government provisions speak of what the First Nation government and people may do, but they do not explain the jurisdiction that will remain with the federal and provincial governments. The 'we will give you this and that, and we will have everything else' approach of government should be a thing of the past. Recent treaties do not deal adequately with potential areas of conflict and do not discuss the interaction between the various jurisdictions.

I suggested that, as with any International treaty, the rights and jurisdiction of all the parties, and the rights of all those who would be affected by them, be recited. To be more specific, I suggested that the rights of the First Nation, the rights of the federal government, and the rights of the provincial government, along with the rights of third parties and the rights of Canadian citizens, all be spelled out. Certainty, I suggested, can be obtained by the careful exposition of the rights of each party and those likely to be affected by a treaty.

On the thorny question of the extinguishment of Aboriginal rights, I recommended that treaties start by recognizing the existence of historic and current Aboriginal rights, without trying to recite them. The detailed description of the rights of each party would describe the rights to be protected and preserved by the treaty. I said that a recital of rights the parties do not have is unnecessary.

My report also recommended that all possible conflicts or disagreements about the interpretation of a treaty, be dealt with in the treaty document. I recommended they include a process of re-negotiation, mediation, and finally, binding arbitration. A Board of Arbitration could contain one or more persons appointed by the First Nation and one or more by government, with an independent chairperson selected by those representatives, possibly from a list to which the parties had agreed in advance.

My report was published by the Department of Indian Affairs and Northern Development as "A New Partnership" in English and "Un Nouveau Partenariat" in French. It suggested a new and positive relationship be established between First Nations and the federal government.

This review is intended to answer some of the questions members of the public ask. It is also meant to indicate that claims now being advanced by Aboriginal people are not new claims. They are legitimate claims, solidly based on history and on principles of domestic and international law, supported and confirmed by the Canadian Constitution.

4

Discrimination

Discrimination comes in many forms. We usually think of it as not wanting to associate with or just not liking some people because of their language, their colour or their ideas. We hear of discrimination in hiring and in rental practices. Aboriginal people are familiar with these issues, but are also disturbed by other matters that some of us would not even think of as being a form of discrimination.

For example, I am often asked: "Don't you think it would be a good idea to close all the reserves?" I asked one person why, and they said: "Well, if the reserves were closed, Aboriginal people would have to assimilate with other Canadians and that would get rid of all sorts of problems." He then quite seriously added, and as if the thought had just occurred to him, "and it would be better for them as well."

I didn't tell my friend that assimilation, in a number of forms, has been tried for 150 years and that all attempts to force it upon Aboriginal people have failed. Nor did I tell him that Aboriginal people consider these suggestions to be a major insult and an affront to their very identity. The problem with that sort of explanation is that it is unlikely to change people's minds and is likely beyond their comprehension. They mean well and don't realize the pain they cause.

If reserves were closed, that would bring Canada's treatment of Aboriginal people full circle. We started by removing Aboriginal people from their land and from other Canadians. We then tried to civilize them to the ways of others. We broke up their families and sent their children to separate schools. The next step was to remove the children from their homes and place them for adoption in non-Aboriginal homes. If we closed the reserves we would be back to where we started; Aboriginal people would be free but they would have no land, no compensation for it and no right to the protection of government.

The most recent attempt to eliminate Aboriginal rights and their independent status was in 1969 when the federal government issued its White Paper on Aboriginal policy. It spoke of the need for a break from the past and measures that would gradually lead away from different status to full social, economic and political participation in Canadian life. Aboriginal leaders saw this as a government attempt to abandon its fiduciary and guardian responsibilities to them. The government shelved the approach and it is interesting to note that it was the same government, in 1982, that brought in the Constitution that guaranteed the protection of Aboriginal and Treaty rights.

The Supreme Court of Canada decision in *Calder v. British Columbia* was undoubtedly the impetus for the change as it affirmed Aboriginal rights and title. Judson J. stated at p. 328:

"...when the settlers came, the Indians were there, organized in societies and occupying the land as their forefathers had done for centuries. This is what Indian title means..."

Indians gave up their lands in return for Treaties and for the protection of government. The Canadian Constitution now makes those rights inviolate.

Apart from the legalities that prohibit it, forced assimilation won't work. Some Aboriginal people would be left alone in the wilderness. Others would move with their problems to the towns and cities. The current efforts of Aboriginal people to improve themselves and their communities would be lost and there would probably be demands for the return of the land and independence given up in return for the Treaties. In my opinion there would be chaos.

The Canadian government started its discriminatory approach by keeping Aboriginal people separate and apart from other Canadians. It removed them from their land and their homes and put them on Indian Reserves. It gave or sold the land it acquired from them to the Hudson's Bay Company, the Canadian Pacific Railway and to settlers.

The Treaties were supposed to provide farm land as well as reserves where the Indians were to live. Having achieved its main objective of obtaining their land, government was no longer even concerned to provide all the land it had promised. Treaty Land Entitlement claims for the rest of the land are only now being completed — 130 years later. The government was clearly not interested in making the Indians self-sufficient.

The Treaties were nevertheless the instrument for implementing the policy of separating Indians from others. They spoke of limited benefits but said nothing of the separate enclaves where the Indians must live under strict rules imposed by the government rulers. The Indian Agents were never the agents of the Indians but were the agents of the government and responsible to implement its policies. The Agents, under the authority of the Indian Act, ran their lives and told the Indians what they could and could not do, while Parliament spoke of 'the Indian problem' that confronted Canadians.

The original inhabitants of the land were deprived of their practice of hunting, fishing and trapping wherever they wished. Instead, many live their lives in poverty as inmates of a gulag or quasi-prison run by a foreign power. They were stripped of their independence and deprived of their traditional rituals and practices. Their method of governing themselves was destroyed and their religious beliefs and practices were forbidden. Aboriginal people did not ask to be confined on segregated land, but that is what they received. About all they feel they have left is the reserve and the promises Canada made to them when they gave up their land. They feel that public suggestions they give up what is left, to be discrimination of the worst kind.

To make things worse, many feel that the manner in which they have been treated is no better than the way in which the blacks were dealt with in South Africa, another member of the British Commonwealth. The system of control in each country was apartheid. Strong words indeed, but I use the term to emphasize the horror of the program and its total disregard for basic human rights. It is strange that I couldn't find the word in my two-volume Shorter Oxford English Dictionary, but it is significant that it appears in the Canadian version. That volume defines apartheid as:

> "the South African policy of segregation and discrimination against non-whites and segregation or discrimination in other contexts. [Afrikaans (as apart-hood.)]"

The isolation approach didn't work any better than the attempt to 'civilize' Aboriginal people, but the government was not deterred. In 1879 the federal government received a report from N.E. Davin, who had been engaged to study the American 'aggressive civilization policy' and its racially segregated industrial schools. He reported that the only way to 'civilize' Aboriginal children and to accommodate them to

European culture and values, was to remove them from the disruptive influence of their parents and their community. He said that

> "if anything is to be done with the Indian, we must catch him very young."

The federal government, having co-opted a number of national churches, pressed ahead with its next discriminatory and assimilationist approach — the establishment of residential schools. The ones I saw were large brick or wooden structures set apart from the communities they were near. They were austere if not foreboding in appearance. Driving by, you would either see no sign of activity or a small cluster of children standing in a massive yard.

These exclusive schools represented a strange mixture of government intent. They were an extension of the plan to keep Indians apart from the general population, and were part of the plan to assimilate the children into white society. Even worse, the plan was to convert the Aboriginal children into 'white' citizens.

Many of the teachers assumed they were part of a noble venture to help Aboriginal people and didn't see or didn't question the emotional harm that was resulting from the children being separated from other family members and their disassociation from their culture. They probably didn't see the manner in which the children were removed from their parents or the pressure that was applied by Indian Agents and the police. They may or may not have been aware that the Agents would not permit the parents to visit their children without a pass and that a pass was almost impossible to obtain. They may even have assumed that the absence of the parents indicated a lack of interest on their part.

At school, the children were treated in an entirely different manner than they were by their parents. Instead of the quiet teaching by example, respecting the child as an individual, and teaching cultural practices and beliefs, the school program was directed at having them forget about their parents and former ways. Their hair was cut, they were dressed in school uniforms, and they were forbidden to speak their own language, even in private conversations and brothers and sisters were kept apart. Presenters during the AJI told us that the rules were strictly enforced, supported by corporal punishment on a regular basis.

The Aboriginal culture was denigrated. The message to parents was that they were incapable of caring for and raising their children. The message to the children was that they had an inferior culture and their parents were unfit to care for them. Parents lost their connection with their beloved children and were deprived of the opportunity to instruct and raise them. Children's attitudes toward their parents were likely in a state of turmoil. Many lost all respect for their parents and, more seriously, lost respect for themselves and for their culture.

Although some children were permitted to live with their parents during the summer break, others didn't have that opportunity. When the children who were being conditioned to reject their parents and their culture in their cloistered environment did visit, the visits were strained and it was hard and often impossible to re-establish a normal family relationship. The parents couldn't understand what was happening to their children and the children had trouble knowing whether to accept or reject their parents' instruction. As the years passed, the children became more and more confused and didn't know which way to turn.

The impact on children of being removed from their parents apparently received no attention by the school or by the government. There is now much discussion of physical, and some sexual abuse occurring at the schools. Without discounting those serious allegations, it seems to me that it was the emotional abuse that was so devastating. The disruption in family relationships, the respect due to spouses and the care to which children are entitled, seems to have been lost or severely damaged. Aboriginal people say that the disruption in family unity and in child caring practices is still being felt today. I expect that anthropologists and sociologists would agree that the effect of 75 to 100 years of family disruption would still be visible today, only 40 years after many of the schools were closed.

The government seemed blind to the short and long-term damage it was causing. On the contrary, it seemed pleased with its program. In 1889 the Department of Indian Affairs, in its annual report, spoke of the wonders of the residential schools. It said, with apparent pride, that the boarding school:

"dissociates the Indian child from the deleterious home influences and effect(s) a change in his views and habits of life."

Similar statements were made by government officials for years to come. The mixed messages and treatment received by those who attended residential schools, and their children, remain in the form of disturbed family relationships and in damaged self-esteem. It may be hard for the non-Aboriginal person to believe the effects could be so deep and long lasting, but they are.

The residential school program was a failure and was abandoned in the 1960s. One would have thought the experience would have taught governments and others the folly of the approach, but the ashes on the school program were not yet cold when another attack on the Aboriginal community and its survival, was under way.

Another paternalistic and destructive program emerged. This time it was the provincial governments and child welfare agencies that descended upon Aboriginal communities. The new attack also had a quasi-religious fervour that appealed to many non-Aboriginal people. The battle cry was, once again, to save Aboriginal children from their parents and from the influence of Indian reserves.

After the Second World War, social workers graduated in large numbers and started work with the mainstream child welfare agencies. They also began to visit Indian Reserves that had previously been left to their own way of life, at least subject to the rulings of the government agents. The squalid living conditions and the lifestyle of Aboriginal parents and their children shocked the social workers and the fault for the conditions was incorrectly placed on the shoulders of the parents. The workers were not familiar with Aboriginal lifestyle and child raising practices and decided that the children needed to be protected from their parents and from the squalor. The corporate decision appears to have been that Aboriginal people were simply unfit to care for children.

Thus began what has been referred to as the 'Sixties Scoop.' Large numbers of Aboriginal children were taken 'into care,' placed in foster homes and for adoption, and were never again seen by their parents. Aboriginal leaders leveled charges of 'cultural genocide' and 'selling of babies' and demanded an investigation. In 1982 Associate Chief Judge Edwin Kimelman of the Provincial Court of Manitoba was appointed to examine the Child Welfare System and particularly its adoption practices. In his report, 'No Quiet Place,' Judge Kimelman reported on the number of children who had been adopted into Canadian families, and the even greater numbers that were adopted in the United States.

He recommended that "no child be placed for adoption in a family whose ethnic/cultural background is different than its own until every possible effort has been made to find a home that is ethnically/culturally compatible with the background of the child." My own experience makes me doubt that recommendation has ever been embraced or properly applied. Protocols have been developed that require First Nations to be notified when children from their community were being placed for adoption, but if the First Nation does not respond to the notice, that is the end of the matter and the agency has done its duty. That certainly does not mean 'that every possible effort' has been made to find a culturally appropriate home.

Judge Kimelman also recommended that Aboriginal siblings be kept together, that foster and adopting homes be carefully evaluated and that group homes and institutions assist children to develop pride in their cultural heritage. He called for research to determine the percentage of the population that had been in the care of the child welfare system, and the impact that had on their lives. He recommended off-reserve mandated agencies for Treaty Indians.

This removal of children from their parents and their culture and placing them for adoption with non-Aboriginal families was another attempt at assimilation, although it was not defined as such. It was another example of discrimination. The litany of abuse and depression suffered by the children continues to unfold and has again clearly shown the folly of the approach. The wrenching experience of being torn from one culture and forced into another was painful in itself. The devastating developmental effect on the children and their relationship with their natural parents and their culture continues to surface. The effects of this program will also be felt for generations.

Canadians should shudder at the thought of being classed as racist or having to think their government has embraced discriminatory practices, but in fact government policies of assimilation over the last 150 years have been racist and discriminatory. Aboriginal people have resisted all attempts at assimilation as best they can. They see them as nothing more than a deprivation of their remaining and unresolved historic rights. They feel they are not welcome in white society and wonder why they should be asked to surrender what remains of their homeland, their culture and their way of life.

If the assimilation approach has been tried for a century and a half and has proved to be a failure, one has to ask why the suggestion continues to be made. It is safe to conclude that forced assimilation will not work. Individual Aboriginal people have assimilated successfully but as a result of their own choice and initiative and at their own pace. If Canadian society would welcome Aboriginal people to join their ranks, many might do so if the same society would provide them with the opportunities and benefits that are available to other Canadians.

In the meantime, they will rely on the protections given to them and their Treaties in the Constitution of Canada and its Charter of Rights and Freedoms. Aboriginal people cannot be displaced and Canada cannot close the Reserves or force assimilation upon them, nor can it close its eyes to their continuing needs.

One of the most obvious areas of discrimination against Aboriginal people is in the area of employment. I will start with a story that shows some of the difficulties Aboriginal people face when looking for employment, and some of the devastating effects of their failure to find it.

Robert and his wife Edna were born and always lived on a remote Indian Reserve. They and their two young children occupied a crowded dilapidated house, without running water. There were no paved streets and mud was everywhere. Robert once worked with his father on his trap line that he finally had to give up due to the fallen price of furs, his advancing age, and the cost of skidoos, gasoline, and equipment. Robert then did some fishing but couldn't afford to buy his own boat, nets or other equipment, let alone set up a fishing business.

Edna had once had a job as a receptionist in the band office but she had to give that up when a new Chief was elected. Life was hard, the future looked bleak and they feared their children would lead the same dull and unproductive life they were stuck with. They dreamt of a better future for themselves and their children and were encouraged by the TV showings of the wonders of city life and the newspaper ads showing boundless opportunities for employment. They thought of the many opportunities their children would have, and were encouraged by rumours about how well others who had moved away were doing.

They finally decide to leave the reserve. They packed their clothing and a few possessions and headed for Winnipeg and a cousin's suite where they had been told they were welcome to stay for a month while they got settled. The train ride to The Pas and the bus trip to Winnipeg kept them up for eighteen hours but the excitement of the voyage buoyed their spirits. The children too were excited about their new lives.

The couple was proud that they had expressed their independence and were going to build a better and a happy life for their small family. They believed they were making the move for the benefit of their children and they were prepared to sacrifice their community and the friends they had to leave behind. Robert thought of the job he would enjoy and the education his children would receive. Edna dreamt of financial security, of modern conveniences, how she would dress the children, and how happy they would be.

The reunion with the cousin was a happy event. The next day Robert headed for the employment office to get a job. The first thing he had to do was fill out a form explaining his background and his work experience. He had trouble understanding the form but finally handed it in. The clerk demanded further information and as Robert didn't really understand what was needed, he left the office, planning to ask his cousin for help.

The problem seemed to be with his grade standing and not naming specific employers. He had a grade ten certificate at one time but it was lost. The only people he could name as employers in the last year were neighbours, but they hadn't really hired him — he just helped repair a porch and build a cupboard but he wasn't paid for his work. He may have received some fish and firewood but he didn't consider that to be a payment for the help he had freely given. He had worked on a farm at one time but he couldn't remember the farmer's name.

Robert returned to the employment office the next day and handed in his application in spite of the smirking and shaking of the head of the person at the counter. He wasn't told where to report for work, as he had expected; in fact the clerk said nothing to him at all. He didn't know what questions he should ask and his follow-up visits were no more productive. When he approached the clerk the comment always was "nothing yet."

Robert started reading the board where employers list their needs. One day he took a slip to the counter that offered a job in construction. He was to report to a certain address in St. James the next morning at eight o'clock. He had money for the bus and away he went. As suggested by his cousin, he told the bus driver where he was going and asked to be let off at the right place. When he got off the bus he walked back and forth on Portage Avenue but couldn't find the name of the street that was on his slip. He had no idea how to find the address himself so he tried to stop people to ask them for directions. His efforts produced "Don't bother me," and "I don't know." More often, people just ignored him and refused to stop or talk to him at all.

He finally walked the five miles back to his cousin's home. On his next visit to the employment office he was told that he wasn't reliable and that he would never be sent to another job. He didn't think the clerk believed him when he said he couldn't find the place where he was to work.

After wondering what he should do next, someone suggested he apply for upgrading and for skills training. He went to an office to apply but was told there was no course to fit his needs and that there was no space in any event. To make things worse, a test he took did not support the grade ten certificate he had received years before. His writing and mathematics skills were weak but he began to wonder if his appearance was limiting his chances.

He went to a private day-employment office and was sent out on a job. He was to help pour cement at a construction site. He found the place and worked all day and was pleased to be working. He thought he had done a good job and hoped the boss would give him a permanent job. No such luck. He was paid in cash and that was the end of the job. He kept going to the same office but wasn't sent out on another job and after several weeks he stopped going back. He had to start facing the reality that he wasn't going to find a job.

The cousin was having a hard enough time getting by and couldn't support his relatives much longer. He suggested that Robert go to the City Welfare office to see if they would help him find their own place. Robert went and faced the same grilling he had experienced when looking for a job, although he told the welfare person he was willing to work and asked them to give him a job. He was told that was not their responsibility but he was finally put on welfare and given a limited amount of money and a budget to follow.

All he could afford to rent was two rooms in an old apartment building. There was a small bathroom but the plumbing didn't always work. The neighbourhood was poor and there was a lot of yelling and fighting in the nearby park. The building was noisy and people were drinking and fighting every night. He didn't want to live there but had no choice.

He quickly found he couldn't live and provide proper food and clothing for his children on the amount provided by welfare. His children needed clothes for school and he wanted them nicely dressed, like other kids he saw on the street. He knew that Edna deserved a better place and a better life. She was a good mother and he wanted her at home to look after the children. Edna would have liked to find a job but she didn't want to leave the children and she was very unhappy with how things were going. She finally decided to get a job and to leave the children in Robert's care, but couldn't find one. She had little formal education and no skills that qualified her for a job in an office or factory. She took a course through a support agency but that didn't produce any job prospects either.

Edna wanted to return to the reserve. The children came home crying, partly because they were lonely for their friends and partly because the other kids were mean to them. Robert was unhappy too, but was too proud to admit defeat and to go home. In any event they had given up their house when they moved to the city and there would be nowhere for them to live on the reserve. People wait for years to get a house on a reserve. He couldn't even turn to the Department of Indian Affairs because his cousin told him that Indians aren't covered by that department once they move to the city.

Robert and Edna started to take their frustration out on one another. At first their fights were verbal, then Robert started to slap and then to beat her. He started to hang around with men whose lives were also in a mess. They offered him companionship but they also shared their substitute liquor and gasoline soaked rags with him. He was able to forget his misery for a time but would wake up to the horrible reality and his slide into depression made the family situation even worse.

Robert and Edna made some friends in the building who were generous and friendly, but the form of their generosity only made the situation worse. Now both were drinking in frustration or to find some temporary escape from their problems. Both began to lose control over their actions and started to take their anger out on the children. The children were going to school in dirty clothes and with bruises on their faces.

One day a teacher referred one of the children to the school nurse. She suspected physical abuse and reported her suspicions to the Child and Family Services Agency. An agency worker went to the apartment in the company of a police officer, saw the mess the parents were in, saw bruises on the children, and immediately took them to the hospital for examination. They were not returned.

Aboriginal people unfortunately face a whole different level of problems in finding a job, and even a place to live, than others moving into Canadian cities. It is too often the continuing onslaught of racial prejudice and discrimination and the degrading expression of rejection that limits the progress to which they aspire.

They are ready and willing to work, even if the tasks are difficult and demanding, but they need others to provide them with the opportunity. They need employers who are prepared to go out of their way to employ them and they need policies of government that will require that to be done. If employers will not act on their own, they need government to require their employment as a condition of receiving a government loan or contract.

Attempts have been made by government over the years to see that Aboriginal people are employed in the major hydro-electric construction projects of Crown Corporations, but even where there are employment requirements in the contracts, they do not appear to be rigidly enforced. It appears that contractors are permitted to avoid some of the employment requirements by saying they have to bring in skilled tradesmen, rather than training Aboriginal people to perform the work.

Excuses should not be accepted. Government should insist that the terms of the contract be adhered to at all times. Penalty provisions should be inserted in the contracts to ensure enforcement. Employers should not be able to wiggle out of their commitments, and if workers need training, the government or the employer should provide it. If absence from work is an occasional problem, some accommodation should be made until the person becomes used to a different life style and to the demands of the particular business or industry.

In some situations a company can adjust its requirements. I recently had a conversation with an employer who had hired an Aboriginal caretaker. He extolled the dedication of the man and explained how careful he was and how he worked more hours per day than he was required to. He then added, "but he will have to learn to conform to the demands of business." The employer was upset because the employee was supposed to start work at 9:00 a.m. but didn't show up till 10. I believe I shocked him when I said, "Can't you alter your requirements to suit his needs?" I thought to myself, "Is it better to have a mediocre caretaker who starts at nine, or a gem of a caretaker who starts at ten and puts in a full day?"

Unfortunately, many Canadians place the blame for lack of employment on the Aboriginal people themselves. The comments I hear on an all too regular basis show little support for Aboriginal employment. "They should get off welfare and get a job. They're lazy and never show up for work. They get too many handouts now." I also hear the other side of the coin; "They shouldn't take our jobs." The message is pretty clear to Aboriginal people. Most employers don't want to hire them.

In remote communities it is not unusual to find 80 or 90 percent of the population unemployed. The rate for Métis and non-status Indians living in remote communities adjacent to Aboriginal Reserves is similar. In Winnipeg, the unemployment rate among men who have moved from reserves, according to my best estimate, is between 70 and 90 percent, depending on the age of the people. Where Aboriginal youth have limited education, their unemployment rate is about 70 percent. It is impossible to extract accurate figures from the statistics but these estimates are what I hear from people looking for work.

Apart from working for the band, there is almost a complete absence of employment opportunities in reserve communities. Even in communities that are not isolated, such as northern towns and cities, unemployment is a serious problem. Thompson is a northern mining town with a population of 15,000 of which 40 percent or 6,000 are Aboriginal. It is the commercial centre for dozens of reserve communities and its daily population is swelled by Aboriginal people coming to shop or for medical and legal reasons.

While walking through one of the Thompson malls during the AJI, Judge Sinclair and I discussed the apparent absence of Aboriginal employees. We decided to do our own unofficial survey and again walked past every store and counted the number of Aboriginal staff we could identify. We saw only three out of the hundred odd employees who appeared to be Aboriginal. Even stores that specialized in Aboriginal artefacts and clothing had no Aboriginal employees. This fact supported the stories that Aboriginal people in the north told us of being unable to find employment of any kind.

I had the same concern about The Pas, and when there on court business, I did my own walk-through survey at the Otineka Mall that is located on the Opaskwayak First Nation on the north side of the North Saskatchewan River. Although the First Nation owns the mall, I saw no Aboriginal employees in the bank, the variety store or the restaurant. There was not even an Aboriginal person in sight in the store that sells Aboriginal clothing.

This is not to say that all companies in the north refrain from employing Aboriginal people. The Hudson's Bay Northern Store at Island Lake, for example, apart from the manager, had only Aboriginal employees. The manager was happy with his Aboriginal staff and told us of his efforts to train them to assume managerial positions. The difference is that almost all the residents in the Island Lake area are Aboriginal.

Government employment statistics are of course inaccurate if not fraudulent. Canada and the provinces should blush from shame whenever they are reported, rather then bragging about the low rate of unemployment. It is known, though seldom mentioned, that the reported unemployment statistics only refer to those who have filed a job application during the period under review. The massive numbers of unemployed Aboriginal people, whether they live on a reserve or in cities, are not included. Many have long since given up hope of finding employment and no longer attend the employment office to go through the useless process of formally applying for a job. In any event, those in remote communities have no access to an employment office.

Some employers with whom I have discussed Aboriginal employment, say they only hire the most qualified applicants. That is not good enough. There must be entry-level jobs where employment can be provided to Aboriginal people, along with on-the-job training to provide opportunities for advancement. If every corporation would set aside a number of places for Aboriginal employees, the numbers of unemployed would quickly diminish. There will have to be a greater acceptance of responsibility by government and business if the crisis in unemployment is going to be resolved.

During the AJI we occasionally had an Aboriginal employee leave us for what looked like a permanent position with the provincial civil service. They were qualified for the work, but quit within a month or two. Each gave the same reasons for leaving - they felt lonely and isolated. Their fellow workers were all white, did not talk to them and did not include them in their conversations. They were ignored and felt out of place. The more serious reason was that other employees made stereotypical and impolite remarks about Aboriginal people, which they believed they were intended to hear.

If employers would engage a 'group' of Aboriginal employees, that would overcome many of these problems. If Aboriginal employees have other Aboriginal people to associate with in the workplace, they feel more comfortable and are more likely to be productive. Some resource industries engage a group of Aboriginal workers and assign them to an Aboriginal foreman. They find the group to be productive and the foreman can handle any problems in communication that arise.

A sub-contractor we engaged when building our home had an Aboriginal crew that was among his most productive.

At the time of writing, jobs are available in the garment industry, in the building trades and in the restaurant business and there is talk of bringing workers in from foreign countries to fill the void. That solution is almost unbelievable when there is 50 percent unemployment among segments of the Aboriginal workforce that could be hired and trained to do the work. If this type of employer is seeking government grants to import workers, the government should respond with a resounding "NO" but should offer funds for training Aboriginal Canadians.

I know there is criticism when a number of spaces are set aside for Aboriginal people. Three office workers berated me when the Winnipeg Police Service was making a number of positions available for qualified Aboriginal applicants. "What about my son?" one demanded. "Why should an Aboriginal person have a benefit he doesn't have?" Their criticism of preferential hiring might have had more merit if Aboriginal people had been participating on an even playing field for the last hundred years. If they had not been excluded from employment because of overt or systemic discrimination over the years, they would not need to catch up.

The police are only one example, but Aboriginal people should, at least as a matter of fairness, have an equal opportunity for education, job training, and employment. They, like others in our society, need education and training in order to have productive employment. Opportunities need to be provided to them if Canada is to say it treats its Aboriginal population as well as it treats others.

I agree that pro-active employment policies and targets to ensure the employment of a fair number of Aboriginal employees should not be necessary, but they are. Even if the public wants to consider Aboriginal employment as a means of reducing the costs of welfare and their own taxes, that would be a justification in itself for finding employment for this part of our society.

Aboriginal people are not happy that so many of them only survive with the help of the public and they resent being regularly reminded of their plight. They want to work but many are not equipped for employment in business or industry. There are few jobs to be had on Aboriginal reserves and a paucity of employers ready to employ them in the cities. The frustration of Aboriginal people about their inability to obtain employment is mounting. Chief Louis

Stevenson and his supporters forced their way into the opening session of the Manitoba Legislature in April 1999 with a sign saying,

"Give Us Jobs Not Welfare"

Aboriginal people are ready and anxious to work at improving their lives, but they cannot do it alone. They need the help and support of the non-Aboriginal community. Canadians at large can help. They can start by refusing to use any of the deleterious comments to which I have referred and suggest to others that such comments and attitudes are grossly unfair. They can help by supporting Aboriginal programs that attempt to instil feelings of pride in their people. They can help by encouraging Aboriginal people in their efforts to overcome their poverty, to improve their education, to obtain productive employment and to improve their place in Canadian society.

I do not want to give the impression that efforts are not being made — just that there are not enough of them. Some forestry, mining, oil and gas and other resource industries throughout Canada are working with First Nations in the development of partnership and joint venture agreements. Some guarantee a certain percentage of Aboriginal jobs and provide job training and scholarship opportunities. In urban areas, organizations such as the Manitoba Business Council are directly addressing the under-employment of Aboriginal people. Community colleges have expanded their number of Aboriginal students and upgrading programs are preparing them for entry into employment-oriented institutions. Education and business incentives support stay-in-school programs and recognize education as the key to the future.

One program to enhance the employability of Aboriginal people for the mining industry has been evaluated and shows the benefits to government and to the public generally of supporting training programs. The Multi-Party Training Plan (MPTP) is a 'training to employment' initiative supported by the Federal Government, Province of Saskatchewan, Aboriginal organizations and by the mining sector. It is open to northern residents, 87 percent of who are Aboriginal. An analysis of the program shows the displacement of welfare costs and the return of investment through taxes. Government is relieved of its welfare costs in a matter of months from the commencement of employment and there is eventually a complete return of all training and related costs.

A number of joint venture programs between resource industries and Aboriginal communities guarantee a certain level of Aboriginal employees. The BHP Ehati Diamond Mine's employment policy, in spite of unsettled land claims and some overlap in negotiated agreements with the Dogrib, Akaitcho, Inuit and Métis gives preference to Aboriginal residents of the Northwest Territories. The agreement includes jobs, training, and scholarships, related business opportunities and some pre-employment training. In 1997, roughly 50 percent of all company purchases were made through northern businesses, including 25 percent from Aboriginal owned businesses.

The Province of Quebec earmarked $3 million over three years for the creation of mining funds for the Crees, Inuit and the Montagnais. The Musselwhite Mine in northern Ontario, owned by Placer Dome Inc. and TVX Gold Inc. was developed on traditional lands of North Caribou Lake First Nations containing small Aboriginal communities of 400 to 700 people, where the unemployment rate had been 80 to 90 percent. Its agreement respected culture and heritage and set a minimal employment level of First Nation people at 25 percent.

Aboriginal students are now graduating with degrees in social work, engineering, law, medicine, dentistry, social work and in the Arts and Sciences. They are making valuable contributions to the professions and businesses they join. Most of them, in one way or another, are working with other Aboriginal people in an attempt to improve their situation and their prospects. In 1969 when the federal government introduced the White Paper, there were about 80 Aboriginal people in post-secondary institutions. Today there are 27,000 small businesses owned and managed by Aboriginal people throughout the country.

The employment of Aboriginal people is increasing because of their own initiative and special efforts by many employers. Some of the success stories are dramatic. The employment of Aboriginal residents of the Sagkeeng community near the Pine Falls paper plant was at a low ebb ten years ago. Then the plant became employee-owned and is now part of the Tembec Group. Ten to 15 percent of its 600 employees are now Aboriginal and in the pulp cutting and hauling part of the operation, 85 percent to 90 percent are Aboriginal. An Aboriginal person is a member of the local Board of Directors.

My intent in discussing the horrors of unemployment, and the prospects employment brings, has been to highlight this issue as one that requires the immediate and continuing attention of all Canadians, their businesses, industries, and governments. In spite of the progress that has been made, the lack of attention to the issue is still a black cloud hanging over Canadian life and Canada's standing in the world. It is that serious.

The individual efforts of Aboriginal people to find employment on their own, are often stymied by widely expressed assumptions about them as a race. The assumptions are generally untrue and inaccurate, but are stereotypical generalizations that hurt their chances of getting a job. Some run into more direct expressions of racial prejudice. I do not wish to rail against those who express damaging sentiments but I would like to bring to their attention the damage their comments to one another cause to Aboriginal people.

I find that the deepest and most personal attacks result from thoughtless comments made by otherwise kind and thoughtful Canadians. It is so unfair to pre-judge an individual by wild comments about the community to which they belong. From the standpoint of the listener, it is hurtful to hear your whole race and society put down because of someone's assumptions or because of one unpleasant experience. It is hard for Aboriginal people to understand why such hatred is directed towards them. I assume that most Canadians do not appreciate the extent of the harm their comments and attitudes are causing.

PART II

The
Gavel

5

Existing Courts

T he gavel is associated with the courts and the administration of justice, although Canadian courts don't actually use gavels. I use the term here, when referring to the regular courts and the services they provide, to contrast them with the Aboriginal courts I will later discuss and their softer feather approach to sentencing and incarceration.

Courts are confusing places. Most people who have to go to one are lost without the guidance of a lawyer. The procedure is steeped in tradition and some of the expressions that are used are unknown in common parlance. Many clients I had over the years had no idea what level of court they were in. They wanted to be polite, but didn't know how to address the judge. As a judge, I was called everything from Your Worship to My Honour to Your Eminence. Unless the client was a fan of Rumpole of the Bailey, they probably never heard of a judge being referred to as 'Your Lordship.'

Provincial judges are referred to as Your Honour and judges of the higher courts as Madame Justice, My Lady, Your Ladyship, Mr. Justice, My Lord or Your Lordship. These terms, as well as other traditions that are followed in court, come from the courts in England. In Quebec, the terms Monsieur le juge, Madame le juge and Votre Seigneurie are used. There is now some discussion about doing away with these historic forms of address. I am not too excited about the idea, as I hate to see our courts become casual, as the American ones are portrayed on television.

In Canada, lawyers stand when speaking to a judge or jury and they and the judges wear outdated and sometimes colourful gowns that nevertheless add dignity to court proceedings. It is amazing the influence television has on some young counsel. During my early days on the bench I had a number of lawyers interrupt another lawyer or a witness and make a comment from their chairs behind the counsel table. Following the tradition of E.K. Williams and Izzy Nitikman, I would always say, "I can't hear you Mr. So-and-so." Some of them would raise their voice and repeat the comment, and I would repeat mine. Seasoned clerks like Al Rouse or Benny Moroz would then say, in a whisper that could be heard in the hallway, "Stand up." The lawyer got the message.

I agree that the term 'My Lord' is unwarranted in Canada but it is a term we inherited with the English courts. In England the term is appropriate, because when a barrister is made a High Court judge, the appointment carries with it an appointment as a Lord of the Realm. When I was in England some years ago examining the operation of their courts, I watched a High Court judge conduct a case in court and was then invited to his Chambers where he had a discussion with counsel. I was amazed to find that the lawyers referred to the judge as 'My Lord' in court and 'judge' in his chambers. At his Inn of Court, where we went for lunch, he was called 'judge' by everyone we passed and by his first name by those who apparently knew him on a personal basis. I asked him about the various forms of address and he explained that the formal designations are reserved for use in court.

Only one lawyer I knew consistently followed the British practice. The late D'Arcy McCaffrey Q.C. never called me anything but 'judge' out of court, unless it was 'Al.' As a retired judge, I am not entitled to use any designation other than 'The Honourable' but many non-legal friends seem comfortable calling me 'judge,' although some lawyers who used to appear before me, still call me 'My Lord' when I pass them on the street. Some ask, "What do I call you?" Depending on the person, I must admit that I either give them my first name or say judge.

In addition to the use of unusual language, many of my clients were confused by the whole court process. When a trial was completed, some would ask, "What happened?" My reply might be "You got off" or "We have to come back next month." "Oh!" was the usual response. If, however, an accused was convicted he would know it, as the judge would have him stand, give him a lecture, and impose sentence. If a jail sentence was imposed, the offender would know that too, as he was escorted from the courtroom by a Police or Sheriff's Officer.

Because of these experiences, and before dealing with the structure of an Aboriginal court, I thought it might be helpful to review the courts that now exist and the services they provide. The court structure is also a mystery to the vast majority of Canadians and the levels of courts, their names and the extent of their jurisdiction is confusing. The differences may be taught in Law School but I am uncertain how the general public acquires its understanding of them, particularly when the media reports are often wrong. My comments may also be of interest to any Aboriginal people contemplating the establishment of their own courts.

The Parliament of Canada enacts the criminal law of the land. It and the Canada Evidence Act, drug and firearms laws and the Young Offenders Act appear in the Criminal Code of Canada, which contains the laws most often referred to in court. The federal government establishes and administers the Supreme Court of Canada, the Federal Court, the Tax Court and a number of administrative tribunals. The Federal Minister of Justice appoints the *puisne* (*puis né*, or next named) judges of the provincially established Superior Courts and their Chief Justices and Associate Chief Justices are appointed by the Prime Minister of Canada, as are all the judges of the Supreme Court of Canada.

The provinces also pass regulatory and quasi-criminal laws governing liquor, traffic, fishing, hunting, resource protection and many other matters within their jurisdiction under the Constitution. The provinces establish the courts that function exclusively within their territory and give them their names. They also appoint all the judges of their Provincial Courts. The names of the Provincial Courts are quite similar but the names of the superior courts vary from The Superior Court of Justice of Ontario, Cour Supérieure de Quebec, the Supreme Court of (name of Province,) and The Court of Queen's Bench of (name of the Province.)

The provinces are responsible for the prosecution of breaches of provincial and most federal legislation. The provincial Department of Justice, with its cadre of prosecutors, lays or approves criminal charges and sees that they are processed in a timely manner. They decide who to charge with what offence. If a trial decision does not find favour with the Crown, appeals may be taken in an attempt to obtain a different result.

The terms 'lower court' or 'higher court' indicate the extent of jurisdiction a court has in relation to another court. A lower court decision may be appealed to a higher court and the Supreme Court of Canada (the highest court) gives direction to all the lower courts. The term 'superior court' is used in a similar manner to indicate that it is the court in a province that has the greatest degree of authority.

The judiciary hears cases that are brought before it by private citizens or by government, including criminal cases instituted by the Crown. The role of a judge is to listen to the evidence and the arguments of counsel and to render a decision based on established principles of law. It is important that the judge be seen as the protector of everyone's rights and judges make every effort to be even-handed and open to persuasion. 'Convince the judge' is one of the tasks of the lawyer. The persuasiveness of their arguments and the legal authorities they cite often makes the difference between winning and losing. In criminal cases it may be the skill with which witnesses are questioned that will raise a reasonable doubt or seal the fate of an offender.

The judiciary is the third order of government, the others being the legislative and executive branches. The intent, in establishing a democratic form of government in this manner, was to maintain a balance of authority. Parliament establishes the laws and the Executive (or Cabinet) sees that the government departments apply and administer the law. The judiciary plays a supervisory role to see that the legislative and executive branches operate within the limits of their authority. Courts may strike down a law that is beyond the jurisdiction of government but parliament still has the right to amend the law if it wishes, to correct any problem the courts have identified.

An independent judiciary is a bulwark of justice that balances the rights of the individual with the authority of the state. Judges consider the demands and submissions from ordinary citizens on an equal basis with those of the wealthy or powerful. The courts provide a level playing field where litigants on opposite sides of every case have an equal opportunity to have their cases independently assessed. There are many unfortunate countries that do not have that balance, where the decisions of the army or a dictatorial government apply, and where the public has no access to an independent court.

Provincial and federal governments recognize the need for an independent judiciary. On occasion, Ministers of the Crown have had to step down from office for writing to a judge about a case and, directly or indirectly, attempting to influence the outcome. It is important for all citizens to see that the judiciary remains independent and free to make difficult and sometimes unpopular decisions if that becomes necessary. To perform its function in society, the judiciary must be free of the influence of government. That is not to say that government does not have an important role in the administration of justice, or does not influence decisions judges make, but that influence is only applied by passing or amending laws.

A practical and obvious example of the need for an independent judge is that the Crown (the government) is one of the parties to every criminal prosecution. When a citizen is charged with a crime (breaking a law parliament or a legislature has enacted) it is the Crown that goes to court seeking a conviction. The judge must be able to deal with the case without bias and without fear of government pressure or reprisal. The judge must decide whether or not the charge has been proven, based on the evidence, the statute law and broad principles of justice.

There are several levels of courts in Canada. Justices of the Peace are usually civil servants who are appointed by the provinces and have very limited authority. They may be authorized to accept pleas of 'guilty' to traffic and other minor offences, and they assess and recover fines based on a predetermined schedule which recommends a certain fine for the amount by which the speed limit is exceeded. The province has the authority to set, extend or limit the authority of these officials.

Magistrates also have limited jurisdiction and do not have to be legally trained. They may accept pleas of guilty to a wider variety of offences and impose fines. If a trial is likely to be required, or if a jail term is being sought by the Crown, the case is usually transferred to be heard by a judge of the Provincial Court. Magistrates regularly admit accused persons to bail, again following limitations developed by the Provincial Department of Justice. Some Aboriginal magistrates are being appointed to perform some of these functions but in the same places where the Provincial Court sits. This arrangement is intended to clear the dockets of less serious offences but does not provide judicial services to the isolated Aboriginal communities whose residents still have to travel to the place where the court party sits.

Provincial Courts have extensive criminal jurisdiction. In addition to hearing a wide variety of criminal cases, they have jurisdiction over young offenders who are twelve to seventeen years of age at the time an offence is committed. The Act recognizes that young people should not be held accountable for their actions in the same manner as adults, or suffer the same consequences, but should still bear responsibility for their actions. It emphasizes the need for supervision, discipline and control and that young people require guidance and assistance.

It stresses the need for rehabilitation and provides the option of taking "no measures, or measures other than judicial proceedings."

A youth may be discharged absolutely or conditionally, ordered to pay a fine up to $1,000, or be required to make restitution or pay compensation for any loss or damage that has been caused. Youth may also be put on probation or incarcerated for up to two years.

In the case of certain severe crimes, there is provision for the transfer of a youth to an adult (Supreme) court for trial. The trial then takes place in the superior court and may be before a judge sitting alone or with a jury. If the youth is convicted of a charge where the adult penalty is life imprisonment, the youth may be incarcerated for up to three years. If a conviction is for murder, the sentence may be up to ten years, with a maximum of six years in jail and the balance under supervision in the community. If a conviction is for second degree murder, those times are reduced to seven years, with a maximum of four years in jail.

A Youth Court is often a separate specialized court but in rural and northern areas it is common for the same Provincial Court judge to hear all adult and youth matters during the same sitting. The only distinction is that young offender matters are usually left until the adult cases have been disposed of.

In the adult court judges deal with charges varying from traffic offences to manslaughter. They hear a wide variety of criminal cases as a matter of right and the more serious offences if the accused consents. In spite of this broad jurisdiction, they cannot hear a murder trial or any indictable offence where the accused has elected to be tried by a judge and jury. They nevertheless conduct a preliminary inquiry in cases where trial by jury has been chosen.

Provincial Court judges are really the only judges seen by Aboriginal people in the north. They sit to hear criminal cases in central Aboriginal communities while those from other reserves travel to its monthly sittings. The Provincial Court sits in a number of centrally located Aboriginal communities but does not sit in the vast majority of them. The majority of accused enter a plea of guilty but the length of the dockets may require several trips before even that can be dealt with. The judge has to hear the facts of the case and listen to the arguments of the lawyers, before imposing a penalty. If an accused has a lawyer, there is often some negotiating (plea-bargaining) with the Crown attorney or a request by the judge for a pre-sentence report and those proceedings also result in prolonging the final disposition of a case.

The court dockets (lists) in Aboriginal communities are long and may be backlogged for months. The court usually has poor facilities that hardly exude an ambience of decorum or solemn justice. The judges fly in to a community with the lawyers and sometimes the police and are immediately tarred with suspicion. The suspicion escalates if the judge is seen talking to the police or to a Crown attorney in the courtroom before court begins. The conversation may be about the length of the list or the number of matters that will be going to trial, but onlookers don't know that. The effect on the reputation of the judge is devastating when he or she has to announce that cases on the list will have to be remanded for a month and the accused, their parents, and witnesses, have to come back once again.

The scene in the courtroom would be comic if it were not so tragic. The judge, in his black robe, sits behind a collapsible table. A similar table, where the Crown Attorney and the police sit, is placed at one side of the judge's table, at right angles to it. A table for Legal Aid and defence lawyers sits opposite. There are then rows of seats for people waiting for their case to be called, for onlookers, family members and witnesses. The seats usually remain empty as people congregate at the back of the room or outside, waiting for their case to be called.

The acoustics are not good and those at the back of the room cannot hear what is being said between the judge and the lawyers. An even greater problem is that even if they can hear, most can't understand what the judge and lawyers are talking about. Technical legalese like 'disclosure, loss of jurisdiction, or *locus*,' is unknown to them. When they don't understand, there is no one to ask and no one to explain what is happening.

There are other problems facing Provincial Courts in the cities. They often schedule cases that are expected to last for several days. Plea-bargaining intensifies as the date of trial approaches and sometimes the most serious discussions do not take place until the morning of the trial and it is common for a settlement to be reached at the last minute. The judge is advised there will be a change in the plea from not guilty to guilty, or guilty to a reduced charge. Counsel then request a remand to a later date so they can prepare to speak to sentence. The case is adjourned in fifteen minutes or so and the judge may be left with nothing to do for the rest of the day.

Courts do some double booking in anticipation of these last minute changes but it is hard to do that with a limited number of judges. In the meantime, many Aboriginal accused remain in custody and wait the six or more months until their case can be scheduled. If there is a preliminary hearing, they may wait a year or even three years before their trial is heard.

Another problem facing the Provincial Court is having to make judges available to sit on Preliminary Inquiries. The purpose of the hearing is not to determine guilt or the absence of guilt, but to hear evidence for the sole purpose of determining whether the Crown has a case worth sending to the superior court to try. The only issue is whether there is enough evidence to put him on trial or whether he should be set free.

In my opinion the whole process is unnecessary and a waste of valuable judge time. It keeps accused people and witnesses on hold and also seems to be an insult to the integrity of the Crown. In England, in the distant past, it might have made sense to have this type of screening before the Justice arrived in the circuit town to hear cases, but it makes no sense today. The Provincial Judge has limited jurisdiction and is really being asked to second-guess the Crown office that has laid or approved the laying of the charge. Surely in this day and age, the Crown can be trusted to bring to court only those cases that should be there. The Crown does have jurisdiction, if it wishes to exercise it, to lay a direct indictment and proceed to trial without a Preliminary Inquiry, but that authority is seldom used.

Another change in recent years that makes the Preliminary Inquiry redundant, is the heavy onus on the Crown to disclose the particulars of its case to defence counsel well in advance of a trial. The defence now has a much better idea of the case it has to meet than it did a decade ago. Nevertheless it has been the lobbying of the defence bar that has persuaded the federal government to refrain from abolishing the Preliminary Inquiry. Counsel like to use the process as a form of discovery similar to an Examination for Discovery in a civil case. They like to see how key witnesses stand up under cross-examination. If the Crown witnesses are strong, defence counsel may recommend that the accused enter a plea of guilty. If the witnesses are weak, the defence may decide to take its chances and proceed to trial.

A Provincial Judge should not be tied up to enable counsel to play these games. Accused, often Aboriginal people who are in custody, should not have to wait for this procedure to be followed, but should be entitled to be tried within a reasonable time. If the federal government thinks it appropriate to permit some preliminary questioning of Crown witnesses, that could be done before a Court Reporter or Special Examiner. The evidence need not be transcribed as counsel will have been able to assess the witnesses, but even if a transcript is needed for cross examination at trial, the process could be shorter than it now is and Provincial Court judges could be free for other duties.

The Charter of Rights and Freedoms guarantees a trial within a reasonable time, but that is not happening. The courts, including the Supreme Court of Canada, have permitted so many exceptions that cases drag on for years. Former Chief Justice Lamer tried in vain to speed the process. Again, it is often the Aboriginal people who are denied bail and who are kept in jail that suffer the most.

The Provincial Court does have some family law jurisdiction in parts of the province where there is no resident Queen's Bench Family Division judge. They hear child protection matters as well as separation, support and custody issues but have no authority to deal with the division of family assets or a divorce. Provincial Courts do have criminal jurisdiction that ties in with family issues. Their judges issue restraining orders under its Criminal Code and Family Law jurisdiction in the hope of preventing abuse, but because of the court's busy schedule these orders are difficult to obtain in an emergency and are usually impossible to enforce.

Superior Courts are the courts in each province with the greatest jurisdiction. Some are trial courts and others are Courts of Appeal. The term 'superior court' comes from a technical term of long usage, 'criminal courts of superior jurisdiction,' which is still used in the Criminal Code of Canada.

In most provinces it is only Superior Court Judges, sitting with juries, that have the authority to hear murder and other serious charges. Juries may hear any indictable charge where the accused has elected to be tried by a judge and jury. In those cases, an accused may change his mind and decide to be tried by a judge sitting alone and without a jury. A Superior Court judge then hears the case.

There are judicial centres at numerous places in the provinces where the superior trial courts sit and offer a full range of civil, criminal and family services, including jury trials. Some centres have resident judges and others are circuit points served by judges on a rotation basis. I am not aware of any superior courts that sit in Aboriginal communities although they have the jurisdiction to sit in any location approved by the Chief Justice.

Superior Courts have unlimited jurisdiction to hear civil cases. That includes all matters that are not criminal. A civil case may involve a claim by one person or corporation against another for the recovery of a debt, for damages for personal injury or for the interpretation of a disputed contract. The interpretation of wills or statutory provisions, bankruptcies, real estate cases, injunctions and labour disputes are heard. Divorce, the custody of children and the division of family assets and spousal support are included in the civil law jurisdiction of the court.

In some provinces, Provincial Courts have authority to hear civil cases involving up to five or ten thousand dollars. In Manitoba that work is done by the Court of Queen's Bench Hearing Officers, subject to an appeal to a judge of that court. Apart from the distant and expensive higher court, Aboriginal reserve residents really have no court to which they can go to present a claim for a debt, to seek compensation for an injury or to have a legal document interpreted.

There are, however, civil claims that arise. During my time on the Court of Queen's Bench I had a civil case where a home had been sold in the non-reserve part of Norway House. It turned out that the house was not located on the land both the vendor and purchaser thought it was. A neighbouring house was also found to be on the 'wrong' piece of land.

The case had to be heard in Winnipeg, no doubt at considerable expense as the lawyers called local people who were aware of the history of the community and the lands in question. Although it was a struggle to find an applicable principle of law, let alone a legal precedent, I ordered that the boundaries of the lots be re-drawn so the titles in the Winnipeg Land Titles Office would have the two houses on the land each owner believed was theirs.

During the AJI we heard of disputes about the theft of a canoe and another about the theft of a coat. The cases arose in a criminal context as there was no civil jurisdiction available. In the case of the canoe, the person who took it said he only borrowed it and intended to return it at some point. He argued that Aboriginal tradition permitted a person to borrow something that was not in use and that it was not a crime to do so without the consent of the owner. In legal terms, the argument seemed to be that, because of tradition, there was an implied consent.

The coat had been abandoned and was lying in a field. A person picked it up and refused to return it to the previous owner. The argument was that the coat had been abandoned and that the finder was entitled, in Aboriginal tradition, to claim ownership. If there had been an Aboriginal court with civil law jurisdiction, it would have been interesting to hear the result.

I mention these matters, not to suggest that the Court of Queen's Bench hold court in remote Aboriginal communities, or that Provincial Courts have civil jurisdiction, and sit there as well, but to indicate that litigation does emanate from them.

Each province has its own Court of Appeal with a Chief Justice and some have an Associate Chief Justice as well. A single Justice of Appeal may hear interim and procedural applications, but panels of three or five judges, assigned by the Chief Justice, hear full appeals. The responsibility of the court is to review decisions of lower courts and to consider whether they should be confirmed, amended or reversed.

The appeal court will usually have a transcript of all the evidence that was presented in the lower court and a copy of the oral or written reasons of the trial judge. It will also have received written arguments from the lawyers in advance. At the hearing of the appeal the lawyers summarize their position, introduce additional arguments and answer any questions the judges ask. In clear cases, the appellate judges will give an immediate oral decision, but in more complicated ones they will reserve their decision and release a written decision later on.

The judges of appeal will examine the manner in which a trial was conducted, will study the evidence, and will see whether the trial judge properly applied the law and arrived at the correct decision. This may include a consideration of whether the provisions of the Charter of Rights and Freedoms were properly interpreted and applied, and may include an examination of case law that has dealt with similar circumstances in the past. It will consider the statutory or case law to make sure it was properly applied to the facts.

The Court of Appeal may hear further evidence if it wishes but that is seldom done. The appeal is therefore not a new trial but is a review. Appellate judges rely upon the 'findings of fact' and assessment of the credibility of witnesses the trial judge has made. On matters of fact, appellate courts often say "the decision is not one the facts would reasonably bear," or "we see no reason to interfere with the decision of the learned trial judge." Many appeals deal with sentencing and the appellate court attempts to maintain some degree of uniformity, depending on the type and severity of the offence and the record of the offender.

Courts of Appeal are mindful of the effort, and sometimes agonizing time trial judges spend trying to arrive at a fair and just decision. Many of them have been trial judges in the past and are aware of the fine distinctions that have to be made in deciding which evidence to accept. They have a different role to play as judges of appeal, but their objective is the same as the trial judges, to arrive at a fair, proper and just resolution of the cases they are called upon to hear.

Most Courts of Appeal sit only in the provincial or territorial capital although the statute creating the court leaves it up to it to decide when and where cases will be heard. The larger provinces have branches of the court in two or more cities. Although the trial courts regularly sit in a number of cities within their territorial jurisdiction it is unusual for a Court of Appeal to do so. While there are valid monetary considerations for not sitting in a variety of centres, it is a fact that vast areas in Canada, particularly in the north, have limited access to that level of court.

Rural litigants and their lawyers are less inclined than their city colleagues to appeal cases. One factor that limits the number of rural appeals is the cost. It is one thing to walk to court for a two-hour appearance and another to travel from a distant part of the province. Litigants from a distance have travel and accommodation to consider and the rural lawyer's costs either have to be passed on to the client or absorbed. Some appeals, that would be taken if the court were more accessible, are not taken at all.

The televising of trials and appeals is an alternative worthy of consideration. If court proceedings were telecast that would bring the court and its responsibilities and manner of operation into the living rooms of citizens in the most remote parts of Canada. It would show the solemnity of the Canadian courts and the difference in practice from the U.S. courts and from Hollywood productions.

As long as a judge has the right to turn off the camera when sensitive or embarrassing evidence is being presented, or when discussions take place in the absence of the jury, I believe that using this method of inviting people into the courtroom would serve a positive educational purpose. I would even favour having comments from trained and knowledgeable commentators to explain what is happening as a high profile trial or appeal proceeds.

Superior Courts never sit in Aboriginal communities but many have their own closed circuit TV channel. A distributor of programs or the northern Aboriginal stations should be able to select and provide coverage on trial and appeal cases dealing with aboriginal issues. In addition to supporting the image of a thoughtful and listening judiciary, it would be valuable for Aboriginal people to see the vigour with which lawyers present arguments on cases affecting their lives.

This will of course not provide these communities with access to the courts themselves.

The Supreme Court of Canada is the highest court in Canada and is its final court of appeal. Prior to 1949 appeals could be taken from the Supreme Court to the Judicial Committee of the Privy Council in London, England. The change was requested by Canada and made by the British Parliament in recognition of Canada's increasing stature and independence.

The Supreme Court is established by federal legislation and holds its hearings in Ottawa. There are nine judges, made up of three from each of Ontario and Quebec, two from the western provinces and one from the Maritimes. The Prime Minister of Canada appoints the judges and they, like other superior court judges, may continue in office until age seventy-five. While I am sure that inquiries are made to find the best candidate to fill a vacancy, there is no public inquiry system like that of the United States where committees question nominated candidates. Most of those appointed to the Supreme Court have been judges of provincial Courts of Appeal. Occasionally a lawyer who has never been a judge, but who has a respected record, is appointed directly from the Bar. The Chief Justice is usually selected from among the other judges of the court but there have been exceptions to that practice as well.

I have heard no serious objection to the present method of selecting the judges, or the Chief Justice, nor am I persuaded that a public screening or selection process would do better. I do think it is preferable to name judges to the Supreme Court of Canada from judges of provincial trial or appellate courts (just as I think it appropriate to appoint judges to provincial Courts of Appeal from judges of the superior trial court) as the authorities will then have the person's judicial performance to consider. It is important to keep partisan politics out of the process as much as possible and to select judges for the abilities they possess. I would not favour the selections being made by a committee of the bar. There would be allegations of bias or selecting people because of their popularity, or their service to the bar association. The selections made by Prime Ministers of differing political persuasions have generally been well received.

The questioning of a prospective judge by some sort of committee would be demeaning to the individual being questioned and to the high office as well. Questions such as "How do you feel about the abortion issue?" or "How would you rule on same sex marriages?" are totally inappropriate. Any response would have to be: "It depends on what the statute provides." Mere fishing expeditions by an unqualified questioner would not advance the search for a qualified judge. The search should be for a person knowledgeable in the law, who will consider all issues in a fair and careful manner, and will apply an independent mind to each case and issue.

The task of the Supreme Court of Canada is basically to review decisions of the provincial Courts of Appeal. Because of the large number who wish to appeal, and due to the limited number of cases it can handle, the Supreme Court screens the cases it hears. Before a case is accepted for hearing (with some exceptions in serious criminal cases) counsel must present an application for leave to appeal. Panels of three Supreme Court judges hear those applications and either accept or reject the application. In general, as I understand the practice, cases to be heard are limited to unusual ones that cry out for review or ones that involve an important point of law of national importance.

Parliament has the right to ask the Supreme Court of Canada for an opinion on the validity of federal legislation. Social issues with which parliament appears reluctant to deal also find their way onto Supreme Court dockets. The court has no option but to consider these matters and cases involving the Charter of Rights and Freedoms consume much of the court's time.

The court usually has seven or nine judge panels hear cases. Lawyers are assigned a limited amount of time to present their arguments. Judges ask questions to clarify points of argument or to focus counsel's attention on specific issues and it is evident that the judges have read the material in advance of the hearing. The court usually reserves its decision until draft opinions are written, exchanged and discussed by all the judges who heard the appeal. A decision may be unanimous or there may be a number of written decisions that support or differ from the majority.

One of the particular services of the Supreme Court is to give a definitive analysis of points of law. On occasion, courts of appeal in two or more provinces have come to different conclusions on the interpretation or application of the same provision of a statute, or on the applicability of a principal of the common law. The Supreme Court's decision is final. Its decision provides the basis by which lawyers and judges can approach a subsequent case where the same principle arises. The court usually sticks to the narrow point of law that has been raised by a case and declines to wander afield to deal with subsidiary issues. It provides guidance in the wording of jury charges and it will describe the manner in which damages are to be calculated, and the method to be used in calculating child support. This sort of guidance is of inestimable value to the lower courts and to lawyers.

Occasionally, decisions of the Supreme Court can cause some confusion for judges and juries. When trial judges charge juries after the evidence and submissions of counsel are completed, they spend some time explaining principles of law in great detail. They have to do that because Courts of Appeal and the Supreme Court, in examining charges to juries, suggest that a trial judge should have used other language and should have covered other parts of the evidence or explained principles of law in greater detail. On many occasions they have found that the principle of reasonable doubt has not been adequately explained.

As the years have gone by, trial judges have to spend more and more time preparing their charges to make sure they have covered every possible issue that might trouble a Court of Appeal or the Supreme Court of Canada. They go over the evidence in great detail as the court has said they must review the evidence. They spend hours, and occasionally days, addressing juries, instructing them in their duties, defining principles of law and reciting the various conclusions to which they may come. Jurors find it difficult to maintain their concentration for such a long time. Some jurors visibly tire and, if not asleep, have certainly lost their ability to follow what is being said. Something should be done to shorten or simplify the process.

As one who has considerable faith in the collective wisdom of juries, I would respectfully suggest that they are able to decide what happened and whether the accused should be found guilty or not, without having to consider intricate details of the law. The Supreme Court would provide a valuable service if it would devise a charge to the jury that could be delivered in half an hour. It would be helpful if the court could say, particularly for the shorter cases, that a short simple charge like the following would suffice:

"You have heard the evidence. Your task is to decide whether the accused killed the victim. If he did not, you will find the accused not guilty. If the accused did cause the death, if the act was planned and intentional your verdict will be guilty of murder. If the death was wrongful but unintentional, your verdict will be guilty of manslaughter. If you have a doubt on any evidence, or about your decision, you must give the benefit of the doubt to the accused. You have heard the facts and the law discussed by counsel. I have no argument on the law as they described it to you. Please retire and consider your verdict."

The Chief Justices and Associate Chief Justices in Canada make up the Canadian Judicial Council. The Chief Justice of the Supreme Court is the Chief Justice of Canada and the Chairperson of the Council. The Judicial Council is responsible for the operation of the office of the Commissioner of Judicial Affairs. It also has a number of committees dealing with matters such as court administration, judicial remuneration, judicial education and the independence of the judiciary. With members from every province and territory in Canada it is a clearing-house for innovative management techniques.

It receives complaints from the public on the conduct of superior court judges,' notifies the judge in question and obtains an explanation. If the complainant is still not satisfied, an inquiry can be held and a report made to Council. The Council can reject a complaint or, in cases where it is of the opinion that a federally appointed judge should no longer remain in office, it can report that opinion to the Government of Canada. Only if the House of Commons and the Senate pass a joint resolution to that effect, can the judge be removed from office.

6

Child Protection

I have spoken of the devastating effect of the removal of children from Aboriginal parents and their culture, and I have suggested that it can still be seen today. There is no area of the law where this is more evident than in today's Child Welfare system, more specifically in child protection cases.

Combined, as it is, with dysfunctional families and spousal and child abuse, there is also no other issue that so clearly defines the unfortunate relationship between Aboriginal people and the justice system. In spite of the development of innovative ways of dealing with the issue by Aboriginal agencies like the Awasis Agency of northern Manitoba, the courts and the non-Aboriginal agencies are not addressing the needs of Aboriginal families.

The term 'in need of protection' is defined in Child Welfare statutes. Section 17(1) of the Manitoba Child and Family Services Act provides:

> For the purposes of this Act, a child is in need of protection where the life, health or emotional well-being of the child is endangered by the act or omission of a person.

Section 17(2) gives illustrations of when a child is in need of protection:

(a) is without adequate care, supervision or control;
(b) is in the care, custody, control or charge of a person
(i) who is unable or unwilling to provide adequate care, supervision or control of the child, or
(ii) whose conduct endangers or might endanger the life, health or emotional well-being of the child, or
(iii) who neglects or refuses to provide or obtain proper medical or other remedial care or treatment necessary for the health or well-being of the child or who refuses to permit such care or treatment to be provided to the child when the

care or treatment is recommended by a duly qualified
medical practitioner;

(c) is abused or in danger of being abused;

(d) is beyond the control of a person who has the care, custody,
control or charge of the child;

(e) is likely to suffer harm or injury due to the behaviour,
condition, domestic environment or associations of the child
or of a person having care, custody, control or charge of the
child;

(f) is subjected to aggression or sexual harassment that
endangers the life, health or emotional well-being of the
child;

(g) being under the age of twelve years, is left unattended and
without reasonable provision being made for the supervision
and safety of the child; or

(i) is the subject, or is about to become the subject, of an
unlawful adoption under *The Adoption Act* or of a sale under
section 84.

In its application, the term in need of protection almost always
means — in need of protection from their own parents. The statute
gives Child Welfare Agencies broad authority to remove children from
their homes and parents and to do whatever they wish with them
thereafter. When a case goes to court and the agency becomes a child's
guardian, it has almost total authority and influence over the child's
life, and the natural parents have none.

The paternalistic approach of many agencies is often no better than
the century-long approach of the Department of Indian Affairs. The
agency believes it knows what is best for the children. One belief is that
it is best to remove children from what is seen as the destructive
influence of parents who may be suffering from poverty, substance
abuse or inappropriate conduct.

It often seems that an agency believes it has completed its task
when it takes children away from their parents. It does not apply the
same zeal in looking after the interests of the children thereafter. The
deep personal, psychological, and developmental problems of the
children, caused by their removal from their parents, are usually not
addressed. If problems arise later on when the children are rebellious
or in trouble with the law, it is too late to reverse the damage that has
been caused.

The Child and Family Services Act of Manitoba, and the agencies, like the residential school policy, are undoubtedly well meaning. The statute even opens by declarations of the highest principles. Some of them are:

The best interests of children are a fundamental responsibility of society.

The family is the basic source of care, nurture and acculturation of children and parents have the primary responsibility to ensure the well being of their children.

Children have a right to a continuous family environment in which they can flourish.

Families are entitled to receive preventive and supportive services directed to preserving the family unit.

Families are entitled to services with respect to their cultural and linguistic heritage.

Aboriginal people do not see these principles being applied by non-Aboriginal agencies. Instead, they see social workers from another culture applying their own standards and their own beliefs. They see mainstream principles being argued in court and do not feel their concerns for their children are being heard or respected.

The statute which gives the agencies their authority is seen as a brutal instrument in the hands of one of the most powerful and independent organizations in the country. Seizures over the years have shattered Aboriginal families and have destroyed the lives of children as they are moved from one foster home to another. The agencies exercise enormous authority and Aboriginal people are afraid to go to them for help. They are afraid that if they do, the agency will decide they are unfit to care for their children and will apprehend and remove them forever.

When an agency apprehends a child it must take the child to a place of safety where the child may be detained for examination and temporary care. Some safety! In 1997/98 an average of 37 children in the care of the Winnipeg Child and Family Services Agency were kept in hotel rooms due to the lack of foster homes. In 1999 the number varied between five and 20 per night. It is not hard to see the effect on the Aboriginal community when 70 percent of all children in care in

Winnipeg are Aboriginal. Apart from what happens later, the treatment of children at the front end of the system is in chaos.

The next step in the process is also traumatic for children and for their parents. The agency has the authority to return a child to its parents pending a hearing but my experience was that children were always 'in care' when a case came to court. The agency must file an application for a hearing within four juridical (working) days of an apprehension and the case itself is supposed to come on for hearing within seven days. That never happens. The Court of Appeal, a number of years ago, ruled that those times could be extended by adjournments, and the intent to avoid keeping children and their parents in limbo for long periods of time, was circumvented.

Even with the best court management techniques, cases seldom get to trial within six months of an apprehension. That length of time would not be unreasonable if the children were not in the custody of the agency and in limbo, but during that time children may live in several foster homes.

The agency has almost unfettered authority to decide whether the parents may visit with their children pending a hearing. I can't recall a case where an agency would allow parents to visit for more than an hour once a week. The visits had to take place in the agency office and, at least until the agency felt the visits were going well, a supervisor had to remain in the room at all times. It was clear that the agency believed that the parents were unfit and could not even be trusted to have normal visits with their children.

When parents applied to court to extend the visits, the standard answer of the agency was that their staff time was very limited and they didn't think it safe to allow the parents to take the children out on their own. This limitation of contact between the parents and the child was of course damaging to the child. I cannot imagine how anyone could suggest that keeping children away from their parents could possibly be in their best interests. The agency, of course, had already passed judgment on that issue as well. Children have a right to be protected and to be removed from abusive parents, but they also have a right not to be left alone or placed with abusive foster parents.

As they wait for a trial, the antagonism increases as the parents accuse the social worker of acting without just cause and the workers define the parents as uncommunicative and uncooperative. With the assumption that they are guilty and are unworthy to even talk to their children, it is not surprising that the parents are frantic at the thought of losing their children and see the agency as a foreign and oppressive force.

When a case is finally gets to trial, the judge's hands are tied by other provisions of the Act. One of the major problems with the process established by the Manitoba Act is the limitation it places on a judge's ability to examine the whole situation at one time. Section 2(1) of the Manitoba Child and Family Services Act provides, and I italicize the limiting phrase:

> The best interests of the child shall be the paramount consideration of the director, the children's advocate, an agency and a court in all proceedings under this Act affecting a child, *other than proceedings to determine whether a child is in need of protection*, and in determining the best interests of the child all relevant matters shall be considered...

Two weeks of trial time can be expended as witnesses describe why a child is in need of protection while the judge is supposed to steer clear of considering what is in the best interests of the child. A succession of witnesses invariably deals with the conduct of the parents and signs of abuse that have been found on the children. If the judge finds that a child is in need of protection, the agency expects to receive an order of Guardianship. No one suggests that another hearing be held to see if that is in the best interests of the child. If a placement in a foster home is likely, or if adoption is mentioned, the judge is not supposed to explore those matters until the initial finding is made. By that time it is too late — the witnesses have left. The judge should be able to examine all the issues upon which he will eventually have to rule, as the case proceeds.

Agencies and their counsel, in cases I sat on, often took the position that their decision on what they would do with a child if the agency became its guardian, could not be considered by the judge until a finding on whether or not the child is in need of protection is made. Then, when an order of Guardianship is made, they argue that what is to be done with the child is beyond the jurisdiction of the court. That meant, in practical terms, that the judge was foreclosed from examining the plan of the agency even though evidence had not been lead on whether the plan was in the best interest of the child.

That is an intolerable situation, and surely one the legislature never intended. The judge is there to look out for the interests of the child and should be entitled to make whatever inquiries the situation demands. Some judges ignore the limitation but most leave the presentation of the case to the lawyers. It still plays a part in the sort of evidence the agency will present. I understand that agencies are now more prepared to discuss their plans and in some cases a proposed foster parent is called as a witness. That is as it should be, but the legislation should be amended to clearly expand the authority and responsibility of the court.

The law should be amended to require agencies to have a plan in place before they come to court. A judge should be able to balance the seriousness of the parents' problems against the type of home where the children will be placed. He or she should know the background of the proposed foster parents, the number of children they care for, what they plan to do about schooling, recreation and child development.

If the proposed foster parents are non-Aboriginal it would be important for the judge to know their experience in dealing with Aboriginal children and what, if anything, they plan to do to make certain the children maintain contact with their culture. Their plans to keep the children in touch with their parents and other family members, should also be explored. All of these matters should then be weighed in the balance before a judge makes a decision on whether the children are in need of protection from their parents.

The hearing should not be compartmentalized by separating the issues a judge has to consider. Doing so places too much emphasis on whether children are in need of protection and not enough on what is in their best interests. The court needs the assistance of experts who have studied child development, and evidence on the trauma the removal of children from their parents may cause should be presented. Witnesses should then be available to discuss these issues with the judge.

The judge should also be entitled to put conditions on an Order of Guardianship. He should be able to require visits with the natural parents and to require the child's participation with his extended family and in cultural activities. To enable that to be done, the statute would have to be amended to alter the provisions that give the Guardian the authority of a parent. Parental responsibilities can be defined by the court in other types of custody cases and I see no reason why the court should not have similar authority when dealing with guardianship.

Cases that go to trial usually deal with the diametrically opposed positions of the parents and the agency. The parents say they have overcome their problems and can properly care for their children. The agency says the parents are alcoholic or abusive and cannot be trusted. Throughout these trials, the gulf between white and Aboriginal values is often evident. Neither trusts the other to deal with the children in an appropriate manner.

If a judge decides to return the children to their parents, which seldom happens, he should have the authority to impose conditions on the parents that would guarantee their good conduct towards the children. That would enable a judge who is not impressed with the plans of the agency, to give it specific authority to supervise the conduct of the parents (even if it has that authority under the Statute.) He might prefer to take a chance on less than perfect parents, rather than to rely on foster parents from another culture. He might even adjourn the case to see if the parents are willing to make changes in their life-style. The case could be brought back to court if the parents default.

In my opinion the whole concept of a 'foster home' where children are raised by strangers, should be done away with. In its place the court should have the right to order where the children are to live for the time being. In that event the judge could impose conditions that would soften the blow to the children and do something to maintain their connection with their culture such as placing them with grandparents, uncles and aunts or with other extended family members.

In 1996/97 the Manitoba Child Protector received over 500 complaints. The greatest number of them dealt with the placement of children in foster homes — too many or inappropriate placements. About 25 percent of the complaints came from CFS workers and almost 50 percent from other professional workers or agencies. The other 25 percent came from children, family members and others. Out of a total of 133 children whose racial origin was determined, 101 were Aboriginal.

In my latter years on the bench, I kept statistics on the results of the pre-trial conferences I conducted. In 1992 my settlement rate of all cases was 84 percent and the settlement rate in Child Protection cases was 90 percent. Many did not settle during the conference but I traced the subsequent history of each case and marked a case as settled if it did not go to trial. The conference may have only raised some options for the parties and their lawyers to explore but the results convinced me of one thing: If the parties can enter into a free discussion of the issues under the direction of a mediator, albeit a judge, there is an excellent chance that mutually acceptable solutions can be found.

I found that the compulsory pre-trial hearing or settlement conference before a judge in the presence of the parties and their lawyers was often the first time the conduct and concerns of the parents and the agency were discussed in a quiet rational way. The hearing forced the parties to turn their attention to the vital question of a solution that was best for the children.

That result also caused me to believe that if mediation can be applied to all the issues as soon as children are apprehended, many cases can be kept out of the courts altogether. After taking the mediation course at Harvard I offered to attempt mediation of child protection matters at an early stage (without charge) but no one accepted my offer. In any event, where Aboriginal people are involved, it would be best to have an Aboriginal Peacemaker or mediator try to resolve any problems that exist and to identify family members who can assist the parents. That mediation should take place before court cases are commenced and the mediation should be outside the court process.

During a child protection settlement conference some years ago, I did have the opportunity to mediate a solution. The social workers for the Agency had mentioned the possibility of having the two children placed in a foster home or placing them for adoption. The parents were beside themselves at the thought of adoption. With some prodding, they admitted they couldn't care for the children themselves and wouldn't be opposed to the children living with a relative until they got themselves straightened around. When the Agency workers indicated that would be fine with them, discussions about an acceptable relative began.

The social workers said they would speak to the suggested relative and agreed to consider continuing contact between the parents and the children. The parents were clearly aware they would have to change their lifestyle. The case was adjourned and I never heard of it again, presumably because it was settled to everyone's satisfaction.

Aboriginal children are regularly placed in non-Aboriginal foster homes. While an Agency may think that is in the best interests of children, that objective is seldom achieved. That is not to say that many apprehensions of children are not necessary or that many foster parents have not been supportive and helpful to Aboriginal children.

Opikihiwawin, (of which I was a Board member for a time) is a support group for non-Aboriginal people and the Aboriginal children they have adopted. It has done an excellent job of seeing that the children are well cared for, remain connected to their Aboriginal culture, and are supported by both cultures. In the vast majority of cases however, where there is not that sort of support, a great deal of damage is caused by removing Aboriginal children from their parents. Many are placed in a stranger's home with different cultural attitudes and values.

The question I ask, particularly with respect to Aboriginal children, is: is this whole process in the best interests of the child? The paternalistic answer the system has always given seems to be a resounding 'Yes,' but only because the child is removed from what is assumed to be the negative influences of the parents. That assumption may appear valid when one looks at the superficial facts, but it is usually not when the lost advantages are examined and the effects of dislocation are considered.

Whatever the reason, the existing child protection system is not working. Aboriginal children are ending up as victims of the system and their young lives are in turmoil. They are removed from people who, even if they have problems and face an uncertain future, love and want to care for them. Some are abused in inappropriate foster homes. Others are given bed and board but are emotionally neglected. Many turn to inappropriate conduct and fall under the influence of young offenders and of gangs.

The Child and Family Services Act should undergo a major revision. The authority of agencies should be carefully spelled out. Attention to the cultural needs of children should be addressed from their perspective and procedures should be put in place to avoid the damage that is currently being caused to them. The court process should be amended to make it less legalistic, less confrontational and more mediative in its approach to cases. The assistance of experts on child development and how children's needs can be addressed, should be sought. Aboriginal professionals should participate in the search for a more compassionate and effective system.

Two very specific changes should be made to the Child and Family Services Act. One is that Aboriginal children should be left with their parents until a child protection hearing is held. I would guess that the parents would be on their best behaviour during this period. The other needed change is, that if children, following a hearing, have to be removed from their parents, they should only be placed with members of their extended family. One way or another, whatever arrangement is made, the one and only goal should be to do what is in their immediate and long term benefit.

In October 1993 I met with a group of 60 or so Aboriginal inmates at Stony Mountain Penitentiary as part of a church visitation program. I had been asked to speak to them but hadn't prepared anything in advance. I decided, almost at the last minute, to give them an opportunity to talk about themselves. I introduced a number of topics and kept notes of their comments. It ended up that I was taking a rough survey.

We talked about their experience with lawyers and judges (which wasn't that bad) and their history with the legal system and with jails. It became evident that most of them had started getting into trouble with the law as young offenders, had spent time in youth facilities, provincial jails and finally in the penitentiary. Many were there for the second and third time and almost all had received parole at some point and had their parole revoked.

Near the end of my questioning I asked how many had been involved with the Child Welfare system. They broke out in laughter and I asked, "What's so funny?" One replied, "We all have been." On more careful questioning it turned out that a few had not been removed from their parents, but 90 percent had been. Although I found the answers significant, I was aware that my 'survey' wouldn't stand up to academic scrutiny.

It was therefore gratifying when, in November 1999, the Hon. Tim Sale, the Manitoba Minister responsible for Child Welfare, and the Hon. Eric Robinson, the Minister responsible for Aboriginal Affairs, provided funding so a more scientific study of the connection between the child protection system and subsequent criminal conduct could be done. Professor Doug Skoog, a sociologist and criminologist at the University of Winnipeg, devised the study and instructed the interviewers engaged by Sharon Perreault of the Ma Mawi Chi Itata Centre Inc., which managed the project. The questions were discussed with Ms Perreault and myself and finalized by Professor Skoog.

The subjects were 100 inmates, half Aboriginal and half non-Aboriginal. Their answers showed a marked difference in the experience of the two groups. The most startling difference was the extent of their involvement with the child protection system. When they were five years of age or younger, 64 percent of the Aboriginal group lived with their parents, compared to 90 percent of the non-Aboriginal participants. During the same period, 20 percent of the Aboriginal inmates were in foster care, while none of the non-Aboriginal inmates were. By the age of 12, over 50 percent of the Aboriginal group lived away from their parental home and by age 18 only one in ten was at home.

The inmates were too young to have experienced a residential school, but by age 12, 24 percent of the Aboriginal group and 10 percent of the non-Aboriginal had spent time in custody. During their teens the numbers grew to 70 percent of the Aboriginal respondents and 42 percent for the others. The study showed that 12 percent of the Aboriginal group and 10 percent of the others had been adopted. While it was impossible to separate the answers for this group, Professor Skoog reports that it is unusual to find such a high percentage of adopted people in a group of 100 when there are only 7000 adoptions in all of Canada each year. Their removal from parental care was likely a factor in their involvement in crime.

Exactly 50 percent of the Aboriginal inmates reported having been abused while in foster care and 40 percent said the care they received in foster homes was worse than the treatment they had received in their own home. No non-Aboriginal inmate rated the care as worse. Twenty-eight percent of the Aboriginal subjects also reported the level of supervision while in foster care to have been low while zero percent of the non-Aboriginal subjects said so. Fifty-six percent of the Aboriginal respondents reported that none of their foster caregivers were from the same background.

By the time the respondents were between 13 and 18 years of age the number of each group ending up in jail became more distinct. Seventy percent of the Aboriginal respondents had been in jail, compared to 43 percent of the non-Aboriginal group. During the same ages, 24 percent of the Aboriginal youth were in foster care compared to 10 percent of the others. By the time they were 18, Aboriginal youth had been in closed custody twice as many times as the others. Fifty-two percent, as compared to 28 percent, had been sentenced to open custody, although the number of sentences and the length of them were about the same for each group.

Professor Skoog drew a number of conclusions from the survey. He suggests that the net effect of removing children from their homes and placing them with strangers through the child protection system increases the probability of their coming into contact with the criminal justice system. A poor quality of care in that system magnifies the problem.

He also refers to other writings which have found that children who are removed from their parents are less likely to form strong attachments with others, resulting in a lesser level of social control and an increased likelihood they will break the law. Placements in a number of homes will reduce the opportunity to bond with responsible adults. Children who receive less than adequate care or who are emotionally rejected or abused tend to view the world as hostile, have feelings of suspicion and fear, and have little motive to cooperate or follow adult guidelines for conduct

The numbers of Aboriginal people in our jails must reflect, at least in part, the devastating effect of so many children being taken from their parents during their formative years and placed with strangers who, intentionally or not, contributed to their abnormal development. All those who were interviewed had been in trouble repeatedly with the law and were in jail at the time of the survey, but it was the Aboriginal group that had the greater involvement with the child protection process.

The legacy of the disruption of Aboriginal people in their past, their treatment as individuals at the present time and their floundering in our system of justice, is the staggering number that fill our jails. Before solutions are considered, it is important to know how bad the situation really is.

The Aboriginal population in the Stony Mountain federal penitentiary is reported to be approximately 48 percent, the Provincial Jail numbers (those sentenced to two years less a day) are even more startling. They indicate a massive disparity in the incarceration of Aboriginal people. As I thought one set of figures might be a distortion, I obtained figures for random days in both 1998 and 2000. The 1998 figures only show the total population of each jail and the percentage of Aboriginal inmates. The 2000 figures show the total jail population, the number that are Aboriginal and the percentage they are of the total population:

Institution	1998		2000		
	Total	Ab%	Total	Ab	Ab%
Headingley	250	80%	331	275	83%
Brandon	150	80%	178	140	79%
Dauphin	55	85%	50	43	86%
The Pas	55	80%	55	47	85%
Egg Lake	40	100%	40	40	100%
Milner Ridge	145	85%	126	108	86%
Portage (Women)	48	90%	54	43	80%
Winnipeg Remand Centre	300	75%	315	252	80%
Manitoba Youth Centre	180	80%	156	125	80%
Agassiz Youth Centre	120	90%	115	100	87%

At the time the 2000 numbers were taken, 95 youth were awaiting sentence in the Manitoba Youth Centre. A sampling of their time in custody, without having been sentenced, indicates the seriousness of their situation.

Youth	Days on Remand
1	70
3	82
4	82
5	124
6	266
7	92
8	95
9	75
10	152
11	129

The average percentage of Aboriginal people in provincial jails in 1998 was 84.5 percent and in 2000 was 85.4 percent. This situation will be the reason for many of the comments and suggestions I will ultimately make.

Whether the reason is the manner in which Aboriginal youth were treated by parents with long standing emotional problems, by a child protection system that is not meeting their needs, or other societal causes, the result is a tragedy and a disgrace. The causative factors need to be examined and steps must be taken to correct them.

PART III

Hope in
the Mist

7

Education

I have entitled this part "Hope in the Mist" to indicate that good things are happening but they are elusive and hardly indicate an established trend. They nevertheless indicate some possibilities and show that systems can be developed by and for Aboriginal people that are of value to all Canadians.

Good news. Gains are being made as Aboriginal youth excel with the help of more and more educational opportunities. They are staying in school longer and are graduating from high school and universities in increasing numbers. They are assuming positions of responsibility in their home communities and in organizations that are providing services to Aboriginal communities, on reserves and in the cities. More and more young people are graduating with university degrees and are taking their place alongside non-Aboriginal professionals.

There is a thirst for education where the opportunity to absorb it in a positive setting exists. Well-educated youth want to help other Aboriginal people who are less fortunate. They want to play an effective role in rebuilding the society from which they come. They are interested in modern methods and look forward to the day they can play a part in Aboriginal government. They understand the problems facing Aboriginal people on reserves and in the cities and they want to devise solutions.

In spite of improvements that are being made, the Auditor General of Canada indicates that there is still a long way to go. He reports that the Department of Indian Affairs is not devoting enough resources to education and points out that only 37 percent of Aboriginal people in Canada have a high school diploma, compared to 65 percent in the general population. Manitoba is the lowest of all the provinces with only 22.8 percent of the young adult population enrolled in post-secondary programs.

The need for the education of Aboriginal people is only going to increase. Aboriginal youth now represent the fastest growing segment of Canadian society. According to federal statistics, there are 811,000 Aboriginal people in Canada and that number is expected to exceed a million in twenty years. Approximately 10 percent of Winnipeg's population, or 60,000 people, are now Aboriginal and 62 percent of them are less than 29 years of age. There are 61 Aboriginal reserves in Manitoba and 65 percent of their population is under 25. The overall numbers and percentage of Aboriginal residents is high in western Canada but the percentages of young people are equally dramatic in other parts of the country as well. Fifty percent of the residents of the Big Cove Mi'kmaq reserve at Moncton, New Brunswick, are under 18.

With the percentage of Aboriginal unemployment on reserves ranging from 65 to 85 percent, and in the cities about 50 percent, Canada faces a serious challenge to reverse these figures and to address the future. Aboriginal youth want no more but no less than other Canadian youth. They want an education that teaches them their history and their heritage, that provides them with the tools to survive in a modern age, and they want to obtain employment and to advance in accordance with their abilities.

Young people would like to play an effective role in improving the lot of other Aboriginal people. They know that goal can be achieved because they see Aboriginal people who have succeeded and play a significant part in Canadian society as professionals, businessmen, artists and actors. They admire these people and hope to have similar opportunities. They take pride in observing their accomplishments and yearn for the day when they can make a similar contribution.

To put these aspirations into context, Aboriginal youth have a large stake in the quality of the education that is provided to them. They need the tools to succeed but they also know that a great deal of education is needed to acquaint the non-Aboriginal population about their abilities and about their need for acceptance in Canadian society.

The general public will only benefit as the level of education of all youth increases. As youth become employed they not only contribute to the productiveness of their employer, they begin to pay income taxes and are no longer the recipients of public assistance. It is in the best interests of the Canadian public to do what it can, and to urge government to do what it can, to improve the education of Aboriginal youth and to see that they become productive citizens.

It will be the young people who become the next generation of Aboriginal leaders. They are anxious to take on that responsibility and it is in the best interests of all to see they are well educated and prepared for that substantial responsibility.

As a result of the University of Manitoba and governments ACCESS program, Aboriginal students are able to take graduate programs leading to degrees in faculties such as Medicine, Engineering and Education. Some students enter from the public school system, while others who have been working or raising a family, are drawn back by the opportunity for higher education. Bursaries and scholarships provided by business and industry also encourage them to excell.

These investments are productive. Young people who might otherwise have trouble finding employment, become employed. When good employment begins, the former public support can stop. When a livelihood is earned, income tax is paid and a positive contribution to the wealth of Canada is made. Although they only represent a small part of the solution that is required, there have been a number of positive developments in the field of education in Manitoba, some of them going back twenty-five years, and others of more recent vintage.

The Brandon University Northern Teacher Education Program, commonly known as 'BUNTEP,' has been in place for more than 25 years. It is a community-based education program that provides graduates with concurrent Bachelor of General Studies and Bachelor of Education degrees. It is open to all northerners who live in selected communities, but the vast majority of the students are Aboriginal.

In the 1999-2000 academic year, courses were delivered at eight locations — Cranberry Portage, Lynn Lake, Oxford House, Pukatawagan, Sioux Valley, Thompson, Wanipigow and Ste. Theresa Point. When the five-year course is completed in one community, another is selected. Professors travel to one of the communities each week and deliver the same courses they teach on the university campus. After four or five weeks a new professor arrives and the former one goes to a different community, while the students remain in their home community.

When not in class, the students work in the local schools as teachers' aids. As most speak the local Aboriginal language, they provide valuable support to the non-Aboriginal teachers. They are able to understand and speak to the children in the language with which they are most comfortable. They are also able to communicate with the parents and advise them of the education that is being offered and tell them how their children are doing.

Of the 359 teachers that graduated prior to 2000, 308 are teachers, eight are principals, four are vice-principals, five are university faculty members, 15 are in educational administration, three are post-secondary counsellors and ten hold other staff positions. A number are also involved in their local governments. One is a Chief, one a Vice-Chief, one is a Mayor and one is a Band Administrator. Two have positions with Indian Affairs.

The courses taught by the visiting professors include teaching and communication methods, oral narratives, native studies and linguistics. One course schedule that I saw included courses on Canadian and World History, Social Studies, Literature, Economics, Geography, Mathematics, Science, Child Development and Learning. The students receive the same courses and the same professors they would have if they took their classes at the University in Brandon and they write the same exams.

The Children of the Earth School in Winnipeg is a unique example of what can be accomplished when attention is given to the particular needs of Aboriginal students. The school opened in 1991 under the jurisdiction of Winnipeg School Division No. 1. Its establishment, as the first all-Aboriginal high school in Manitoba that is part of the public school system, was recommended by the Urban Aboriginal Advisory Committee of the Division's Race Relations Task Force. A student suggested the name.

A joint committee was created to oversee the school's operation and to give direction in school management. The committee is made up of two students, two parents selected by the Niigiigoog Parent Council, a teacher, a non-teaching staff member, a school superintendent and the school principal.

The school's published goals are to prepare students for the future by:

▸ Providing cultural programming, demanding high academic achievement, developing positive self esteem, and developing skills in communication,

- Adapting the curriculum to reflect Aboriginal cultures and values by implementing programs that meet the needs of the students,

- Seeking and involving parents and the community in the life of the school through volunteerism and support for the implementation of the cultural and academic programs,

- Ensuring the preservation of Aboriginal languages by offering Cree and Ojibwe language instruction.

The school applies Medicine Wheel teachings to address emotional, mental, physical and spiritual needs. It views the student as a capable, worthy, gifted individual who has the potential to develop into a caring, committed, responsible human being. Activities include retreats to traditional healing lodges, healing ceremonies, cleansing and healing sweats, healing and talking circles, along with teachings from respected elders. The students experience smudging, sharing circles, full moon and pipe ceremonies and learn their significant place in Aboriginal culture. Family members are encouraged to participate and to assist in the education and development of the students.

It also follows the curriculum required by the Department of Education, and must provide its program within the budgetary limitations applied to all high schools. In addition to the core subjects, the school pays special attention to the history of Aboriginal people in North America, to how the various tribes survived, how they adapted to the land they occupied and how they governed themselves. Their particular place in the exploration and development of Canada is also explored.

The school has its own code of conduct that sets its expectations of the students. It includes an attendance policy that is strictly applied. If a student fails to show up for a class, the parents are immediately contacted to determine the cause. It contains rules to cover regular or continued absences that permit the suspension and ultimate expulsion of offenders.

At the present time, all the students come from families who live below the poverty line. Some of the students are single mothers and the school has an 'Infant Lab' to care for their children. This recognizes the fact that some students have children but it is not an invitation to have more. In the 1998-99 school year, there was only one pregnancy among the student body. These programs and the approach of the administration, indicate the sensitivity of the school to the community it serves.

In my years as a school trustee, including my time as the first president of the Manitoba Association of School Trustees (MAST), I never come across a school with such a diverse program of studies, nor a school with such a record of success. It was an exciting experience to listen to the dedication and aspirations of the principal, Jan Breland. The statistics speak of the success of the school and its approach to education:

▸ Eleven of the 15 graduates in 1999 were going to university. Statistics Canada reported that in 1997 only 22.8 percent of Manitobans between the ages of 18 and 20 were enrolled in university or at a community college. The percentage of these students was 73.34.

▸ The 1999 provincial average in mathematics was 68.5 percent. This school had an average of 86.8 percent.

▸ The provincial average in English was 68.5 percent, while in this school it was 88.6.

Starting in September 1999, in partnership with the University of Manitoba, the school planned to offer a transition year program for students, including mature students, who were having difficulty adjusting to a post-secondary urban institution. Assistance in the use of libraries and labs and orientation to university teaching was planned, as were introductory courses in mathematics, psychology and Native Peoples of Canada parts I and II. On successful completion, students will earn 15 credit hours towards a university degree.

The Children of the Earth school recognizes that the education of Aboriginal students requires more than presenting them with a standard curriculum and throwing them into a learning environment. It reflects the importance of self-esteem and the support of parents and the community. It should be the model for all schools in Aboriginal communities and its history courses and teaching of Aboriginal history and tradition would be a valuable addition to the curriculum in the regular schools.

It is surprising to me that this success has not lead to the establishment of similar schools, with a similar curriculum, at other locations. It should also be possible to introduce parts of this school's program in other schools, either as an option for Aboriginal students or to augment the understanding of all students.

8

First Nation Government

The state of First Nation government is probably the single most important issue facing Canadian governments and Aboriginal people today. It was the destruction of the Aboriginal societal structure in the first place that caused the problems we see today. The effects of that destruction have yet to be repaired.

When the Treaties were being negotiated and signed, it was understood that the Indians would be removed from much of the land they occupied and that settlers would move in. I referred earlier to the promises that were made to obtain the Treaties and particularly to the commitment that their way of life would not change. It was the breach of that promise that began the disruption of the Aboriginal way of life. The Indian Act and the dictatorial powers of the Indian Agents replaced the Chief and his authority. They took over the running of the lives of the people in their hived-off and isolated enclaves. The government's actions were an attack on the very existence of Aboriginal people, an insult to their integrity and a direct assault upon their way of life.

I have spoken about the damaging effect of the residential schools and manner in which families and children were dealt with, but the damage began much earlier. The federal government decided that there would be a Chief and Councillors in each community and an Indian Agent, representing that government, to tell them what they could and could not do. The tribal coming together of Chiefs for the making of major decisions (like signing Treaties) was done away with and each reserve was separated from the others and was stripped of any real authority.

The impact of this betrayal by the federal government has had serious consequences. Not only could the community not live as it had before, but its leaders were denigrated in the eyes of their people. They had no say in what was happening and the heavy hand of outside authority quickly eroded the Aboriginal way of life. The people felt abandoned and imprisoned.

First Nation people feel the same way today. They don't believe that the federal or provincial governments care about their plight and they see little or no move to reverse the damage that has been caused. That attitude effects the way they live, the way they are 'governed' by their local authorities, the manner in which they view the federal and provincial governments and the way they view what they consider to be foreign courts.

The AJI report refers to the disruption of the traditional teachings by parents and Elders and how that undermined the families and their beliefs. The new teachings taught the children to scorn their culture as primitive and of no value. The parents and the whole community became depressed as they were stripped of every vestige of independence. The Chief lost his revered position of influence and responsibility. His authority had been removed from him.

Much of this book is not a happy recital of historical events. It talks of the destruction of a nation and the near-destruction of a distinct people. I hope it will also talk of the potential for the "re-birth of a nation."

The answer to so many of the problems I have described is to return to Aboriginal communities, and to their people, the authority they need to manage their own lives and to look after their own problems in their own way. I am certainly not an expert in the complicated area of government, governance and self-determination, so it has taken me some time to come to that realization.

Government has paid lip service to this necessity, and changes are happening at a snail's pace. For the last number of years, government has been speaking of the devolution of authority. That means that the Department of Indian Affairs will gradually transfer its authority for the administration of various services to First Nations. We have therefore seen agreements that transfer some authority over education. Aboriginal School Boards have been established and community members participate in the making of some decisions. Some federal health services are being transferred but the extent of local authority is still restricted. Tribal police services have been initiated in various parts of the country and the tri-partite Child and Family Services Agencies are probably the best example of the transfer of authority from the federal and provincial governments.

While there is the odd glitch from time to time, the Aboriginal agencies are doing an excellent job of looking after the needs of families and are caring for the children who have been removed from their parents. In Manitoba, the service they provide has recently been recognized by the Doer government with the extension of their authority to urban and other centres. This means that once their administrative structure is in place, they will be able to service the problems of the families and children that still have a relationship with their home reserve. The establishment of a province-wide Métis Child and Family Agency has also been approved.

The devolution approach does not permit First Nations to make major decisions such as determining priorities or establishing budgets. It merely gives the First Nations some further administrative authority. They still have to follow the rules and priorities set for them by Indian Affairs. The devolution of authority from Indian Affairs is nevertheless a good beginning to rectifying some of the ills of the past, but it is a minor step. The next step that is needed is to return a full measure of governmental authority.

Things are beginning to change but there is still a long way to go. Apart from the few specific programs I mentioned, and probably a few others, the authority of the local First Nation Government is very limited. All their by-laws have to be approved by the Minister, and many are not. They can deal with matters like ditch cleaning and the hours a pool hall may operate, but nothing of substance

I thought that First Nations had broad authority to make decisions, establish priorities and use the monies allotted to them as they pleased. I now understand that is not the case at all. Instead of the Chief and his Councillors being the 'local government,' they are more like administrators — operating programs and spending money in the manner prescribed by the Department of Indian Affairs and Northern Development. They have little room to exercise authority and to make needed decisions. They have little discretion.

If, for example, a Chief and Council were to decide to spend extra money on improving education by using funds forwarded for another purpose they did not think necessary, they would be in trouble. The expenditures would not be approved by the auditors and an administrator would likely be sent in to reverse the decision. Those who made the decision might even be charged with a criminal offence.

In spite of these limitations there have been some signs that things are beginning to change. The government has published a statement indicating its support for self-government. I find that the term 'self-government' is widely misunderstood and many Canadians seem to take offence at the use of the term. Journalists often describe it as a demand for a 'third order of government.' This is not accurate. The self-government First Nations want is merely the right to run their own affairs on their own land. They want to be able to make decisions that will allow them to progress and that will return their lost dignity to them.

Aboriginal people want to make their own decisions and to have Indian Affairs stop running their lives for them. They are not asking for anything new; they are merely asking the government to allow them to do what was promised to them during their Treaty negotiations. They just want to be able to exercise the rights they say they have always had. If the Indian Act had not been passed, and Indian Agents had not been appointed, they would have been able to live as they did before they signed. First Nations people believe that the federal government has not only taken over what is rightfully theirs, but has done a poor job of looking after them over the last 125 or more years.

Self-government is not a gift or other benefit being sought from government. It is rather a plea for the recognition of the rights that existed long before Europeans came to this part of the world. It is a recognition of the rights that actually exist and it is an attempt to have government finally stop assuming the authority Aboriginal people require to start rebuilding their lives and their communities.

The concept of self-government is nothing new. Self-government agreements have been part of the modern-day Treaties to which I referred. The Nunavut, Yukon and Nisga'a Treaties contain very detailed Aboriginal governmental powers, as does the Sechelt agreement. They have all been negotiated with government and specify the matters on which their governments can legislate. Another thing self-government agreements do is remove uncertainties about the extent of Aboriginal authority.

The Canadian public can take comfort in knowing that self-government provisions apply only to land owned or occupied by Aboriginal people. If the agreements contain any limitations on the rights of the general public, the limitations are no greater than those set out in the Indian Act. The extent of local authority should be settled in negotiations with the federal government and if the First Nation wishes to deal with matters within provincial jurisdiction, the province would have to be involved in the negotiations as well.

Not all Chiefs and Aboriginal people favour self-government. Many want to proceed cautiously. Some believe they are not ready to take on a substantial amount of additional responsibility all at once. Many prefer the policy of devolution which permits them to take on new programs one at a time, so they can introduce and test new services at a measured pace. Some are concerned that if they sign a self-government agreement, that might release the federal government from its fiduciary responsibility to them. Others are reluctant to enter into the world of self-government until the existing system of governance is improved.

Some Chiefs and Councillors won't even speak of self-government and prefer to describe the changes they would like to see as 'taking responsibility.' They are nevertheless anxious to develop programs to meet local needs and want government to give them the authority to do so. They do not want to merely take over programs and administer them in the same way the federal or provincial governments have done. They know changes in approach are needed and they believe they have the people with the ability to develop and administer programs that will meet their needs. They want to do things in their own way and in their own time.

The problem is that it is difficult to get the federal bureaucracy to let go of its historic practice of running the reserves and telling First Nation governments what to do. With the advent of devolution I had assumed that the paternalistic running of the lives of First Nation people was a thing of the past. That too is not so. The belief that government should run the lives of Aboriginal people seems to permeate the Department and to dictate the actions of successive Ministers of Indian Affairs. Instead of continuing this approach the Department should get out of the way and permit First Nations to run their own affairs.

The government has a published policy endorsing self-government in addition to the devolution of its authority. It speaks of community development, but nothing seems to be happening. It seems that the bureaucrats just don't follow through on these policy statements. Funds that appear to be earmarked for programs are not passed on to the communities but get eaten up within the department.

Self-government is but a logical extension of the devolution of administrative authority and should build on the changes that have been made. It should permit First Nations to establish, as well as to administer, its own services. First Nations would then have the authority to tailor the services to their particular needs and to structure them in a culturally appropriate way. They should have the authority to pass laws to govern the rights and responsibilities of their citizens. If they want to establish different election and local government structures they should have the right to do that.

Most First Nations handle their finances carefully and well. They have their own accountants and auditors and file reports with the Department of Indian Affairs on a regular basis. They are hurt by broad allegations of over-expending and poor administration that do not apply to them. The unfair allegations also damage the public support they so badly need. Government has all the power it needs to ensure that funds are properly spent. The real issue is insufficient funding.

The First Nations with which I am familiar have outstanding Chiefs and members of Council. Their financial management is impeccable and their vision is positive, but their authority is limited. Keeseekoowenin, for example, worked closely with the police and provincial agencies to establish a diversion and healing program to deal with offenders in a culturally appropriate, rehabilitative manner. They wanted to include processes to assist families and children who are in need of support. The Federal government refused to be involved if that part of the plan was included. The reason was that while the Department of Justice was interested in the criminal project, it had no authority to include child welfare. Lengthy delays would have resulted if an attempt was to be made to start all over again and involve the Department of Indian Affairs. The project never did get off the ground!

If and when the power to govern their own lives is returned to Aboriginal communities, they will need their own form of government and will need a local court and its supervisory authority to which citizens can appeal if their government exceeds its authority or if legislation requires interpretation. Courts provide one of the checks and balances common to all democracies, but they must have a local presence and be available to act when they are needed. These moves to responsible government can only improve life on reserves and provide the opportunities for improvement for which the Chiefs now fight. The lethargy towards self-government makes its establishment almost impossible for First Nations to achieve.

Many Canadians get upset when they read stories of contention between members of the band and the Chief. Chiefs certainly do things from time to time their members do not approve of. There have been occasions where the members of a First Nation have voted to oust their Chief in mid-term for some impropriety they think he has committed.

When Indian Affairs is asked to support the concern and remove the Chief, it refuses and takes the position that the incumbent is legally entitled to complete his term.

Even worse, when people hear that an Indian Reserve has been placed in receivership they assume some substantial wrongdoing has occurred. That is not likely to be the case. If a First Nation exceeds its budget by eight percent, a receiver will be appointed to manage the reserve for awhile. That shows the power of Indian Affairs but it will not likely correct the local problem and may well make it worse. The cost of the receiver will be charged to the community.

On occasion there are allegations of mismanagement of public funds and members of the public become enraged and ask whether Aboriginal people are ready for the greater authority they seek. Often it is members of the community that bring these matters to the attention of government or to the attention of the media. They want their affairs to be properly managed and they want government to do something if they are not. In most of these situations it is impossible for an observer, such as me, to tell whether the fault lies with the First Nation and its Chief, or with Indian Affairs.

First Nations need the self-government the American Tribal Courts have had for some time. They also need the devolution that goes with it. The department should retain responsibility for the overall budgetary control of monies they are advancing, but the First Nations should have the discretion to decide how their annual allotment is to be spent. The Minister of Indian Affairs and the Cabinet should insist that the bureaucratic power be reduced and that the Aboriginal authority be increased.

First Nations should be entitled to elect their leaders in whatever manner they choose. If they do something that is improper, the electors should be able to remove them from office and elect someone else in their place. If the First Nation had the authority to legislate in this area it could indicate the responsibilities of elected office and provide a mechanism for their Court to hear an application for removal.

Various attempts have been made to restore true self-government in which Aboriginal communities have control over their lives but all have been blocked. The report of the parliamentary task force on Indian self-government was accepted by all parties in the House of Commons, but its recommendations have been ignored. The Royal Commission on Aboriginal Peoples made additional recommendations just a few years ago and these too are gathering dust in Ottawa.

At the present time, the Minister has advised that changes to the Indian Act are being considered and will be presented to Parliament. I am not aware of any consultation with First Nation people and they have no idea what the changes are likely to be. They believe they have a right to be consulted and have their views taken into account and that sounds fair and reasonable to me. A previous Minister did have a consultation process on proposed changes, received many good and workable suggestions, but ignored them all.

The death grip of Ottawa seems almost impossible to break. It seems that the Ministers of Indian Affairs cannot control their monolithic department to see that government policies are put into effect. Instead, it appears that the civil servants in Indian Affairs and Justice develop plans and policies and the Ministers, for some reason I can't understand, allow them to set the agenda. They do not appear to be accountable to either the government or the people they are supposed to help. The sad result is that First Nation communities are going to have a difficult time improving themselves and exercising the initiative that is needed to turn their peoples' lives around.

Canadians may think that billions are being spent on First Nation people. The reality is that the per capita spending on Aboriginal people is less than the per capita amount spent on other Canadians. Most of the billions go for social assistance programs that are available to all Canadians but are separately recorded for First Nations.

The continued paternalism of government will merely keep Aboriginal people in Third World conditions. Paying lip service to Aboriginal government only continues the pattern of subjugation that started with the failure to observe the Treaties. First Nation people are still isolated and are still deprived of the economic development enjoyed by other Canadians. Out-of-sight, out-of-mind.

Aboriginal people need their own form of democratic government. Whether that means self-government or merely letting First Nations make their own decisions, is for them to decide. Funding must be based on their needs and should not be arbitrarily set by some far-away decision-makers on the basis of formulae they like to apply. Economic development and self-sufficiency should become the priorities of government. If government doesn't release its control, the progress all Canadians want for their indigenous people will never be achieved.

If mistakes are made by First Nation governments during the learning process, so be it. All of our national, provincial, municipal and school board politicians make mistakes from time to time, but they learn by doing. Aboriginal communities and their leaders deserve the same opportunity to try. We are never going to get anywhere as long as the tight governmental control remains.

Reserve communities can't improve themselves on the funding that is now provided by government. More monies will have to be provided and government will have to start sharing resources and helping with mineral exploration and other developments that will permit them to become self-sufficient. As the Royal Commission found, spending that money now will be far less expensive than allowing current conditions to fester. Canada simply cannot afford to maintain an entire population in a state of forced dependency, especially given the enormous potential of First Nation people to produce and contribute to Canada's well being.

There was a need for more and better housing in every community I visited. A house built to accommodate four people has eight or ten living in it. Funding for reserve housing is so miserly that many houses deteriorate within ten years and a substantial percentage of Indian Housing would be condemned if health inspectors were involved. When the government enacted Bill C-31 in 1986, tens of thousands of people who had lost their Indian status through marriage or in other ways, regained it. This placed even greater pressure on communities to find accommodation for them.

Chiefs and Councillors recognize the shortage of housing and want to do something about it, but there is little they can do. It is Ottawa that decides whether additional housing will be built, and it is Ottawa that is responsible for the sorry state of housing and other amenities on reserves.

Chiefs exert as much influence as they can by direct discussions with government. They participate in regional Tribal Councils that discuss common areas of concern and make representations on behalf of their members. The 650 or more Chiefs, and their two to 12 Councillors (one for every 100 band residents with these limits) exert as much political pressure as they can through their provincial associations and their national body, the Assembly of First Nations.

Some Chiefs, like those of the Nisga'a, spend a lifetime trying to get a first Treaty for their people. Years of work are required merely to get government to agree to negotiate and years of negotiations to settle the terms and contents of a final document. Few of those who initiated the struggle have lived to see its completion.

Some national leaders have tried the calm persuasive approach with government. Others have been more aggressive and more openly critical about the lack of government attention to their legitimate needs. The decision on which approach to take is not an easy one. If attempts at persuasion continually fail to bring about better policies and needed changes, the leader must consider whether a more aggressive stance will be more persuasive or will only harden government resistance. The leaders are often influenced by their members' demands for aggressive action, and if they fail to live up to the expectations of their people, they will often be replaced at the next election. Government likes to retain control. It seems prepared to make small concessions to leaders who make few demands and to restrict funding for the programs of aggressive leaders who seek fundamental change.

Chiefs are sometimes criticized for attending meetings in some pleasant locale and spending band funds to do so. Such sessions are not unlike the retreats or meetings held by provincial and federal departments and by business and industry. Corporations send their representatives to national and international meetings to make contacts and to pick up new ideas. Most of the meetings of government or industry are supported, directly or indirectly, at public expense.

Certainly, everyone involved in public expenditures or obtaining tax breaks should act responsibly, but First Nation leaders should not be singled out for criticism. They have learned from bitter experience that they cannot just sit back and rely on government to bring about the changes that are desperately needed and they do go abroad from time to time to examine other systems and to consider the approach they should take.

The answer to the vast majority of problems facing First Nations can be solved by providing those that desire it, with a full measure of autonomous government. They will accept and respect the laws of the rest of Canada but they need this local authority to correct the damage that has been caused to them in the past. It, self-government, will allow them to again serve their people in a culturally appropriate way, it will result in a greater degree of accountability to their electorate.

As long as the funding is reasonable, First Nations will no longer be able to blame Ottawa for failing to meet their needs. They will have to assume the responsibility for their own performance and for their own advancement. If they had the authority, they might be able to enter into partnerships with resource industries that would guarantee employment for their people. The development of natural resources could also permit communities to earn the income that is needed for them to shed the yoke of government support. Other spin-off businesses would permit Aboriginal people to become involved in productive activity that will eventually lift them from their lethargy.

If they have their own court as a part of their government structure, they will be able to provide the benefits I will suggest. The return of authority would benefit the First Nations and the rest of Canada at the same time. The transfer of real and effective administrative authority to the local communities and their people is but a first step towards their personal and economic recovery. If the tools are provided it will then be up to them to pursue the re-birth of their nation and the salvaging of their personal lives.

I would like to think that some internal changes are in the making but it is impossible to assess that possibility until each First Nation has greater authority. The manner in which First Nations have come together to form regional police services and child welfare agencies shows a new willingness to work together. Their provincial and regional bodies now consider matters of common interest and are places where Chiefs come together to debate their common concerns and aspirations. If government would relinquish its control there might be more Tribal government and authority. There may be a return to the gatherings of the past where Chiefs came together to make decisions that affect all their people.

If my instinct is right, that movement may eventually lead to local governments with a second layer of regional government to either handle more general matters or to provide a house of sober second thought. If there is a regional court to provide the third order of government, a broad democratic structure would emerge.

As this book was going to press in March 2001, Indian Affairs Minister Robert Nault announced the signing of self-government agreements in principle with Sioux Valley First Nation in Manitoba and Meadow Lake Tribal Council in Saskatchewan. This is a significant development.

9

Existing Aboriginal Systems

C anada is no leader when it comes to developing court systems to deal with the needs of its indigenous people. It is not even a good listener or a good follower. This is in spite of the fact that significant developments have occurred in other countries. One might even say there is a wave of change that is leaving Canada behind.

Canada abandoned its original method of providing court services on Indian reserves with the disappearance of Indian Agents. Prior to that time, the Indian Agents and some Aboriginal people were named as Justices of the Peace and Magistrates. They had authority to deal with offences under the Indian Act and later with some criminal offences as well. Since then, the Provincial Courts sit in selected communities and people from other communities have to travel there if they are required to appear in court.

New Zealand, on the other hand, has made dramatic changes in the way it deals with the criminal and child protection problems of its indigenous people. Both before and after the Treaty of Waitangi of 1840, the Maori had their own ways of addressing problems. They continued those practices after the arrival of settlers, but with the expansion of the general justice system and outside agencies, they had to abide by their rules and procedures. If youth went outside the Maori lands and got into trouble with the law, they had to be dealt with in the country's general justice system and many ended up in jail.

When there was an allegation of parental abuse or neglect, Maori children were taken into care by outside agencies and placed in white homes. Studies found that the children suffered more from being uprooted and placed with strangers than they had when living with their parents. Even in good foster placements, the emotional turmoil from their removal was real, even if it was difficult to measure. The Maori were upset with these 'outside' practices that failed to apply their traditional ways. Instead of the family and community approaches that had once been applied, the youth were swept into a punitive justice system that dealt harshly with them.

The regular system finally came to accept the fact that many of its practices that were intended to help children were creating new and sometimes more serious problems. New Zealand, like Canada today, was filling its jails with Aboriginal youth and was not dealing well with child protection matters. Instead of decisions being made by families and tight-knit communities, they were being made by the police, the courts, and by the child welfare agencies. The emphasis was being placed on proving the unsuitability of the parents rather than on helping and protecting the children.

In 1989, after a broad public and parliamentary debate and an examination of the practices in the Maori and broader communities, the *Children, Young Persons and Their Families Act* was passed. It reduced the involvement of the State and replaced it with greater parental and community responsibility and authority. Family Group Conferences replaced the teams of social workers and their 'case conferences,' and the decision-making authority was transferred to the family and to the community. The objectives of the Act remained the same as those in prior legislation — to see that abused or neglected children are protected and that youth in trouble with the law are held accountable for their actions and do not become repeat offenders.

The Act recognized that the involvement of the Aboriginal family was essential when dealing with both child protection and criminal conduct. The Statute still has its loopholes and escape clauses such as 'wherever possible' and 'wherever practicable' but it repeatedly stresses the need to have children cared for on both a short and long-term basis within the family. If others have to be involved with Maori children, the Act specifically provides that they be people belonging to the same "tribal, racial, ethnic or cultural background as the child, and who live in the same locality as the child."

In the youth justice area, the Act provides that "unless the public interest requires otherwise, criminal proceedings should not be instituted against a child if there is an alternative means of dealing with the matter." It requires that measures be taken to strengthen the family and to foster its means of dealing with offending children.

The results have been so positive that a number of youth jails have been closed for lack of inmates. Family problems are now dealt with in sensitive ways by family members in ways that are more effective than those previously applied by the regular courts and the child welfare agencies. The Family Group Conference became the method of dealing with both types of problems.

Australians have conducted considerable research on the New Zealand process. They have also established their own systems and have experimented with and analysed the Family Group Conference approach. Their aim has been to analyse the processes and to examine the reason for its success. Trainers from Australia are now visiting Canada on a regular basis to explain and demonstrate the process to Canadian police, courts and front-line service providers. Sessions in which I have participated have been limited to its use in criminal matters.

Psychologist John McDonald of Australia, during his visits to Canada, has described the family group conferencing process as reintegrative shaming. The wrongdoer has to go through the humiliating experience of discussing what he did, in the presence of his parents, the victim and others. By the end of the conference the offender's motives and the reason for the wrongful act are understood by his parents and by the victim. The family members who have to enter into the discussion are brought closer together by the support they give and receive from one another.

The process requires the offender to take responsibility for his actions. The family also assumes some responsibility for what happened and shares in the plan to make amends. When a method of repairing the harm that has been caused is agreed to, the offender is usually better understood by his parents and a new feeling of family unity is established. The process is intended to benefit the victim and the community as well, by preventing similar conduct in the future.

The police in Wagga Wagga, Australia were dissatisfied with the ineffective manner in which young offenders were being dealt with by the police and by the courts. A survey found that the sentences being imposed by the courts were considered to be a slap on the wrist, and did not deter anyone from criminal activity. It concluded that young offenders had no respect for the courts, and that their parents didn't care what their children were doing, or that they had to go to court. These findings will sound eerily familiar to the North American observer.

In 1991, the police decided to take matters into their own hands and established a program similar to the New Zealand family group conference. Young people who had committed a criminal act were interviewed in the presence of their parents and a statement was taken. A committee then examined the statement and decided whether the case would go to trial, that no further action was required, that a warning should be issued, or that a 'cautioning conference' should be held.

When holding a conference, the police invite the offender and the victim, and any friends or relatives that either want to be present. A police officer acts as the chairperson and leads the participants through a discussion of what had happened and what should be done about it. The process continues until everyone agrees on the reparation the offender should make.

After two years, the number of young people appearing in court had been reduced by half and only five percent re-offended. The rate of participation in the program was high and the offenders, victims and their families were pleased with the process. The offenders learned that their families were concerned about them and took responsibility for what they had done. The authority of the parents was recognized and strengthened and they took more responsibility for the conduct of their child. The victims felt strengthened by being able to play a part in deciding what should be done about the crime.

The police came to the conclusion that it was their involvement in the process that resulted in the participation of 95 percent of the victims, while the rate in New Zealand was only 40 percent. They suggest that the involvement of the police provides a sense of safety and protection for the victims, and a degree of formality that may be lacking in other conferences.

When in Philadelphia, Pennsylvania, doing some training, Police Sgt. Terry O'Connell from Wagga Wagga was asked to co-ordinate a family conference in a firebombing case that had already gone to court and where the offenders were in jail. After overcoming the reluctance and scepticism of some who had been involved in the trial, he interviewed the victims who were still devastated by the experience and feared for their safety. A conference of 30 people, including the offenders, members of their families, the victims and their supporters, was finally set up and lasted for three hours.

The victims told of how terrifying the experience had been for them, and of the anguish they continued to feel. This recital continued for an hour and a half and had a substantial impact on the offenders as they listened to the victims reliving their experience. The telling of their story also had an effect on the victims as they spoke. Apparently without knowing it, they were dealing with their own need to express their fear and their anger. They came away from the experience relieved of their fears and tension.

The families of the offenders spoke of how they could rebuild some trust between themselves and the community. A psychiatrist who observed the conference spoke of how powerful the process was and how it minimized the post traumatic stress disorder of the victims. The police officer stated that the experience confirmed his belief that the process could be used in serious criminal matters.

The United States of America has the most highly developed justice system for indigenous people of which I am aware. It operates in co-operation and harmony with the state and federal courts and makes a valuable contribution to community responsibility and justice. There are now 558 federally recognized Tribes in the United States. The term 'Tribe' is comparable to the Canadian terms 'First Nation' and 'Reserve.' Tribal governments are firmly established and their jurisdiction is determined in part by federal legislation, and in detail by each Tribe's own laws. As of mid-2000, there were 255 Tribal Court systems, some operating full time and others two to four days a week. There are 327 Tribal Judges, approximately 17 percent of whom now have law degrees.

Although traditional Pueblo Courts have existed since time immemorial, the United States government became involved and began establishing Courts of Indian Offences on Reservations in 1883. These were known as CFR (Code of Federal Regulations) courts and federal civil servants, and later Indians, were appointed to preside in them. The Indian Reorganization Act of 1934, and the 1935 amendments to the Bureau of Indian Affairs Code, authorized Indian Tribes to enact their own tribal constitutions and law and order codes. They were also authorized to establish their own courts, which became known as Tribal Courts.

Tribal Courts began to be established on Indian reservations in 1936. Their development slowed during the 1950s due to a lack of planning and funding and due to the uncertainty of the federal government's commitment to them. In the 1960s however the present federal policy on self-government was adopted and congress authorized the tribal courts to enforce the Indian Civil Rights Act. There has been a massive expansion and rejuvenation of Tribal Courts since 1968. There are presently 33 new courts being developed in Alaska and 16 new courts in California under two inter-tribal systems.

American Indian Tribes, like Canadian First Nations, are inherently sovereign. *United States v. Wheeler* summarized the principle as follows:

> "Our cases recognize that Indian tribes have not given up their full sovereignty. The sovereignty that the Indian tribes retain is of a unique and limited character. It exists only at the sufferance of Congress and is subject to complete defeasance. But until Congress acts, the tribes retain their existing sovereign powers. In sum, Indian tribes still possess those aspects of sovereignty not withdrawn by treaty or statute or by implication as a necessary result of their dependent status."

In 1991 the United States Civil Rights Commission completed a six-year review of the Indian Civil Rights Act of 1968. It concluded that, as the tribes predate the Constitution and the federal recognition and regulation of them, they are not part of the federal government and are not subject to at least some constitutional provisions. In its report, the Commission made the following comment at p. 72:

> "If the United States Government is to live up to its trust obligations, it must assist tribal governments in their development, and must continue to promote the recognition of this authority, as the Congress has previously done by means of the Indian Child Welfare Act."

The situation remains the same today. On November 6, 2000, President Clinton signed an Executive Order renewing the administration's commitment to tribal sovereignty and their government to government relationship. In making the announcement, the President went on to say:

> "The first Americans hold a unique place in our history. Long before others came to our shores, the First Americans had established self-governing societies. Among their societies, democracy flourished long before the founding of our Nation. Our nation entered into treaties with Indian nations, which acknowledged their right to self-government and protected their rights. ...The federal government did not always live up to its end of the bargain. That was wrong, and I have worked hard to change that by recognizing the importance of tribal sovereignty and government-to-government relations."

...We must respect Native Americans rights to choose for themselves their own way of life on their own lands according to their time honoured cultures and traditions. We must also acknowledge that American Indians and Alaska Natives must have access to new technology and commerce to promote economic opportunity in their homelands."

The Indian Civil Rights Act was enacted to recognize some of the differences from other civil rights legislation. It requires that no Indian tribe may prohibit freedom of speech, religion, assembly and redress of grievances. It requires protection from double jeopardy, self-incrimination and the taking of private property without just compensation. It speaks of the right to a speedy and public trial, to be informed of the nature of a charge, to be confronted by witnesses and to have legal representation at ones own expense. It contains provisions against excessive bail, fines and cruel and unusual punishment. It guarantees the right to trial by jury and provides for Habeas Corpus to test the legality of detention.

In 1968 the Indian Civil Rights Act set the Tribal Courts' sentencing limit at a fine of $500 or six months in jail or both. In 1986 the jurisdiction was extended to $1,000 or one year in jail, or both. In spite of this extension some Tribes have chosen to maintain the lower limits, as they have proven adequate. Even with this limited jurisdiction, the systems I am aware of are able to handle 90 percent of all criminal charges that arise on their reservations. This is in spite of the fact that Tribal Courts have no jurisdiction over the sixteen most serious offences covered by the Major Crimes Act. The tribal courts however have unlimited civil jurisdiction.

The Navajo Tribal Court was established in 1959. It now has courts in seven judicial districts throughout the reservation. Each has generalist trial judges and specialized judges who deal with youth matters. As with most tribes, there was little consensus on how traditional systems had operated, so the new tribal courts were modelled on the Bureau of Indian Affairs courts.

The Navajo courts require arraignment within 72 hours of arrest. Trials are then held within 30 days. Cases may be adjourned for that length of time to give people time to get a lawyer. If the attorney they approach declines to act, one will be appointed for them, but appointed attorneys only receive their travelling expenses. In some cases, a trial is held within three or four days of an offence and if there is a plea of guilty, they are sentenced immediately. Most offenders want to get their case over with right away. Both languages are used on arraignments, English for the young, and Navajo for the older people.

Tribal justice systems in the United States appear, at first glance, to be carbon copies of the regular courts. Many have their own police, jails, lawyers, probation officers and courtrooms that look like those in our cities. Prisoners are to be seen maintaining the court and other tribal facilities. The ones I saw wore orange coveralls and reminded me of the 'trustees' (trusted inmates) who used to work around government facilities in Winnipeg. There are however only 70 jails in Indian Country as of 2000, so most of the systems either rent space from a state or devise other ways of dealing with offenders.

Behind the appearance of similarity, there are major differences in approach as each tribe establishes the system it prefers. Some tribal codes provide that "This code shall be interpreted according to tribal tradition." On occasion, elders give evidence on how a particular dispute would have been handled in customary ways. Prosecution and defence lawyers are similar to ours but most are not legally trained.

The adversarial system of getting to the bottom of problems is contrary to Indian tradition and the United States Civil Rights review commission found that many tribes are opposed to the Indian Bill of Rights. Their objections include a belief that it is improper to have a jury composed of people who know nothing about an incident and have no connection with the accused, the victim, or the families that are involved. Indian tradition would not involve outsiders, but would rely upon those who have personal knowledge about what happened and have opinions about what should be done. They expect the wrongdoer, who knows exactly what happened, to tell the tribunal the reason for his conduct and the circumstances of the offence.

The civil right to avoid self-incrimination is part of the same issue. Indian tradition expects a person who has done something wrong to explain himself and take responsibility for his actions. The person or tribunal dealing with a problem can then listen to others as well and arrive at a solution that will satisfy the needs of everyone affected by the wrongdoing. The concept of a disinterested, unbiased decision-maker (judge) was also unknown. The Commission was told that American Indians do not want to have to play the white man's game that permits people to plead not guilty and to force the prosecution to prove their guilt. That practice, they maintain, only interferes with an honourable Indian practice and tradition.

Each tribe has its own criminal and civil code, in other words, their own laws. The codes are sizeable documents that set out all the laws, rules and regulations of the tribe. Civil codes deal with every imaginable issue such as membership and administrative matters, land tenure, estates and succession, elections, liquor, health, safety and natural resources, but some deal only with gaming or public utilities. Family codes define when a child is in need of care, how abuse and neglect are to be reported, the placement of children, court hearings, family protection plans, guardianship, parental rights, adoption, domestic violence, the protection of vulnerable adults and predicting parenting capacity.

Some codes deal with employment contracts, car accidents, personal actions and the rules for instituting them. Suits may be between residents or involve individuals or corporations outside the reservation. One of the Tribal judges we met during the AJI presided over a five-day fatal accident case just after he was appointed. He awarded damages of $1.4 million, which was immediately paid by an insurance company. It was a non-jury case where lawyers from outside the reservation represented the parties.

Criminal codes define each and every offence. These are similar to offences that would be found in our Criminal Code and Provincial Statutes but are written in clear concise terms chosen by each tribe. The description of each offence is followed by the penalty for a breach of the provision so people do not have to look elsewhere to determine the effect of a breach of the law.

The laws of the community establish the court structure and define its jurisdiction and procedures. They set out a comprehensive bail structure. They provide limitations on who may appear to represent litigants, whether they are lawyers admitted to the Tribal bar or individuals asked to assist a litigant. Matters such as extradition, contempt of court and disbarment are covered. They specify the method for instituting criminal and civil proceedings and make provision for jury trials in both criminal and civil cases.

They make as little use of incarceration as possible. Even then, offenders stay in jail for relatively short periods of time, and are released on parole. Jail is not much used for young offenders, primarily because there is often no separate jail for them and the tribe has to pay to have them sent to a jail in the State. Some tribal members consider jail as 'hotel time' and are not anxious to pay for it, particularly if there is a workable alternative. Restitution, working off fines and community service, are preferred sentences. Where incarceration is used, inmates are often released to do community service work. The work may be proposed by a probation officer and approved by the judge.

Some of the smaller Tribes which cannot afford their own court, or do not have enough work to warrant one, enter into contracts with larger systems to supply a judge when needed. The larger systems then make their judges available to hear cases and recover the cost from the smaller tribe. One New Mexico tribe employs a judge from another tribe for a few hours each month. The Salt River court serves the Fort McDowell Mojave-Apache reservation, with a population of 300, on a case by case basis.

Juries are used in most courts and are common in the Hopi courts. Ninety names are called and the usual rules of challenge apply. Some tribes limit peremptory challenges to three. Lawyers from nearby cities represent some accused while local non-legally trained advocates represent others. Everything is recorded and written judgments are usually given, as these are 'courts of record.'

Diversionary procedures are often applied to juveniles. The prosecuting attorney meets with the juveniles and their parents and some sort of counselling or school program may be agreed to. The case goes to court if the prosecuting attorney thinks it should. The emphasis is upon learning the cause of inappropriate behaviour and dealing with it without a prosecution. The Hopi courts have a slightly different philosophy to preventing crime. Their judges are more inclined to sentence a first offender to a short period of incarceration, in the hope that the experience will teach the young person a lesson and persuade them to refrain from any further inappropriate conduct.

Family proceedings, whether related to divorce or child welfare, are also solution oriented and judges try to place children in the extended family. In the Navajo Nation the grandparents decide what will happen to the children if they have to be removed from their parents, and the courts almost always accept their decision. In child welfare matters, the workers are attached to the court rather than to the tribal council.

The pueblos in New Mexico operate on a less formal basis. In several, the Governor of the Pueblo serves as the trial judge. In some, court procedures are unwritten and customary law is applied. Some have no appeal procedure at all, while others have the members of the tribal council decide appeals. In other reservations some civil disputes do not involve the courts but are resolved by members of the Tribal Council on an informal basis.

The most common offences that are dealt with by tribal courts are public intoxication, impaired driving, assault, break and enter, burglary, theft, criminal damage, bootlegging, sexual assault and incest. Eighty percent of the charges are disposed of with a guilty plea. Judges do not get involved in plea bargaining though counsel may jointly recommend the penalty a judge should apply. In the Navajo reservation in 1988, there were 14,060 cases. 14,000 were dealt with in the Tribal Court, 50 in the State Court and 10 felonies in a Federal Court.

I have visited the Inter-Tribal Court System in Edmonds, Washington on two occasions, once in 1988 with Judge Sinclair, and again in 1997. My reason for taking a second look at that system was because it is a circuit court system that serves a number of scattered and independent communities similar to many in Canada. The communities in that system vary in size from 200 to 2000 members. The court serves its own 14 tribes and has a contract to provide court services to two other tribes who are not part of the inter-tribal arrangement. The U.S. government has also given that court jurisdiction over fishing regulations in part of the Puget Sound. The 1996 the government allotment for each tribe in that system was $29,000.

A judge travels to each community once a month, accepts pleas of guilty, refers others to Peacemakers or other services and presides over an average of twenty trials each month, most of which are quite short. Five of the tribes use alternative dispute resolution methods in the civil field, particularly in family and housing disputes. The court's emphasis is on helping people resolve their problems without a trial.

Each of the 14 tribes appoints one member to a court management committee, which works with the Chief Judge in the administration of the court. Chief Judge Coochise, a former prosecutor, was the Chief Judge of the court for sixteen years. He had his own budget and, with the assistance of the court administrator, legal advisor (who doubles as a code writer for the Tribes) and staff, maintained the court's administrative office on the mainland. He was paid about two-thirds the salary of State judges. Since his retirement he has remained active in the tribal court system, helping tribes establish their own courts improving their existing systems and sitting on pre-trials and appeals.

In 1987 the United States Congress appropriated approximately $11.2 million to fund tribal court systems. The 2000 appropriation is about the same although the amount rose to $14 million prior to 1995 budget cuts. If the funds were divided evenly among the tribes (which they are not) that would amount to $40,000 per tribal court. While the support for the courts remains static, government has substantially increased the tribes' law enforcement budgets. A Bureau of Indian Affairs 1975 study showed departmental expenditures varying from $2.98 to $14.19 per capita and from $8.30 to $35.08 per case. Fines that are recovered go to tribal governments or to tribal court budgets.

All the tribal judges to whom I have spoken believe the tribal courts provide a better degree of service than could possibly be provided by State courts. They believe they bring to their work an understanding of their communities and the people who live in them. They are concerned about the individual residents and about the reservation as a whole and see themselves as part of a service that is helping the community deal with its problems. They realize that community residents have to keep living together and want to see their problems resolved in as positive a way as possible.

The judges believe the residents are comfortable with tribal courts. They are not seen as part of a foreign system that is being imposed upon them, but as a community service. People believe they have a say in the manner in which the courts operate, through the laws the Tribe passes and through the administrative authority of the court management committee. Although there are occasional concerns, the judges do not feel their closeness to the community limits their performance, as they are aware of their responsibility to the community in which they work, and the community is aware of the work they have to do. The acceptance of the local courts may also be due to the judges' attempts to interpret the law and to apply it in a manner that reflects community attitudes and cultural beliefs and traditions.

The tribal courts are of course not free of problems. One concern in 1989 was the high turnover of judges, particularly among those who had not been judges very long. There are problems at times because of having to sit in judgement on a relative or another person the judge knows. The difficulty is even greater if a tribal chairman or a councillor is charged with an offence, or is sued in a civil proceeding. In some situations the judges hear the cases in any event, while in others they call on a judge from another tribe to hear the case. By 2000 the turnover of judges had slowed dramatically.

There may, at times, be a potential conflict between the court and the tribal council. Some judges make a point of keeping in touch with the governing body to remind them of the need for judicial independence. The relationship can become strained however if the court is asked to rule on the validity of some law the council has passed. The question of the tribe's sovereignty, reflected to a large extent in the governing body, is on occasion another area of potential conflict. In spite of these issues that arise on occasion I have never heard of a Tribe wanting to get rid of its court. Some judges do however find these pressures too great and they resign.

In its report to the Human Rights Commission in about 1990, the Indian Court Judges Association discussed the problem:

> Removal of tribal judges by councils takes place for many reasons other than "just cause." In some tribes the judge changes whenever a new political faction takes power. Where recall is effected by a simple majority vote, judges are particularly susceptible to removal after making unpopular decisions. Short terms of office, council removal power, and tribal politics combine to make a judge susceptible to pressures from those in power to dispose of cases in particular ways.

Each tribe has provisions for the removal of judges from office. Some may be removed on a simple vote of the tribal council while others require a two-thirds vote. The reasons for removal seem to vary from giving unpopular decisions to being rude or abrupt with those appearing before them, to appearing to favour or to refuse to favour certain litigants. The Northwest inter-tribal circuiting system, by its structure, has avoided many of these problems. It engages its judges on contract and requires a two-thirds vote of its management committee, representing the 14 Tribes, before a judge can be discharged. It also avoided many problems by selecting a judge from Arizona, a long way from the State of Washington.

During a court symposium in Tulsa, Oklahoma, federal government representatives told me of the growing respect for the manner in which tribal courts deal with cases. They also told me that self-government on Indian Reservations, and in Indian Territory, has existed for some time. The federal interest is in 'devolution' — the turning over of government responsibilities to the Tribes. It also enables the Tribes to set their own priorities in their annual budgets. The conference also discussed comity between the State Trial and Appellate courts and the Indian courts, to ensure that one another's judgements would be respected and enforced.

Peacemakers are used in many American tribal court systems. They have not always been known by that name, but the role has always been a part of Indian tradition. The Navajo system uses them in a formal manner as officers of the court. The Northwest Inter-Tribal Court System, on the other hand, uses them in a more informal way.

After meeting with Judge Cadman at Chinle on the Navajo reservation for an hour or more, we were introduced to three Peacemakers. Each Chapter within the judicial district designates one Peacemaker. The Peacemakers were officers of the court and were available to be assigned specific cases by the judge. If litigants want a case referred to a Peacemaker they must apply to the court and pay a $30 filing fee that is eventually paid to the Peacemaker. Both sides of a case or dispute have to agree to have their case referred to a Peacemaker, except that a judge may refer a criminal case whether the prosecuting attorney agrees or not, although their opinion is taken into consideration.

The Navajo Peacemaker system was established in 1982. It was intended to bring together traditional dispute resolution methods and current court processes, "to blend the old with the new." In 1990, 16 cases from the Chinle court were referred to a Peacemaker. Ten were family cases and six were criminal, although most of them were also family related. Peacemakers have the power to subpoena witnesses and to make orders, subject to confirmation by the court. If a case is not settled it is referred back to the court. If it is settled, the Peacemaker advises the court of the terms of the settlement and, if the judge accepts it, the agreement becomes an order of the court. If the judge questions the settlement, he may require the parties to appear before him to discuss it.

One of the Peacemakers we met was a pastor, one a retired teacher, and the other was an experienced counsellor. Each had his or her own method of approaching a case in search of a settlement. The pastor said he tells people of his own experience with alcohol, urges young people to pay attention to their parents, and reminds parents of their responsibility to their children. Each try to determine the cause of the problem, whether it be alcohol abuse or something else, and they have the authority to refer people for counselling. If parents are interfering with a young couple, the Peacemaker will intervene. The judge selects the Peacemaker he thinks will be most appropriate for each case. A judge may also send a case to a Peacemaker even if there is no admission of guilt, particularly in cases of wife abuse.

Judge Cadman gave us an example of a case he had referred to a Peacekeeper. The charge was initially rape, but to get it within the jurisdiction of the Tribal Court, the State authorities suggested the charge be reduced to sexual assault. It was then referred to a Peacemaker as neither the victim nor the defendant wanted to go to court. The Peacemaker spoke to the victim and the offender and then to the parents of each. The accused admitted his actions and the families of both young people assumed some responsibility for what had happened.

The matter was finally resolved in a traditional way by the accused apologizing to the girl, to her parents, and to his own parents. In recognition of their primary responsibility, the family of the offender gave some of its assets to the family of the victim. The Peacekeeper reported to the court that he thought the concerns of the victim had been dealt with and that there would be no recurrence of the offence. The judge agreed with the report and the charge was withdrawn. The only thing the judge said he might have asked about, if the matter had come before him, was whether a restraining order requiring the offender to stay away from the victim was needed.

The Peacemakers were also involved with education and preventive measures. They had the use of the courtroom on Friday afternoons for group counselling sessions with offenders, including some who were still in jail serving their sentence. On Saturdays the Peacemakers conducted education sessions and showed films on a variety of justice matters to members of the community. Their influence undoubtedly contributed to the peace and good order in the community. Its rate of recidivism at that time was only five percent.

The North-West Inter-Tribal Court System in the State of Washington, uses Peacemakers in a less formal manner. They are not officers of the court and do not have to report on their efforts to a judge. The judges nevertheless know who the Peacemakers are and refer criminal and civil cases to them. If the Peacemaker deals with a case before a charge has been laid, he does not even have to advise the judge of the outcome. If a case that has been referred is not settled, the Peacemaker will advise the court officials so it can go back before a judge. It is then up to the court administrator to put the case on a court docket. If a civil case has been referred, it is up to the parties to obtain a consent order if they wish, or to withdraw any claim that has been filed.

There are a number of ways in which Tribal judges are engaged in the U.S. Tribal Courts:

1. By Appointment

Some judges are appointed by the tribal government and others by the tribal Governor. Some are appointed for a probationary period and are then confirmed if they prove to be satisfactory and wish to continue.

If Tribes have a specialized youth (and family) judge, they are usually appointed, even if other judges are elected. One of the youth judges I met was a woman, another was a young man and both had previous experience working with young people.

2. By election

Where judges are to be elected, they are elected at the same time the Chief and Council elections are held. The one and only qualification to be a judge is that the person has resided on the reservation for at least six months. One Chief told me, "You can be a truck driver today and a judge tomorrow."

It appears common for Tribal members who have worked outside the community in a variety of occupations, and feel comfortable about being a judge, to return to the reservation to re-establish their residency and run for election.

Where a vacancy occurs between elections, the Tribal Council or the Tribal Governor will appoint a replacement, and that person will have to stand for election when the next elections are held. As with other American judges who are appointed in similar circumstances, if the appointed judge performs well until election time, he will have a good chance of being elected.

3. On contract

Some Tribal judges are engaged for a term of years. The contract of employment can be terminated by agreement or it can be renewed.

Some judges are engaged on a case by case basis or to preside for a few days each month. The Tribe can enter into a contract with a larger system to provide the judge or can go outside the Tribal system to engage someone. Some judges may be Indian or non-Indian lawyers from nearby communities who have displayed a good understanding of Indian people and their needs.

In 1989 most Tribal judges were elected but by 2000, that had changed to the point where 75 percent were appointed and only 25 percent were elected. Court of Appeal judges are also engaged in a number of ways. Some courts of appeal are made up of the judges from the same trial court that did not sit on the trial. If there are insufficient judges to call upon, a judge from another tribe is engaged to complete the panel. In other cases, judges from other tribal courts are asked to be part of an appeal tribunal. Children's judges regularly sit on civil and criminal appeals in the Navajo system although the generalist judges do not sit on youth court appeals.

The Navajo nation has a fairly permanent Court of Appeal and all its judges have to be legally trained. At the time of our visit, one was a law professor in Tucson, one a lawyer practicing in the State, and the third was a member of the tribe but was a judge of one of the State of Arizona courts. The Court of Appeal sat on the reservation every couple of months.

In South Dakota, seven or so Tribes have established an inter-tribal appeal court system. All the judges are part time and the position of Chief Appellate Judge rotates between the tribes on an annual basis. Each Tribe appoints one judge and sometimes an alternate as well, and the Chief Judge puts together appeal panels as they are needed. The Appeal Courts apply the law of the community where the case arose. In 2000 there were five Inter-Tribal appellate systems in the United States but still only two inter-tribal trial court systems.

Tribal judges throughout the United States often travel a considerable distance to sit in another community either as a trial judge, a member of a court of appeal, or to do pre-trials, although some have their pre-trials conducted by court officials.

Although no particular level of education is required, most judges have a grade twelve education. Some tribal judges were previously involved in the tribal courts as prosecutors or in some other capacity. Often however, judges are elected or appointed with little knowledge of the law.

Once appointed, the judges, prosecuting attorneys, clerks, administrators and other staff receive ongoing training and education. Training for court staff is provided at the judicial training centre in Reno, Nevada, and for judges, in Reno and at the National Indian Judicial Center in California. In addition to formal training in various aspects of the criminal and civil law, judges have the usual legal texts. Some education is also provided at judges' seminars and judges receive from 18 to 20 days of classroom education each year. One of the judges I met, although he had some experience with the court system, went to judge school three times during his first two years in office.

Judge Cadman had acted as an attorney for 15 years. He called on that experience when he became a judge, but after his appointment he took a two-week course at Reno and attended numerous seminars. His opinion was that the tribal court system would lose a lot, and would not be able to be staffed by Navajo people, if the judges had to be legally trained. He said, however, that cases were getting more technical and he thought that in the future there might be a need for more legally trained lawyers and judges. In 1991, at the time of the Civil Rights review of the Indian Civil Rights Act, 53 tribal judges held law degrees.

Some of the offences coming before the tribal courts appear to encroach on state or federal authority but the tribal judges are trained to examine them to make certain the court has jurisdiction to proceed. Judges start with the principle that the tribe is a sovereign entity and has total jurisdiction, but then look to see if their jurisdiction is limited by federal legislation. One judge said they must ask themselves: "Who is alleged to have committed the offence? Where was it committed? What is the type of offence?" If a judge finds a particular charge to be beyond the court's jurisdiction, he transfers it to the appropriate federal or state authority.

The consensus of the Tribal Judges I met was that although some judges start with an ignorance of the law and legal procedure, they become quite sophisticated in legal principles, and are quite capable of dealing with the matters that come before them.

PART IV

"Let
Us Try"

10

Parallel Justice System

Two themes often emerge when I speak to Aboriginal people about their future. Even though they are reluctant to talk about it, they sincerely feel that they are being neglected and put down by other Canadians and that the legal system treats them with disdain. Because they see no change in the attitudes of people who could help them, they feel powerless to overcome the hurdles they face.

I understand and share their concerns. If, as I felt in my Law School and practicing days, the Canadian system of justice is so marvellous, I now have to ask how it can possibly cause so much pain. It must be blind to fail to appreciate that not all individuals are equal in society and that some are not well served by it. The system is particularly hard on Aboriginal people and I don't think it overstates the severity of the situation to say that the manner in which the law is now being administered in remote communities is a travesty of justice.

The solution Aboriginal people propose has been expressed for decades. Aboriginal people say, "we couldn't possibly do a worse job than the existing courts. We know our people and we know what has to be done." The now almost silent and plaintive cry is: "Why won't they let us try?" It is not a loud and vocal plea, but the soft resigned expression of a lost hope, as they don't think that anyone is listening.

Statements like those of the former Manitoba Minister of Justice, Vic Toews, deflate their hopes and smother their aspirations. He said, in forceful tones on more than one occasion: "There will never be a separate Aboriginal Court in Manitoba." The message I took from that was "don't even talk to me about it." Although Judge Sinclair and I thought we made a good case for Aboriginal Courts in our report, the Conservative Filmon government studiously ignored our suggestions. It was as though the AJI never existed.

The newly elected Doer government quickly established the type of review we recommended to see what can be implemented. The report is not yet in and I can only hope that those involved with the study have given careful consideration to the severity of the problem and the massive changes that are required.

In spite of the history of government apathy, opposition, or timidity, I will set forth a detailed plan for the establishment of an Aboriginal Justice System and Courts. It will be based not just on my experience as a lawyer and judge, but also on my many conversations with concerned Aboriginal people. In my opinion a new approach is required and I know that it can work and will succeed. It already exists in other countries. Such an approach, more than any other initiative I can imagine, would provide a simple and efficient court system that will substantially reduce the chaos, reduce the numbers of Aboriginal people in court and reduce the numbers being sent to jail.

The system I propose would complement the existing courts. It would remove much of the heavy workload from the Provincial Courts that they are unable to handle, but would at the same time leave the most serious cases to be dealt with in the provincial or superior courts. It would also do something else that the present courts are incapable of doing — it would have a presence in every Aboriginal community and would be able to deal with the majority of the cases in an Aboriginal language and in a culturally appropriate manner. It would obviate the necessity of people from remote communities making repeated trips to distant courts, spending money they just don't have.

It is not as if we are talking about providing a special service to a few people. In the remote parts of Manitoba 70 to 90 percent of those appearing in Provincial Courts are Aboriginal and 50 to 100 percent of those in jail are Aboriginal as well. Nor are we talking about an economical operation. Correctional Services of Canada statistics show that the average cost of incarcerating an offender in a federal institution is $50,375 a year. While I find it hard to imagine, their figures show that in 1996/97 Correctional Services spent over a billion dollars ($1,107,042,000.00). I hate to think how much the province spends on police, lawyers, court reporters, jails and transportation. I would think that all Canadians would welcome anything that would reduce these numbers.

As I began to write about what an Aboriginal Court would look like and how it would operate, I started to think about what a community wants from its courts. Why do we need courts? What do they represent? What should we expect from them? Are they just an extension of government or the Ministry of Justice? These questions I was asking myself caused me to drift into the realm of philosophy. Philosophy seems an esoteric area but, as I explored the issues, I found that some had a very basic importance to people and their institutions. When I thought about the importance of justice, which everyone demands but which we sometimes take for granted, I had to do some soul-searching. What is justice? How is it secured and how is it delivered?

Justice, I finally concluded, is a concept and it is a reality. In its conceptual form, justice is fairness, the treating of everyone equally and meeting everyone's needs. In its application within a justice system, the emphasis changes to a balancing of competing needs and competing claims; it changes from merely being just, to doing justice. It must of course continue to be just. A society based on the rule of law expects its laws and its administration of them to provide justice to all its citizens. To be just, the law must also be flexible enough to take unusual circumstances into account.

It is the law that regulates a civilized society. Parliament or local governments pass laws to regulate human conduct in every conceivable situation. Laws indicate what people may and may not do so they will not conflict with the rights of others. It is against the law to take the life of another, to rob or beat a person, to break into another's property, or to drive while under the influence of an intoxicant. The corollary of these laws is the right of every citizen to the sanctity of life, to the uninterrupted enjoyment of their property and to safety in their homes and on the streets and highways.

The law is supposed to protect the innocent and the vulnerable and condemn offenders. In that respect it has an almost biblical aura and is as perfect a mechanism as man has been able to devise to regulate society and, at the same time, individual responsibility and conduct. There are of course flaws in the law that are discovered from time to time but until the law is amended or struck down as being invalid, it stands as the foundation and cornerstone of our society. Parliamentarians work to amend the law to meet current conditions and to overcome flaws or gaps that have been unearthed.

Our legal system is perfect in its conception. Justice is portrayed as a blinded goddess who is not blind but wears a blindfold as a symbol of impartiality. In a roguish twist, the logo of our 1950 law class has the blindfold lifted above one eye so the goddess can take a peek. What she sees I do not know, but the symbolism is not without merit. 'Justice' should keep a sharp eye on how her laws and the administration of them are serving people.

Aboriginal people, like others, accept this even-handed approach to justice and to the administration of the law. The Aboriginal society is a just society. It too wants to protect its people and to deal with wrongdoing in an effective way. The problem they see is how that can be done within the confines of a system that does not always appreciate their differences and particular needs. If there are differing needs, and some would dispute that, do they warrant special attention?

To attain justice it is sometimes necessary to take some unusual circumstances into account. In her 1984 Commission Report on Equality in Employment, Rosalie Abella (now Madame Justice Abella of the Ontario Court of Appeal) stated:

> Sometimes equality means treating people the same, despite their differences, and sometimes it means treating them as equals by accommodating their differences.

> Formerly, we thought that equality only meant sameness and that treating persons as equals meant treating everyone the same. We now know that to treat everyone the same may be to offend the notion of equality. Ignoring differences may mean ignoring legitimate needs.

> Ignoring differences and refusing to accommodate them is a denial of equal access and opportunity. It is discrimination.

> Discriminatory distinctions are only those which are unreasonably exclusionary, which are not objectively justifiable by standards of necessity, safety or civility, as opposed to standards of preference, economic exigency or tradition. This includes too the concept of reasonable accommodation imported from human rights jurisprudence; namely, is there an alternative available which is equally conducive to the achievement of the law's or program's purpose which has a lesser adverse impact?

The Criminal Code recognizes the same principle. One of the definitions of discrimination in Section 9(1)(d) is:

> Failure to make reasonable accommodation for the special needs of any individual or group, if those special needs are based upon any characteristic found in subsection (2).

Over the years, my involvement with Aboriginal people has convinced me that they do have special needs when it comes to the law and the delivery of court services. They need help in understanding the law and the legal system but they have more basic needs as well. They need a system in which they can properly and fully express themselves. They need judges who will understand them, their communities and their background and they need culturally appropriate services to help them resolve problems so they will not run afoul of the law.

It is not difficult to understand why the regular justice system fails. It cannot meet the needs I mentioned. The proof is evident in the slow and costly pace with which the system moves and the staggering number of Aboriginal people that are sent to jail. I hesitate to say that again, but it is the final litmus test of the health of the system. Aboriginal people are not in jail because they are aggressive or have a criminal bent. It is largely because they are caught up in a punitive system that fails to meet their needs. As Max Yalden said, they are in jail because the system doesn't know what else to do with them.

Aboriginal people were not always represented in the courts or jails in such large numbers. Prior to the Second World War the percentage of Aboriginal people in the courts was no greater than their percentage of the population. The same applies to the numbers in jail. One has to ask what has caused the change. Have Aboriginal people changed, or is the problem systemic?

Poverty alone is not the answer as Indians have lived in poverty for a long time. Unemployment, the inability to feel like a contributing member of society, may play a part in a current malaise. Substance abuse, a symptom of many personal problems, is probably part of the answer, although Indians were plied with liquor hundreds of years ago. Continuing prejudice and discrimination that prevents Aboriginal people from participating in and enjoying the advantages of modern society must be a factor. The destructive influence of residential schools on individuals and families is certainly a factor in family and child abuse, and probably in personal conduct as well.

A major factor, at least as far as reserve residents are concerned, has been the interference of others with their daily lives. The manner of resolving inappropriate conduct changed from the quiet influence of the community and the family, to the imposition of a rigid charge-prosecute-incarcerate approach. Many still do not understand that what they have done is wrong, or at least so wrong as to incur the wrath of the white justice system.

Large numbers of Aboriginal people don't know how to respond to the authority of the police, the prosecutors, or the courts. They generally trust the police and go along with their suggestions. At times that results in pleas of guilty when they have a valid defence. At other times, they do not come forward with an explanation or an alibi that might stop them from being investigated. Youth give statements without their parents being present when they don't have to say anything at all. All these situations add to the numbers of Aboriginal people being convicted and sent to jail.

Remote communities have no residents who know the court system well enough to give a person who is being investigated, arrested or charged with an offence, advice as to their rights. There is no one to tell them whether they should speak to the investigating officer or not. There are no lawyers, no para-legal people and no court officials to provide even the most basic information about the legal system. When the court party is in the community the Aboriginal para-legal people that travel with it are so busy with those facing trial they don't have time to dispense legal advice to others. In any event I understand that, as they are not legally trained, they are discouraged from giving advice or assisting local residents. Their task is to assist accused people with their understanding of what is happening during their court appearance.

No matter what the cause of the problems is, it is more important to concentrate on solutions. It is my hope that the Justice System I propose will overcome problems with the existing system and at the same time provide the services the Aboriginal communities require. I don't suggest that Aboriginal people should follow my proposals. They are merely offered for them and the federal and provincial authorities to consider. It is for Aboriginal people to accept or reject my suggestions, or to adapt them to suit their particular needs and aspirations.

I should make it clear at the outset that I will be speaking of a 'justice system' and not just courts and Aboriginal judges. Police services, holding facilities, community support programs, healing processes and a different sort of jail are all part of a justice system. They are all needed to provide the effective justice to which all aspire.

Should some think that I am recommending that a First Nation now proceed to unilaterally establish its own court, that is not possible.

Nor am I suggesting that a carte blanche be given to it. Whatever the final arrangement is, it will have to be negotiated by Aboriginal communities and federal and provincial governments.

There are several types of arrangements that would enable an Aboriginal justice system to be established. The easiest is when a new Treaty is being negotiated, as in British Columbia, when the First Nation is already negotiating the extent of its land, its jurisdiction and law making authority. The parties will likely agree that some control over the administration of justice will be included in the Treaty so all that is needed is agreement on the extent of a court's jurisdiction and the community's authority to establish its own court and related services.

For the communities with older Treaties, there are other ways to proceed. One is to enter into a self-government agreement with government. That document can then indicate the extent of the law-making authority and authorize the organization of a court, police and other services.

Another way to proceed is for a community, or a number of communities, to enter into a stand-alone agreement with the federal and provincial governments that will permit the establishment of a regional Aboriginal Justice System. There is a precedent for this sort of tri-partite agreement in Manitoba. Regional Aboriginal Child and Family Services Agencies now exist. They are managed by regional boards on which each participating community is represented, often by its Chief. They engage their own staff to serve all the communities and establish their own priorities and culturally acceptable means of providing service.

An extension of this sort of arrangement could include the First Nation, non-status Indians, Métis and others living within an agreed upon area. There are several advantages of this arrangement. One is that it wouldn't make sense to involve only First Nation people and leave the Métis parts of communities out. They, and others living in-between Aboriginal communities, would still have to go to the Provincial Court. A comprehensive system would be able to replace much of the Provincial Court service with an Aboriginal one in the vast rural and remote parts of the provinces.

Tri-partite agreements would be needed because some of the residents of the regional system would come under federal and others under provincial jurisdiction. Both governments have to be included as Aboriginal Courts would have to apply both federal and provincial legislation. Also, as I indicated earlier, it is the province that has the authority to establish courts, at least those operating outside of Indian reserves.

Another reason for having Aboriginal systems cover a wide area is that if a crime is committed a few miles from a reserve, it would be important to have an Aboriginal court that is able to deal with it. As I will indicate, there would be no problem in having the areas served by Provincial and Aboriginal courts overlap, as it will be the severity of the case that will determine the court in which it will be heard.

Nor do I see a problem if a First Nation wants to establish its own laws and Métis people want the Criminal Code and other Statutes to apply. An Aboriginal Court could easily apply the law, rules and regulations of the place where an offence was committed.

Although I have expressed a preference for regional courts because I am familiar with smaller reserves that have non-reserve residents living adjacent to them, a single court could certainly be established to serve only one First Nation or one Métis community. Such a court could serve only its members, or could provide its services to the surrounding areas as well, without them having to join in a regional system. I can see independent courts being preferred by some of the large First Nations in British Columbia and in other parts of the country.

I want to emphasize that what I recommend is a parallel court system to meet a specific need and to deal with a distinct part of the Canadian community. An Aboriginal Court would augment the services of the Provincial and Superior courts and would take nothing of significance from them. It would operate with three objectives in mind: to deal with criminal and civil matters in a fair and effective manner; to apply culturally appropriate methods; and to stop the incarceration of so many people.

The Aboriginal system I propose would operate without interference from the regular courts but would maintain the superior courts' supervisory responsibility. In addition to benefiting Aboriginal people and Aboriginal communities, it would be of benefit to the regular courts. It would relieve them of what has turned out to be an impossible task — to serve Aboriginal people and Aboriginal communities in an efficient manner.

At one time I thought the same model of court could be applied to all communities. Having seen more of the workings of Aboriginal communities, their intense independence and the substantial differences between them, I am now satisfied that any attempt on the part of government to impose a specific model would doom it to rejection and failure. Some experimentation and changes will be required as systems develop and each community, or group of communities, will have to be free to apply its own traditions and to devise its own solutions.

I have also seen enough of efforts to improve the lives of Aboriginal people to know that the best-intentioned plans of outsiders don't work. Programs that work, and improvements that are made, are devised and operated by Aboriginal people. Help from others is invited and welcomed, but the programs that are effective are administered by Aboriginal people who understand those with whom they are working.

11

Jurisdiction

The manner in which the jurisdiction of an Aboriginal court will be determined, sometimes on a daily basis, will indicate the parallel nature of the system and its relationship to the Crown and to other courts.

Aboriginal people wishing to establish their own system of justice will have to do it with the co-operation of the federal and provincial authorities. I know that many Aboriginal people would prefer to proceed on their own, but there are reasons why that is not possible. Under the Constitution, Parliament has the exclusive authority to legislate with respect to Indians and the criminal law, and the provinces have the exclusive authority to administer the criminal law and to establish courts. It will therefore be necessary to negotiate the Aboriginal court's in personum and in rem authority to determine who the court has authority to deal with and the sort of cases it may hear.

Looking first at those that may come under its authority, I would think it would be obvious that all Aboriginal people living within its boundaries would be covered. They should have no choice but to be subject to the community's laws and the authority of its court. Those who are charged with an offence, or are involved in a civil issue that arises in the community, should be dealt with by the local court. It would be destructive to the integrity of the community and its court to permit a litigant to be tried in an ordinary court for an offence within the jurisdiction of the Aboriginal court.

Non-Aboriginal people who live on a reserve may be married to a Status Indian or may have chosen to live in the community with its approval. They reside on First Nation land and, I would say, have implicitly agreed to be governed by its laws and institutions. If they are charged with an offence they too should be subject to the jurisdiction of the Aboriginal court and should not have the option of being dealt with in the regular courts.

Those who remain members of a First Nation but live off-reserve, are another category of possible litigants. The decision of the Supreme Court of Canada in *Corbiere v. Canada (Minister of Indian and Northern Affairs, May 20, 1999)* confirmed the right of non-resident First Nation members to vote in reserve elections. Some might argue that those people also have the right to be tried in its courts no matter where an offence is committed. My own view is that they do not have that right. The locus of the offence (the place where it is committed) should determine the place of trial. This jurisdiction traditionally belongs to the court that has authority where a wrongful act is committed. In civil proceedings, cases are tried in the jurisdiction where the cause of action arose or where the defendant resides.

Some non-resident members might still apply to have their case tried in an Aboriginal court. The decision on whether that should be permitted, should be left to the Provincial Attorney General to decide. If he thinks there would be a benefit to having an accused dealt with in an Aboriginal court, he should have the authority to transfer the case to it, provided that court is willing to accept the case. The document creating the justice system should deal with this situation one way or another.

Others who are being dealt with in the regular courts, might like to be referred to one of the unique treatment services of the Aboriginal system. It would be up to the Provincial Judge to decide whether or not to refer the individual and up to the particular service to indicate whether it is willing to accept the person as a client.

Another category of person to consider is a non-Aboriginal person who lives in the non-Indian part of an Aboriginal community. This would only arise if the boundaries of the court were limited to a First Nation. The argument in their case may not be as strong. If they insist on appearing before an ordinary court, and are prepared to go to where that court sits, it would be difficult to refuse them that right. In time, the Aboriginal system and its practices in dealing with offenders in a sensitive manner may persuade these people to defer to the jurisdiction of the Aboriginal court. If that option is available, a person who is charged with an offence or is named in a civil action might be asked to make an irrevocable choice of the court that will have jurisdiction in their case. A simpler solution would be to have the broader community become part of a 'community' court.

Another situation that would have to be negotiated in advance, is that of a non-resident non-Aboriginal person who commits an offence on Aboriginal land. If someone is caught speeding, or is involved in an accident on a provincial road passing through the community, or commits theft or assault, they should, in my opinion, be dealt with in the Aboriginal court. One reason this has to be clearly spelled out is that, in the United States, the Tribal courts do not have jurisdiction over non-Indians. That approach does not have to be followed in Canada, but the document that creates the court should make this area of jurisdiction perfectly clear. Another way to deal with these cases, that may come in time, would be to have the province specifically name Aboriginal Judges as Provincial Judges with jurisdiction to deal with certain situations.

In the criminal area, some of the offences that are most likely to arise will likely involve physical or sexual assault, break and enter, theft, damage to property, creating a disturbance, driving offences, being drunk and disorderly, illegally consuming alcohol and taking or dealing in drugs. It is essential to the health of Aboriginal communities, and to their citizens, that these matters be dealt with expeditiously and in an effective manner. If this sort of conduct can be nipped in the bud, there is a good chance of correcting the offender and preventing any repetition of the offence. They should all be included in the court's jurisdiction.

The abuse and neglect of women and children must be included. Women now feel isolated and abandoned by the First Nation government and by the regular courts. They have nowhere to go for help or for advice. If they complain, that may only make the situation worse when the abuser finds out. If they file a complaint and go to court it will take months to get a restraining order that will likely be impossible to enforce. It is virtually impossible to remove the abuser from the home and there are usually no healing processes in the community. If the abuser is charged and arrested, he will be removed from the community for a time, but will return.

Bail is usually accorded to abusers who after a time in detention return to their home. After a short period of contrition they also return to their former ways. Many who breach the terms of their bail are released again and again, sometimes with fatal consequences. A system is needed where a second chance is not accorded and where rehabilitative and preventative programs start work without delay. A process that will provide day-to-day protection for women and children is needed. Unless or until it becomes effective, a second release on bail should not be available. A local process is also needed to monitor any bail that is accorded.

Child abuse jurisdiction is equally necessary. Children need protection, sometimes from one parent and sometimes from both. If they have to be removed from their home, permanently or for a short period of time, there should be facilities and programs in the community that can come to their rescue. Processes need to be developed to determine the cause of the problem and to assist the parents overcome them. There is no system at the present time that can confer the needed authority on the members of the extended family and if they intervene they will likely be rejected. Applying to the regional agency may mean that the children will be removed from the community.

Young offenders, sometimes because of their youthful exuberance, the lack of sports or other activities, their depression with their situation and lack of hope, do things that get them into trouble with the law. The Aboriginal court should be designated as a youth court but I suggest it operate in a slightly different manner than the ones in the regular system.

For one thing, it should make youth hearings as open to the public as any others and should make the names of the offenders known. While I appreciate that the intent of the Act is to protect young people, in the case of a small community, the residents have a right to know who the troublemakers are. I also believe that if the names and the offences are publicized that will have a positive effect on the youth and on their parents. If they are embarrassed, that may well improve he parents' sense of responsibility and improve the conduct of the youth. Additional pressure should have a positive rather than a negative effect.

Civil law jurisdiction, now unheard of in Aboriginal communities, is required at the present time and will be even more necessary as Aboriginal communities improve economically. Contracts made between reserve residents and between them and outside businesses need to be interpreted and enforced. Torts are committed and a victim should have access to a court where a claim for damages and compensation can be heard. The will of a deceased relative occasionally requires interpretation and administration.

An Aboriginal court would need the same jurisdiction in family matters as that exercised by unified family courts. This would include giving orders of separation, awarding custody of children and setting support payments. It would include all of the matters referred to in the provincial Family Maintenance Act and Marital Property Act and the authority to grant divorces under the federal Divorce Act and to deal with the ancillary matters referred to in it.

It should certainly have the jurisdiction covered by the Child and Family Services Act. This would enable the court to deal with child protection matters and adoption. Along with the Criminal Code and the Young Offenders Act, these statutes would enable the court to deal with the greatest volume of work likely to arise in Aboriginal communities.

An Aboriginal government may wish to consider laws that deal with commercial contracts and the seizure of assets in their community. It may wish to consider both the protection and responsibility of members and the encouragement of trade and commerce. Its legislation should specify whether lien holders may come onto the First Nation land to seize articles such as cars where there has been default in payment, and many U.S. Tribal courts now permit entry for these purposes.

If a First Nation is uncomfortable with a blanket authority to permit outsiders to come onto its land, a compromise would be to have the lender explain the situation to a judge and ask for an order permitting entry and the seizure of an asset. An order might make a seizure subject to certain warnings and notices, but whatever the order is, a court order would be required.

Regulatory matters also fall within civil law jurisdiction and challenges to laws and the right to pass them are common in the regular courts. Any community member should have the right to challenge a law that has been improperly passed or that exceeds the local government's authority. A challenge should be possible if it is alleged that a Chief or Councillor has committed an act warranting their removal. The Aboriginal court should have the authority to strike down any law that is beyond the jurisdiction of the local authority, to interpret laws that are unclear and to issue an injunction to prohibit any illegal act. It should also have the authority to remove an elected official from office and to order a by-election.

Having said that, the community laws should afford some protection to their government members so they cannot be sued for actions taken in good faith, and judges should have the same immunity. These protections are given to existing legislatures and courts and are needed to assure independence of action and the freedom to frankly say what needs to be said.

Resource protection will be another important area of jurisdiction for Aboriginal communities. The Aboriginal government will want to pass laws and regulations to protect resources and to define the rights of members with respect to fishing, hunting, trapping and logging. It should formulate offences to ensure compliance by its members and by people from outside the community who are permitted to enter to use the resources. The police should have the jurisdiction to prosecute or to seek an injunction to prohibit illegal activities and the court will need the jurisdiction to enforce compliance.

Each Aboriginal court should have either unlimited civil jurisdiction, as in the U.S. Tribal courts, or begin with jurisdiction of $10,000 or some other agreed upon figure. In view of the fact that other courts with civil jurisdiction are not going to be available to most Aboriginal communities, I suggest the amount should be substantial.

Once established, the Aboriginal court should formulate a complete set of court rules to specify, among other things, how civil and criminal proceedings may be commenced, the forms to be used and any time limits that are to apply. The rules might be prepared by the judges in consultation with the court management committee and legal assistant to make certain that community concerns will be taken into account.

Before leaving the jurisdiction of an Aboriginal court, I want to emphasize the importance of Crown Discretion and how it will operate. It will, in most cases, determine the actual jurisdiction the Aboriginal court will have. I suggested earlier that an Aboriginal court have criminal jurisdiction over the offences covered by the Criminal Code that may be tried summarily or "on summary conviction."

Provincial courts are summary conviction courts, but they also hear indictable cases with the consent of the accused. In some indictable cases they hold a preliminary inquiry before the case goes to a superior court for trial with a jury. In the majority of cases however the Crown does not proceed by indictment but opts to process cases as summary conviction offences where a less severe penalty applies. Most of the offences defined in the Criminal Code of Canada provide the two options.

For example, Section 266 of the Criminal Code provides that everyone who commits an assault is guilty of:

(a) an indictable offence and is liable to imprisonment for a term not exceeding five years; or
(b) an offence punishable on summary conviction.

Sec. 787(1) of the Code deals with the lesser penalty that may be applied to 'summary conviction' offences. It provides that, "except where otherwise provided," a person who is convicted of an offence punishable on summary conviction is liable to a fine of not more than $2,000 dollars or to imprisonment for six months or both. Some of the offences that 'provide otherwise' are: being illegally in a dwelling house, unlawfully causing bodily harm, sexual assault and drug offences under the Food and Drugs Act. Those and other offences permit incarceration for up to 18 months.

An indictable offence is used in the more serious cases where the Crown wants to seek a substantial penalty. The manner in which to proceed will likely depend on the seriousness of the offence and on the previous record of the accused.

To bring a charge within the indictable category, a Crown Attorney prepares a formal document called an 'indictment' in the name of Her Majesty the Queen against the alleged offender. The indictment enables the Crown to seek the greater penalty, while the summary approach is used for less serious matters and results in a lesser penalty. A summary conviction charge is commenced by an individual, often a police officer, laying an 'information' alleging the commission of an offence.

From the perspective of determining the extent of jurisdiction an Aboriginal court would have, these options enable a clear distinction to be made between less and more serious offences. The Aboriginal court would be able to deal with the less serious offences and to apply the more limited penalties. This should nevertheless enable it to deal with most criminal matters that are likely to arise in its communities.

If an offence appears to have been committed, the local police or the RCMP can decide to have it dealt with summarily by the Aboriginal court. If they are uncertain, they would contact the Crown Attorney for the area so he can consider whether he would prefer to proceed by indictment. His decision would determine whether the case would go to the provincial court or be left in the Aboriginal court. I expect the Crown would develop some guidelines it would ask the police to follow.

This overriding Crown discretion should remain in place. That would, I hope, give comfort to those concerned about an Aboriginal court having too much authority or jurisdiction. My expectation is that the Crown would want to hold on to its jurisdiction, where a discretion exists, until it is able to assess the ability of Aboriginal courts to deal with cases. As time goes on, the Crown will hopefully become comfortable with the performance of Aboriginal courts and see that more cases are dealt with by them.

To enable Aboriginal courts to have the jurisdiction of a summary conviction court, there would either have to be a provision in the agreement or Treaty establishing the court, or the definition of a summary conviction court in Section 785(1) of the Code would have to be amended to include an Aboriginal court.

12

Police and Holding Facilities

There are two prerequisites to the establishment of an effective Aboriginal Justice System. One is a police service and the other is a holding facility in which offenders can be held for a short period of time. If these services are not available, the Aboriginal court would have to rely on outside services and in that event delays and unnecessary expense would result. Worse yet, charges would likely have to be laid and proceedings set in motion, something that could otherwise be avoided in many cases.

Police are needed to fulfil the usual police functions of enforcing laws and protecting citizens and, by their presence, deterring potential troublemakers from committing illegal or unacceptable acts. They are also needed to help residents resolve disputes and strained relationships. If the intent of an Aboriginal court is to divert cases to community services whenever that is feasible, it is important to have police with a similar attitude who are prepared to do the same thing.

The reduction of crime will best be achieved by officers whose main approach is preventive policing. They should be involved in community activities and have the trust of the residents. They will have to become acquainted with the Elders, Peacemakers, Circle leaders, and others in the community who can be asked to become involved in a troublesome situation. They should be prepared to participate in healing and sentencing circles, and to be involved in or chair community justice forums. They should become respected community leaders and be good role models for young people.

These principles are the same as those now being developed by many mainstream police forces under the rubric of 'community policing.' In fact, retired officers tell me that was the approach to policing many years ago. The key element is to have police officers with an intimate knowledge of the community and its resources and who understand its residents.

It is important that the officers believe in a non-punitive and rehabilitative approach to law enforcement. The type of policing that will be required will be quite different from that seen in Aboriginal communities in the past. There would no longer be the charge-prosecution-conviction-incarceration cycle that has become all too familiar. The approach of the police would be to protect the community and victims, and at the same time try to rehabilitate offenders so they will change their lifestyle and refrain from offending in the future.

At the same time, a change in the community attitude must be fostered so residents see the police as working for 'us' not 'them,' and be seen as friends and servants of the community. One of the tasks of the police force and of the Chief and Council will be to bring about that change. Many Aboriginal people have seen the police as agents of a foreign justice system that has applied foreign values, and a considerable amount of public relations work may be needed to change those attitudes. If there is a good explanation of their role and their approach to law enforcement, the community will hopefully be more understanding of their unique role and be supportive of them.

In Scotland, one of the first things the police do with young offenders is take them home and have a discussion with their parents. If a plan of reparation or penalty is agreed to, the parents are responsible to make sure it is put into operation and that it is enforced. If the plan works, the youth can be kept out of the court system. This sort of option involves family members working out solutions that will benefit victims and offenders, and incidentally the whole community. It makes the role of the police less confrontational and more effective and rewarding.

To make that sort of approach work in Aboriginal communities, the police should be fluent in the local language. They need to become familiar with the various services that exist or are being developed and who to contact to get help for a particular wrongdoer. They need to be familiar with the families and understand how traditional principles can be brought to bear on a problem.

There will be cases where, because of the nature of an offence, the RCMP will have jurisdiction and will attend, conduct an investigation, and report to the provincial Crown who will decide whether or not to lay a criminal charge. In their investigation they will likely seek the assistance of the Aboriginal police officers. The effectiveness of the Aboriginal police will become apparent to the RCMP through joint investigations and should result in more work being done locally and in the gradual withdrawal of the RCMP. I would expect that within a few years of being established, the Aboriginal police would do the majority of policing, while the RCMP could concentrate on major crimes.

As difficult as it may be, the Aboriginal police should assume another responsibility during joint investigations. They should make certain that justice is done and that the rights of accused people are respected. If a resident is being questioned by an RCMP officer from outside the community, they should make certain the person knows they do not have to answer any questions if they don't want to. If questioning proceeds, the local police should make sure the person understands the questions and that the responses are understood and accurately recorded. If necessary, the officer should help people fully explain themselves. They should insist that a parent is present if a youth is being questioned. If the person wants to talk to a family member, friend or lawyer, the officer should put the person in touch with them.

This suggestion is not intended to be a criticism of the RCMP but it is at this stage of an investigation that Aboriginal people often get themselves into trouble with the legal system. They sometimes say things they do not mean or refrain from saying things they should say. At other times they misunderstand questions and give answers that incriminate them. There will be no lawyers in the community and, even if there were, the communication with one might not bring out all the relevant facts. This is a heavy responsibility to place on the shoulders of local Aboriginal police but they should be able to carry out the task.

If this approach is taken, it might be well to advise the RCMP and the Attorney General so there will be no suggestion that the Aboriginal police are trying to subvert the law or interfere with an investigation by another police force. The RCMP may try to provide the same protections, but in my experience, difficulties in communication or an overly aggressive officer stand in the way of that being done.

Regional justice systems might wish to establish regional police forces similar to the Dakota Ojibway Tribal Police Service in Manitoba. No doubt there are other changes that should be made to make a Tribal police force a welcome addition to an Aboriginal justice system. The territory covered by a regional police service could be the same as the regional court system, or a Tribal force could serve several justice systems.

A regional force, as opposed to a separate one for every community, would be able to be flexible in the assignment and reassignment of officers. Where an unusual problem arises in one community, police from other communities could be sent to help. If problems continue, the numbers of officers could be increased until the problem subsides. The volume of work will no doubt vary from time to time in all communities and a regional force could adapt to current needs. If sensitive investigations are required in one community, officers could be brought in from other communities so the local officer need not be involved.

It is difficult for an Aboriginal person to be a police officer in an Aboriginal community, particularly in the one where they live. The concept of one person having so much authority over friends and relatives is difficult for residents to accept. The whole idea of having someone watch others, report on them, and arrest them if they are doing something wrong, is contrary to the traditional concept of non-interference. Aboriginal people are supposed to be responsible for their own good conduct and others are not supposed to jump to conclusions or condemn their actions. It will take some time to turn these attitudes around.

Matters such as vacancies, vacations, and training courses could be accommodated more easily in a regional system. If there are problems of acceptability of certain officers, or if they have to be strongly judgmental on occasion and conflicts arise, the officer could be moved to another area. Another advantage of the flexibility of a regional force is that specialties such as photography, exhibit handling and crime scene analysis could be developed and the specialist could be brought in to a community when a case requires some particular knowledge and experience.

A Chief of Police should be engaged to manage each regional system, and to assign, instruct and supervise the police. It would be important for him to have a good working relationship with the RCMP and provincial police. He should visit each community that is served by the regional service from time to time to answer questions the community may have and to make certain the police services are satisfactory.

When a number of regional police services are in place, it would be possible to establish a province-wide Aboriginal Police Commission to perform many of the same tasks as the regional police forces, but on a province-wide basis. It could assume the responsibility for police training and have disciplinary authority over police officers in situations where it would be difficult for local or regional authorities to act.

It would be to the advantage of regional police forces and to the RCMP, to have Aboriginal officers professionally trained. It would likely be possible to enter into an agreement to have the RCMP do the training. To reciprocate, Aboriginal justice systems could provide RCMP officers with some of the cultural training being provided to Aboriginal officers. This cross-cultural approach should benefit all police officers and the communities they serve.

When the AJI was in God's River on November 2nd, 1988, we heard a horror story about the manner in which a 14-year-old girl had been treated on October 7th. The girl lived with her parents and attended the local school. That evening, she and several other girls took a shotgun and shot out the windows of the school. She and two others were arrested and flown out of the isolated community. When the parents spoke at our Inquiry hearing, she was still in custody. Her father had flown to God's Lake Narrows on October 8th at a cost of $250 to visit his daughter who was still being held by the RCMP. He found her and the two other girls on the floor of a police cell containing beds but no mattresses.

He was unable to secure her release. He was told that she would be flown to Winnipeg, but couldn't be taken out of the area yet as "they hadn't given their statements," a travesty of justice in itself. The girls were subsequently moved to Winnipeg and some time later were flown north again, this time to court in Thompson. The parents were frantic about their daughter's welfare and had to charter a plane to get to court so they could be present at the promised bail hearing. The plane cost $577 one way. Two of the girls were released but their daughter was denied bail as the Crown Attorney told the judge she was a danger to the public.

The parents told us they had been brushed off five times as they tried to get help from Legal Aid, and were not allowed to speak in court. They wanted to tell the judge that they were responsible non-drinking parents and that their daughter had agreed to stay at home twenty-four hours a day. The parents had to spend a further $250 for food and hotel rooms during their stay in Thompson and $284 for a plane to take them back to God's River. They said that, as poor people, they couldn't afford to spend so much money on the court system, but that they had no choice and had to borrow the money.

I have no idea what additional amounts they had to spend to attend subsequent court hearings but I heard sometime later that the girl had been charged with break and enter, mischief, and a firearms offence, and that her case was ultimately disposed of without any incarceration being imposed. In the meantime, she was kept in custody at the Manitoba Youth Centre in Winnipeg, hundreds of miles from her home and family. Both the Chief of the God's River community and the parents told us they could have dealt with the girl and with the damage to the school if she had been left in the community.

The Manitoba Youth Centre is no place for a 14-year-old girl who has never even been to a city. It contains male and female youth who are on remand, others who have been sentenced to open custody and many serving sentences in secure custody. Many in each category are repeat offenders. She will be fortunate indeed if she has escaped without some permanent damage to her attitude to law and justice.

Several years later when visiting Aboriginal inmates at Stony Mountain, I told them this story and asked why they thought the girl had shot out the windows of the school. The reasons given by the inmates were: boredom, anger, lack of self-esteem, frustration, alcohol abuse, racial discrimination, she didn't know how to survive, no identity, taught to lash out, no future and no hope. I thought the inmates' answers were quite perceptive and that a sociology or criminology class in university couldn't have done any better; but of course my 'control group' had personal experience to call upon.

If there had been an Aboriginal court in the community, it might not have been necessary to arrest the girl. Even if that was seen as necessary, if there had been a holding facility in God's River, all the flying back and forth and the imposition of the heavy hand of the law, could have been avoided. The ends of justice would have been satisfied if the girl had been held overnight and then returned to her parents. If the police and the courts had to be involved, she would have been available to go to court. Absolutely nothing was gained by her removal from the community and a lot of harm was caused.

Many incidents arise and offences occur in Aboriginal communities when adults become intoxicated, and it is often a close friend or relative of the offender who becomes the victim. If there is a death or serious injury the offender is arrested and charged, and even if the danger to the victim and others has passed by the time the offender sobers up, the offender is flown out of the community.

The Intoxicated Persons Detention Act does not appear to be used where an offence has been committed, probably because the RCMP are not jailers and are more inclined to lay a criminal charge, keep the person in custody and transport them to a provincial jail. If the Act were used, an intoxicated person could be taken into custody by a peace officer and held for twenty-four hours. If the person agrees, they could then go to a detox centre after the twenty-four hours has expired and the Statute places no limit on how long the person may remain there. Many Aboriginal communities now have detox centres.

When at the detox centre, or when released from it, community resources or an Aboriginal court could deal with any wrongful act that may have been committed. In any event the person would remain in the community, rather than being removed to some distant jail. If offenders can remain with their families they would be able to seek their support and advice on how to deal with their behaviour. In cases where another form of diversion appears appropriate, the availability of the offender would permit any support program to begin without delay.

At the present time the only temporary holding facilities that exist in reserve communities are owned by the RCMP. They are usually trailers where offenders are held until arrangements can be made to transport them to a provincial jail or remand centre, or in the case of young offenders, to the Manitoba Youth Centre in Winnipeg. Apart from the fact that the offenders are removed from their parents, spouses or friends, my understanding is that a charge has to be laid or the detention centres won't accept the 'prisoner.' Documents have to be provided when a person arrives at an institution and again when they are returned to the police or to a Sheriff's Officer.

The impact of this situation is far reaching. As there is no one in the community who can grant bail and release people, they remain in custody until they appear before a Provincial Judge in the regional centre where they will eventually be tried. The charge isn't likely to be dropped unless the Crown Attorney believes it should not have been laid in the first place, and that would be embarrassing for the police. The case will likely be remanded a number of times before it is finally disposed of and often the offender has to stay in custody.

The costs attached to interim proceedings are substantial. At the time of the AJI we estimated that two million dollars was being spent every year on the transportation of young Aboriginal people from the north to Winnipeg and back again. A one-day, round-trip from Winnipeg to Thompson, including meals for an offender and an escort (assuming commercial rates apply) is in the neighbourhood of $1,500 dollars. If five trips are required in a single case the cost would be $7,500. The cost of housing people in jail pending their trial should also be considered. It costs $114 a day to care for a young person in the Youth Centre and $84.50 a day for an adult in the Remand Centre.

I assume the cost of building and maintaining the facilities is not included in these figures.

At one time RCMP used their own aircraft to fly officers and prisoners back and forth to remote communities. This cost was considerably in excess of the commercial rate if the maintenance and operation of the plane and the salaries of two pilots is included.

Some changes in the method of transporting prisoners have been made. A person who works in the jails told me that if a youth is in custody in Winnipeg and has to attend court in Thompson, two Winnipeg Sheriff's Officers drive the person in a van to Grand Rapids, a little over halfway to Thompson. There they are met by another van and two officers who drive the rest of the way, while the first van is driven back to Winnipeg. In other words, the salaries of four officers, fuel and meal expenses have to be paid to get a youth to court. If bail is still not granted, the process is repeated.

One of the objectives of an Aboriginal court would be to deal with criminal acts or wrongdoing as quickly as possible. It would want to begin to deal with an adult who has caused harm to another, or a young offender like the girl I mentioned, while the facts and consequences are fresh in everyone's mind. It might want to involve substance abuse counsellors, a community justice forum, child and family services, or a healing program. That is not possible if the individual has been taken out of the community.

If each community that is part of an Aboriginal justice system had a temporary holding facility, that would enable most people who appear to have committed an offence, to be released when they are no longer a danger to anyone. In some situations no criminal charge would have to be laid. In others, the Aboriginal court would be able to assess the situation and decide what should be done. The attitude of the offender, and possibly parents, may indicate the approach that should be taken.

I not only recommend that holding facilities be established in each community, I say that their establishment is an essential pre-condition to the successful operation of an Aboriginal court. If they are in place, they will enable the massive removal of suspected offenders to stop. They will serve the immediate need to protect others and will allow the Aboriginal courts to begin their work. Of equal importance, they will keep hundreds of people out of the jail system and will save young offenders from influences that may permanently damage their lives.

A holding facility in a small community could be a house, a room in a house, or a building converted for the purpose. There would have to be secure rooms where intoxicated people could be left without being able to cause damage to themselves or to others and there would have to be separate places for women, female youth, male youth and male adults. Some communities might decide that a single building should be used and have separate rooms to accommodate the different classes of offenders. In any event, the facilities should not be under the authority of the police, but should be one of the services provided by the Aboriginal justice system.

It should not be hard to find community residents who would be glad to earn a per diem allowance for caring for other community residents for short periods of time. Someone would of course have to cover the cost of renovations or construction to make sure the holding rooms are suitable for their intended purpose. My assumption is that the holding facilities in smaller communities would not be required very often and possibly only for those who are intoxicated. In most cases offenders are not going to 'escape' and leave their homes and family.

If God's River had had its own justice system, its own Aboriginal police and its own holding facility, the girl's actions could have been explored while she remained in the community. The anxiety of the parents, the Chief and Council and others in the community, and the thousands of dollars expended on her case, could have been avoided.

13

Planning

Before Aboriginal communities consider establishing their own justice system there are a number of matters they should explore. The first might be to consider whether they need their own court at all, but it may not be possible to answer that question without analyzing the sort of services they now receive and considering whether they can be improved upon.

It seems to me that there are at least two studies that should be undertaken. One should be an analysis of the Provincial Court services now being utilized by the community and the other should be a survey of the programs that exist within the community that might tie in with a local court if one were created.

I have suggested that there are problems of access to the Provincial Courts which don't sit in every community, and I have spoken of delays, repeated remands, transporting youthful offenders out of the community and the overuse of jail. Each community should do an analysis of their situation to see whether these comments are correct and whether they apply to them.

To do that it will be necessary to establish a local planning committee or to ask Tribal or provincial associations to assist with local efforts or to conduct a province-wide study. Using Manitoba as an example, Tribal Councils or provincial organizations such as the Manitoba Keewatinowi Okimakanak (MKO) or the Assembly of Manitoba Chiefs (AMC) might also undertake a study and help with the preparation of survey documents. The Métis Federation might survey its members and its communities as well. The Manitoba government will already have many statistics but might be interested in gathering more if the possibility of a parallel system is being explored.

Questionnaires should be prepared and circulated to every family in an Aboriginal community, whether it is a First Nation, Métis or non-status one, and people should be asked to respond. To obtain as much information as possible, and to avoid embarrassing those who may have a criminal record, respondents should not have to give their names.

The survey should be as complete as possible and I only suggest some of the information I think would be valuable. People might be asked to list the number of times they had to go to court as an accused, victim, witness or as a parent of a young offender. They should be asked to list the type of offence in each case, the number of remands that were required, the overall time from charge to final disposition and the sort of sentence that was applied.

They should say whether they gave a statement to the police or not, how they were treated by them, and how they were treated in court. They should indicate whether they had a legal aid lawyer and how that worked. If they were sentenced, they should indicate the nature of the sentence, and if they were jailed, for how long and in what institution. They could be asked to comment on the services they received in jail and whether they were granted probation or parole.

If they had to travel to attend court, it would be of interest to know the cost to them of doing so. The means of travel might also be recorded and an indication of any problems they had in getting to court. If they missed court due to the weather or any other cause, they might indicate what if anything happened to them.

At the same time the local study is being conducted, statistics should be gathered from the court records to indicate how it has been dealing with cases emanating from each community. It would be important to know, for example, how many cases in the last calendar year came from Garden Hill, Red Sucker Lake, Wasagamack and Ste. Theresa Point. The reason I have selected those communities is that they are some distance apart but are all in the same part of Manitoba, but the court only sits in Garden Hill.

The Ministry of Justice has statistics from each place where the Provincial Court sits and it would be possible to do an analysis that would show where the cases came from, whether there was a trial or a plea of guilty, how many cases were dealt with summarily and in how many there was an indictment. The records would show, I expect, whether those appearing in court were in custody at the time, were on bail or appeared without being arrested.

Court records would show how many had a trial, and of those, how many were convicted. They would also show how many pleaded guilty and how many adjournments were required before each case was disposed of. They would show the sort of sentence that was applied, so it would be possible to calculate the number who received a suspended sentence, a fine, or were sent to jail. The length of the jail sentence that was imposed would be shown although I expect that the date of release would not be noted.

Young offender statistics would reveal the length of time it took to process cases, the number of times an offender and a parent had to appear and whether the youth was kept in custody or released on bail. They would show how many youth were sent to the Manitoba Youth Centre between hearings, the place of eventual confinement and whether the sentence was to open or closed custody. The record would also show the community from which the youth came. Some place in the system, there would be a record of the cost of transporting youth back and forth from the north to holding facilities in the south.

Statistics would show the places where the court sat and the regularity of its attendance. The number of adjournments would indicate whether the court was able to deal with matters on its dockets when they were set to be heard. It would be possible to determine whether the court was able to keep its work current or was badly backlogged. Actual court dockets would confirm or expand upon the statistics.

Communities wouldn't commit themselves to proceed with the establishment of an Aboriginal court merely by gathering information, but the information would be of considerable value if a court was later established. In the meantime, it would help communities make an informed decision. It would at least provide a starting point for considering the extent of work an Aboriginal court might anticipate, even if it hopes to reduce much of the duplication and the number of cases going to trial. Incidentally, they would show whether my estimates, and some of the stories of delay we heard during the AJI, were accurate.

The same or another survey might examine people's experience with the existing courts. They might be asked to indicate whether they have ever faced a criminal charge, the nature of it, the number of remands and the eventual outcome. Their names need not be recorded but the figures and the attitude of those who have been involved with the courts would be important to know.

While these studies are being done, either locally or on a provincial basis, an inventory of services that exist in each community should be prepared to document the helping or healing programs that exist. It should record all the services and include a statement with respect to each, indicating what they are, how they operate and how people may take advantage of them. The document should show the type and extent of the police service that exists. It should say whether there are band constables and whether they are part of a Tribal police force. It should indicate whether there is a local RCMP police detachment and, if not, where those services come from.

It should list the counselling programs, child care, healing circles, sweat lodges, alcohol treatment programs and justice committees that function in the community. There may be detoxification programs, a 'Flying on Your Own' abstinence one, Justice Committees, Family Group Conferencing, Child Care and nursing. The manner in which child welfare services are delivered should be included.

Those doing the interviewing should inquire, particularly of women, about the extent of spousal and child abuse in the community and what women do when they occur. The same questions should be asked about the abuse of children — what sort of abuse is it, who does it and what is done about it? Women who have been abused should be asked what they did about it and how effective they found Provincial Court orders were in protecting them and their children. They could be asked if abuse caused their separation from an abuser and what happened to the children. They might also be asked if they had ever been involved in a healing circle that dealt with their abuse or knew of one that dealt with an abuser.

They should be asked whether they have turned to family or friends when abuse occurred and whether they have been helpful. It would be important to know if extended family members ever come forward and offer to help, or if it is common for a call for help to be rejected. They might be asked if they think a healing circle, a Peacemaker or an Elder could help and whether there are people in the community that could fill those roles. They could be asked what they think of the concept of a Family Conference where extended family members are asked to offer their wisdom and support, and whether they would be willing to participate in one.

Those doing the questioning or taking the survey would have to be provided with some material or be briefed on the manner in which court connected services operate so they can describe them to those being questioned. The role of a Peacemaker and the functioning of a Community Justice Forum and a Family Conference should be known by them.

Community residents might be asked where they turn if they need help in understanding the law or what may happen in court. They might be asked if they have ever obtained legal advice, and from whom. They could be asked if they think it would be helpful to have para-legal services in the community. It might be explained that para-legal advisors would be able to obtain pamphlets and advice on every aspect of civil and criminal law and procedure.

An inquiry should be made to determine whether there are people in the community who could act as Peacemakers, Court Registrars and Court Officers and whether Peacemakers could be of assistance in resolving disputes. These facts and opinions would be important for judges to know if a court is being organized.

These are questions, and there are certainly more, the answers to which each community should have before moving ahead. They also provide the type of information a management committee would require when setting up a court system and determining the number of judges and court personnel who would be required. Statistics will also provide valuable comparisons with the work later done by an Aboriginal court, if one is put in place.

While this fact-gathering process is under way, Tribal Councils might establish discussion sessions and planning committees to consider how court services might be delivered. They might even establish a regional exploratory process to see which communities would be interested in joining together to form a justice system. Local planning committees, including those from Métis and non-status communities, should be asked to participate in the study.

In its examination of the sort of justice system that might be established, there are two types of court I think warrant consideration. One is be a stand-alone court that would serve only one community, and the other is a regional court that would serve a number of communities and the area between them. Individual communities could conduct this part of the study, or a number of them with common interests could study the matter together. In either case they might appoint a management committee so that any decisions can later be used if an Aboriginal court is created.

First Nation communities with a sizeable population and adequate financial resources may be able to establish their own justice system. It could have its own judges, police, Peacemakers and Court Officers. It would need its own court administrator, court clerks, para-legal advisors, legal assistants and judges. A large community would be able to develop all the support services and other programs the court would need. The only difference between this and a regional justice system would be that all the justice services would be located in the one community.

A large single-court system might require more judges than one serving a number of small communities but it would also permit some specialization. One judge might deal with young offender and family matters, while another might deal with adult criminal cases. A third might concentrate on commercial and civil issues. If the court did serve smaller communities, an advantage to them might be that they could make use of the specialized judges when required.

After this sort of court becomes well established and has developed expertise in dealing with Aboriginal people with their legal problems, it could expand its operation in one of two ways. It could join with smaller communities as part of a regional system or it could provide its judicial and other services to smaller communities on a fee-for-service basis.

A regional court, on the other hand, would serve a number of communities that do not have enough people or financial resources to warrant their own police, judges and court personnel. A regional system involving a group of communities would provide all the benefits and services of a larger system but it would be done by having judges travel on circuit and hold court in each member community on a regular basis. It would have a central office and the local services I will later describe, as well. In that way each community would enjoy a full range of civil and criminal judicial services and, except for serious offences that are beyond the jurisdiction of the court, there would no longer be a need for residents to travel to another community to attend court.

Regional systems could serve all the communities in a defined geographic area. The communities themselves should decide how many of them could share services yet maintain their independence. To make the system viable in a cohesive geographic area, they would want to consider how to involve all Aboriginal residents, be they Indian, Métis, or non-status Indians. Each community would still have its own court personnel, its own court hearings and its own diversion programs. I don't see how Aboriginal courts can be established unless all these people are served by it.

I am aware that it may be difficult to have First Nation, Métis and non-status people come together to establish a regional system, but I can't see how an Aboriginal court can be established if large numbers of Aboriginal people are excluded from it. My recommendation is that all Aboriginal people in the area that is agreed upon, join together to establish a common justice system.

The only workable exception I can envisage is to have justice systems established by First Nations on the understanding that they would make their courts and other services available to all other Aboriginal people who live in the defined area. This would be a matter to be discussed and negotiated with all those who would be effected and with the provincial and federal governments.

Nothing would prevent large and smaller communities from joining together in one court system if they wished. Communities like Norway House with its large First Nation, Métis and non-status population, might agree to join with smaller communities on the east side of Lake Winnipeg. Communities like Churchill, which has no First Nation, might join with Tadoule Lake, Brochet and Lac Brochet, or with communities on the Hudson's Bay rail line. Where there is a large Métis community like Camperville, it might develop a system in conjunction with the adjacent Pine Creek First Nation and might serve other Aboriginal communities as well.

Another benefit of a regional court is that each community would be involved in the operation of the court in their community by having its own Registrar, Court Officer and a place for court to be held and each could have a representative on the committee responsible for the operation of the system. If juries are established, members of the community would be involved in deciding the guilt or innocence of offenders, and if traditional sentencing circles were established they would be involved in determining the penalty to be imposed.

Regional justice systems would have the benefit of a large system by pooling their resources to engage judges and other personnel. They might have the additional advantage of having judges who do not reside in any of the communities being served, so they can maintain their independence. That would reduce the possibility of a conflict of interest arising from personally knowing members of the First Nation government or others appearing in court. Another benefit would be that if judges were employed by a management committee made up of one representative from each member community, there would be greater security of tenure for the judge.

The planning committee would have to discuss with each community whether, if it wants to go to the next step, it wants to look at establishing its own system or join with others to form a regional one. It should have talks with the First Nations, Métis and others to see how a regional system might work. Each community would likely have questions of its own, such as what the financial contributions of each would be and where the funds would come from. Questions of representation on the management committee and an equitable representation among the judiciary and the court staff might arise.

The final matter communities will want to consider before they decide to proceed, is the services an Aboriginal court will be able to provide. Members of the planning committee, judges and administrators from existing systems, or others with a background in Aboriginal courts, should meet with the Chief and Council and with the residents of each community to discuss these matters and to listen to their needs and suggestions. The management committee, when it is established should take their concerns into account.

Financial resources for the operation of an Aboriginal justice system would likely come from several sources. The First Nation communities may have funds in their budgets that relate to justice programs that can be transferred to it. These may relate to healing, diversion programs or justice committees that have already been established. There will be some revenue from fines imposed by judges or resulting from tickets that are issued by the police. Until local resources generate employment and income, the remaining funds will have to come from the federal and provincial governments.

There would certainly be substantial savings to the provincial government once an Aboriginal system is in operation. The need to send Provincial Judges and a whole court party into Aboriginal areas would be reduced. The cost of the permanent staff would probably be less than the amount it costs to pay and transport judges, police, lawyers, clerks and court reporters on a regular basis. If young offenders no longer have to be kept in detention pending a court appearance, and be transported from the north to a southern youth centre, and back and forth, the annual savings will be in the millions of dollars.

If cases are diverted from the courts to community support services, the need for a court will diminish further. If cases that do go to court are dealt with quickly, and are no longer remanded from month to month, the overloaded court lists will diminish. If the holding of adult offenders in custody is either eliminated or the time in custody is shortened, the cost savings will be enormous. If fewer convicted people are sent to jail, the savings will increase. The Aboriginal courts should also be less expensive to operate. The savings can be used to develop and support the local support programs.

The federal government would be a beneficiary as well. The annual $50,000 a year cost to house a federal inmate will be saved for every person that can be dealt with without having to be sent to a penitentiary. It may take a while for the impact of an Aboriginal justice system to reach that level, but my expectation is that it will eventually reduce the overall degree of incarceration in all jails and penitentiaries.

If these benefits do result from an Aboriginal system, it would be possible for the federal and provincial governments to finance its operating costs from the savings they enjoy. The net result would be that the addition of a parallel Aboriginal justice system would not cost a penny.

When Aboriginal systems come into effect, statistics should be kept by the courts and by the Centre for Justice Statistics in Ottawa so comparisons can be made with continuing systems using the regular courts. A statistically supported cost analysis would be valuable as the creation of further Aboriginal systems is contemplated. When a variety of systems are in place, comparisons could be drawn between differing models.

The manner in which the revenue the system receives from fines should be settled in advance. The issue will require agreement between the Aboriginal system and the province in particular. It would probably not be difficult to agree that where an offence is committed within the territorial jurisdiction of the court, the revenue from a fine imposed by an Aboriginal judge, or paid as a result of a ticket issued by a member of the Aboriginal police force, or from the forfeiture of bail, would go to the Aboriginal justice system.

There may however be situations that are not as clear and where negotiations will be required. There would have to be an agreement on where fines would go if a ticket is issued by a provincial officer on a provincial road or highway that runs through an Aboriginal community, or if a ticket is issued by an Aboriginal officer outside the territory. The decision might turn on where the offender was required to report or who was paying the police officer.

A similar issue might arise with respect to hunting and fishing infractions. If a charge was laid by an Aboriginal officer within the territory and the person was called to appear in the Aboriginal court, the revenue should go to the system. If the offence occurred outside the

Aboriginal area, or within a joint conservation area, but is laid by a provincial officer, the result may not be as clear. The agreement that establishes the system should settle what would happen if the arrest was made by an Aboriginal person who held an appointment as a provincial police or conservation officer.

I have no suggestions to make as to how these issues should be decided but merely raise them for discussion in the planning stage and in any discussions with government that may follow. There are a number of modern treaties and other agreements where these matters have been dealt with and they might provide some options to consider.

The other issue in dealing with revenue from fines is an internal one but it should also be considered in advance. Whether an Aboriginal court serves a number of communities, a decision would have to be made as to where, within the system, the revenue would go. One option would be to have the fines go to the community where the fine was imposed. Another would be to have the revenue go into the budget of the committee that manages the entire system and a third, less attractive possibility, would be to have it go into the court's own budget.

Even if an Aboriginal court establishes and administers its own budget, I suggest that the revenue from fines not go directly to the court. The judges, it is to be hoped, will pay more attention to restitution and the compensation of victims than to imposing fines. Even so it might be considered unseemly, if not a conflict of interest, for a court to impose a fine and receive the revenue from it as well. The revenue from fines imposed by the court might better go to the court management committee as it will have a budget of its own and will be the employer of the police and court personnel.

I assume that a court management committee appointed jointly by all the communities which are members of a regional justice system, would assess the costs of operating the system among the member communities on the basis of their population, the amount of court activity in each, or on some other equitable basis. Instead of each community having to receive provincial or federal financial assistance for operating the justice system, the funds could go directly to the system itself to be disbursed by the arms-length management committee.

If the management committee receives the revenue from fines, it could go to reduce the contributions the particular community would have to make but if the communities contribute on a pro-rata basis, the income from fines would benefit the overall budget on a pro-rata basis as well. The only factor that might interfere would be if a provincial highway passes through only one of the communities. It might then be necessary to determine whether that community, or the overall system, would pay the cost of the additional police.

If communities decide to proceed to establish a court, I hope that government will encourage their initiative and embrace their desire to develop solutions to their problems. Some communities will decide not to proceed immediately, but will want to wait and see how others are doing. That wish should be respected. They will be able to watch and see how other systems operate and will be able to assess their effectiveness. They will be able to join a system when they are ready to do so. At that time the terms of their participation can be negotiated with the original participants. While this approach might delay the ultimate objective of having comprehensive systems, I believe it is necessary to permit communities to proceed if and when they are ready.

I will present a model of an Aboriginal court that I believe will work; however it is merely an example for Aboriginal communities and government to consider. There can be many variations to it and communities can choose to adopt it, some parts of it, or develop something entirely different. If communities decide to proceed with the establishment of a justice system, another level of planning will be required, and I will deal with that when discussing the work a management committee might do.

PART V

The
Court

14

Administration

If a First Nation or a group of Aboriginal communities decide to
proceed with the establishment of a justice system they should join
in the appointment of a Management Committee. Its task would
be to see to that police are available in each community and that
holding and jail facilities are provided. It would be responsible to hire
the court staff and to appoint or employ the judges and would have
to prepare and administer the system's budget.

The committee should be composed of representatives from the
participating communities. I suggest that if there are 12 participating
communities in a system, the committee consist of 12 people. They
could then select one of the members as Chairman and appoint a
couple of others to be part of an Executive committee to be
responsible for the day to day operations of the system. The whole
committee would deal with matters of policy and matters effecting
the communities.

The committee would have to see that court offices were
established in every community and a central office as well. It would
have to consult with each community and provide a location where
court can be held. It might have to be the authority to enter into final
discussions with government to settle questions of jurisdiction and
financial support.

An early task of the committee should be to follow up on the
inventories that were compiled in each community and to look at
them from the standpoint of the number of judges and other
personnel that will be required. They should assess the support
services that exist in each community and the others that will have
to be established. They will have to make an initial assessment of
the number of judges, police, holding facilities and jails that will
likely be required.

The severity of the criminal cases going to the regular courts from the area should be examined to determine how many are likely to fall within the jurisdiction of their court. A rough assessment could then be made of the number that might result in a plea of guilty, the number that might be referred to a community resource and the number that would likely require a trial. Child Welfare and child protection services will already exist but they should be examined to see how they would work in conjunction with the local court. It would be important to know the number of child protection cases in process in each community, the number of foster homes that exist, and whether extended family members are active in helping couples who are having problems.

The committee should establish local holding facilities and identify those who are willing to care for overnight residents. The cost of adding to or renovating homes or buildings should be estimated. It should, at least tentatively, consider the establishment of wilderness camps and healing lodges and proceed with their establishment as the court gains experience and can determine the numbers who would benefit from them.

Decisions will have to be taken as to whether each community will have its own police officers or whether a regional police system should be established. Police officers may have to be engaged and all police may require training in community policing and the conduct of community justice forums. Training might be arranged with other police forces or from the RCMP. They should also receive instruction from Elders in traditional approaches to dealing with troublemakers and how local healing programs work.

The next task of the committee will be to engage the first judge. I would suggest that person have experience with the manner in which courts operate and have an acceptable vision of what an Aboriginal justice system needs and how it will operate in a culturally appropriate manner. The first judge will have some unusual administrative responsibilities, possibly as the Chief Judge, and should be able to help the committee and the communities establish the court.

I suggest that the committee engage the first judge on contract after a search and advertising has taken place. Later on, the committee may want to consider how other judges should be engaged, their terms of office and their remuneration, but it might choose the first judge on the understanding that he will assist in establishing the court, selecting the administrative staff and any additional judges that are required.

The committee should see that an appropriate method of establishing and controlling the costs of the system is put in place and auditors should be appointed to oversee the establishment of the necessary records and statistical systems. It should establish methods of receiving financial support from government or for assessing the member communities if they receive the revenue.

The chief judge should work closely with the committee in the preparation of the budget and in setting priorities. Judges must have the necessary financial and other resources with which to function. The management committee should be aware of the rules of court and its practices, that are developed by the judges, but it should not interfere with the manner in which judges perform their duties and in the day to day operation of the court.

The management committee and the first judge, in consultation with each community, should appoint the Local Registrars, Peacemakers and Court Officers. I include the judge in the selection process as these employees will be officers of the court and have to perform tasks the judges assign to them. The location of a central office will have to be determined and the committee will have to engage the court administrator, a full or part time lawyer, and other staff.

Whether the planning committee has held public meetings or not, the management committee and the Chief Judge should hold meetings in each community to explain the work of the court and to receive questions, concerns and suggestions from the residents. Similar meetings should be held annually so the communities can see what their court is doing and how problems are being addressed.

The committee should provide initial and ongoing education for the staff who run the court, and for the judges. The training might be arranged through the provincial government until numbers warrant the formation of an Aboriginal-specific educational authority. Conferences of staff from various Aboriginal systems should be encouraged to meet and to consult with one another. For specific training on court procedures, some Aboriginal people who are familiar with the regular system and with cultural history and traditional practices might be engaged as instructors. An alternative to conferences might be to bring people into the region to provide training.

The management committee can help the court communicate any concerns it may have to the communities. It can also receive concerns from the communities, their governments and members of the public, and pass them on to the Chief Judge. That communication will be important in maintaining a high level of court service that meets the needs and concerns of the communities. The committee should act as a buffer between the court and the community and yet maintain a good level of communication with both.

A skilled Court Administrator, acting as the chief executive officer, will have to be appointed and be responsible to both the court management committee and to the Chief Judge. A central office will be required. It will be the central registry for court documents and provide office space for the judges, a lawyer and the administrative staff. The Administrator would have to see that sufficient staff is engaged to do the record keeping and to provide secretarial support for the judges and the legal assistant. Assistance will also be required to help each community establish its court office and to engage the Local Registrar and Court Officer.

The Administrator should be able to provide information and advice to the public and to the Local Registrars. He or she would have to help the less experienced Local Registrars establish their office procedures and recording systems for Peacemakers and the Court Officer. A system would have to be put in place that would enable Local Registrars to provide para-legal advice to the residents and information on the method to be followed in launching court proceedings or responding to ones commenced against them. The court Administrator might have to obtain advice from the legal assistant or a judge in procedural matters and discuss it with the Registrars.

The Administrator will have to work closely with the Chief Judge to establish the rota and estimate the length of time each sitting will take. The ability to do that will improve with experience but this sort of information is essential so the committee can add judges to the system or engage additional part-time judges to keep the work of the court up to date. He will also have to follow-up on orders made in court to obtain reports from a Court Officer, Peacemaker, or a local program to which an offender has been referred. Sentence re-hearings will have to be worked into the schedule on the dates they are required and probation reports may have to be obtained.

The Administrator should probably be a person with business experience in keeping books, statistical records and making reports. An annual statistical and financial report will be required. It would be valuable to have a person who knows the communities being served and the potential of the local programs. Where support programs are not yet in existence, an Administrator may have to help the communities organize them. Some travelling will be required to enable the Administrator to visit the communities and travel elsewhere to improve his management skills and to learn of programs and procedures that exist in other systems. There are now many Aboriginal men and women working in the regular courts who would be able to administer the type of Aboriginal court I have described.

A staff lawyer would be an important part of the court's administrative and legal establishment. In the early stages of development, the lawyer could help the communities draft their local legislation and agreements that would provide the legal basis for the court's establishment and operation. Local criminal and civil codes might have to be developed if the community is to define its own laws. The alternative would be to have the lawyer adapt federal and provincial laws to the approach the communities and the court wants to take.

The lawyer should be involved in the development of forms, procedures and court rules in consultation with the Chief Judge. He should visit the communities to help the Local Registrars assume their duties. He should instruct them on legal matters and establish a communication procedure so he can be called on to provide information for the Registrar to pass on to members of the public. The lawyer could also be of value to non-legally trained judges and provide the type of services given to lay Magistrates in England by a legally-trained 'clerk' who provides advice on the law that applies to cases they are hearing.

In view of the isolation of many communities and the difficulty and expense of having lawyers fly in to provide assistance to accused persons, the legal assistant could participate in all court sittings to act as a 'friend of the court.' In that role the lawyer's task would be to see that all relevant facts are brought to the attention of the judge. In representing the position of the prosecution he would be responsible to present facts to secure a conviction, as would a Crown Attorney, but he would also have to speak to the accused and present his position in as favourable a light as possible. In summing up, he would not take an aggressive stance on either side of the case, but would point out the facts and arguments for the prosecution and the defence the judge should consider.

If an accused engages his own lawyer, the legal assistant could concentrate more on the case for the prosecution, but could still urge a solution that would be fair and reasonable to all concerned. The same principle would apply to a civil case where the opposing positions of the litigants require resolution. He might suggest the appointment of a Peacemaker or mediator in some cases, to enable the parties to arrive at their own solution.

This role of representing both sides in a dispute is not as difficult or dangerous as it may appear. There does not have to be any conflict of interest as long as the lawyer is fairly representing the interests of both sides. When I practiced in two communities with populations of about one thousand people in the 1950s, (Roblin and Melita) I acted for both sides on almost all commercial matters. If a case became contentious, I told each party to get their own lawyer, but I can't remember having to do that very often. Criminal cases were different, but only because there was a Crown Attorney acting for the prosecution.

I can recall contentious civil cases later on where I acted for only one side in a dispute. One was a fence-line boundary dispute between farmers. Each spent a lot of money going through trial and appeal. The dispute involved 'the principle of the thing' and not the financial benefit or loss that would have resulted from recognizing that the fence wasn't in quite the correct location. Families fighting over the proceeds of an estate, where one felt he had not been well treated, increased the animosity within the family rather than resolving the differences.

Both cases would have been better settled with the help of a mediator. I see now that the Aboriginal way of a gentler dispute resolution process would have been preferable. In a new system, one lawyer representing both interests in a criminal trial — applying an Aboriginal approach to justice — would be an unusual but positive change. Accused persons who object to this procedure would have the right to engage their own lawyer and decline to accept any of the Court's diversion options.

The Charter of Rights would apply but there would undoubtedly be some who would not be prepared to participate in a mediative approach, and they should have the right to refuse and to have a more standard type of trial. On the other hand, I believe that many Aboriginal people would be more comfortable with a conciliatory approach that is closer to their traditions.

The reality of the situation should be recognized. If a 'summary' trial is to be held in a small remote community, the participants are not going to be able to afford lawyers and it would be difficult and costly for them to attend. There would often be no road and no scheduled airline. In any event, every effort would likely be made to avoid a trial and have the issue dealt with by a diversion program. Having a neutral lawyer involved in Aboriginal courts is not new. It exists in the North West Intertribal Court System referred to earlier, and it works.

A local Court Registrar would be something totally new and unheard of in Aboriginal communities in Manitoba, and most parts of Canada. The person would nevertheless be essential to the operation of an Aboriginal court. A permanent, full time Registrar should be appointed in every community where a judge will hold court. The Registrar should have an office equipped with telephone, computer, fax and internet capacity, connected to the office of the Court Administrator. The office should be private, or contain a private room, so that people will feel comfortable discussing an upcoming case, laying a complaint, initiating a claim, or seeking advice.

The Registrar would have a number of responsibilities to the court. He or she would be the Court Clerk and sit in court when it is in session. He would see that evidence is recorded, that witnesses are sworn, exhibits are marked, and that a record of the rulings of the judges is kept. When court is over, he would see that the orders are forwarded to the appropriate place. If a referral to a community service has been made, an appointment would be arranged so the person would know when and where to go.

He would have to keep track of the cases that require a hearing, prepare the docket for each sitting and estimate the length of time that will be required. In doing this he would have to be in constant contact with the court Administrator at the court's head office. In preparation for a hearing, he would have to assemble the relevant files and make certain that those who are to appear in court are aware of the date and will attend.

The Registrar will also have to check to see what is being done by any program or Peacemaker to whom a matter has been referred, and report to the judge at the next court sitting. If personal or community service has been ordered, he will have to instruct the Court Officer and follow up to make certain the work is done. If action is not being taken, the person will have to be brought back before the judge.

The Registrar should have authority to release people on bail. Most bail would be almost automatic where the amount of bail for particular offences is established in the First Nation legislation or self-government agreement. But for other cases, the judges might develop guidelines so the extent of the Registrar's authority is clear. In unusual situations, the Registrar could speak to the Administrator or to a judge, to obtain directions. In some cases the Registrar might think it unsafe to release a person and in that event would have him remain in the local holding facility overnight or until a judge can hear an application for release.

The Local Registrar would also have responsibilities to the community at large. Basic information on the rights of people who are being sued, on options that are available when a person is being questioned by the police, the effect of a plea of guilty, the benefits of a trial or the process applied by Peacemakers, should be provided. If a person is concerned about family abuse they could be provided with information on the various options that are available to them, and how to initiate proceedings if that is their wish. If residents wish to go directly to a Peacemaker, and not go before a judge, the Registrar should make the necessary arrangements. If they would like the assistance of a healing process or family gathering, the Registrar should put them in touch with those who can follow up on the request.

The Registrar would be the community para-legal advisor and be able to provide a wide range of information and advice to people in the community. In the beginning, answers to queries might have to be obtained from the Administrator or from the legal assistant. The Registrar should certainly provide advice on what is happening in a case that is before the court, the responsibilities of parties, witnesses, hearing dates, and other court related information. The Registrar should not, of course, tell a person what to do, but should provide enough information so the person can make an informed decision.

The Registrar could help the community establish meetings on a variety of legal topics so those with experience could attend to discuss them with the residents. In co-operation with the Administrator, he might develop connections that would enable the local TV outlet to run informational programs on the law and on the Aboriginal legal system.

A Court Officer will also be needed in each community who would, as an officer of the court, be responsible to see that orders made by a judge are carried out. He should monitor any personal or community service that has been ordered and see that those referred to a community program have shown up and are participating in a positive way. If a person is having trouble living up to the terms of a court order, the Officer should assist them to understand the order and to make arrangements to complete it. If the person still fails or refuses to obey the order, the Court Officer should advise the judge of the non-compliance and bring the person before the judge at the next sitting of the court. If there is a problem with the conditions of the order, the Court Officer might explain the problem to the judge and suggest a variation of the order. If an accused has been ordered to pay restitution to a victim, the Court Officer would see that is done.

A record should be kept of every case and every order. The Court Officer will not only help the court keep its work up to date, but will enable it to see how effective its various orders and practices have been. Unless the Registrar or the police have assumed the responsibility, the Court Officer should see that justice forums and family gatherings that have been ordered or agreed to, are held without delay. If an order for the removal of someone from a home is made, the Court Officer would make sure the order is respected. If it is not, he can call on the police for assistance or recommend that a criminal charge be laid. The Officer should also assist in the delivery of subpoenas and the empanelling of juries.

The Court Officer would work under the direction of the Court Registrar. It will be that person who will be dealing with the judges and the Court Administrator on a regular basis and will be the local person responsible for the operation of the court.

All these court officers are needed for an Aboriginal system to function properly. Quite apart from the court operation, they will provide valuable services to members of the community. They will provide services that have never existed in Aboriginal communities. They will also provide information the citizens are entitled to have.

15

Judges

Judges hold an unusual position in society and their approach to cases may not be well understood. Some people think of judges as fierce, sober and unbending servants of a punitive legal system, bent on punishing the poor and disadvantaged. Others classify them as bleeding-heart liberals, always giving breaks to criminals. Most judges see themselves as referees who merely resolve disputes when no one else has been able to do that. The 'buck stops here' approach of President Truman somewhat defines that role.

In Aboriginal culture there is no such person as a judge. It is, in fact, contrary to tradition to have one person sit in judgement on the conduct of another. Each person is supposed to be responsible for his own conduct and to clearly state what he has done and what caused him to act as he did. Non-interference is the rule, rather than having someone rule on another's conduct, condemn it, and inflict punishment.

Some of these attitudes and perspectives have affected my definition of the role of an Aboriginal judge in an Aboriginal court. I would like to see the Aboriginal judge well received in the communities he serves and would like to see him exude a less authoritarian and more supportive demeanour than some Aboriginal people have observed in judges they have had to appear before. There should be no fear of judges, rather they should be seen as servants of the communities and the people they represent.

Judges of an Aboriginal court will certainly have a different responsibility than their counterparts in the regular courts. Not only will they have to hear witnesses and decide cases, but they will be expected to introduce and apply a wide variety of restorative procedures. They will have to be knowledgeable about traditional methods of dealing with wrongdoers and learn how their court can apply traditional concepts of healing and rehabilitation.

They should be committed to trying every possible alternative to incarceration. That is different than 'considering' alternatives referred to in the Criminal Code and the Young Offenders Act. Considering alternatives only means that a judge turn his mind to the possibility and decide whether an alternative is worth trying. My suggestion is that an Aboriginal judge not just consider, but actually attempt to apply an alternative approach in each and every case.

One of the initial tasks for the Aboriginal judge will be to do something judges of the regular courts do not do. He (or she) should visit the communities he serves and make it clear that he is committed to serving their needs. He should visit and become familiar with each community in the court system, and all the support services that exist. He should understand each program, how it operates, and the benefits it can provide to offenders and to victims. If a program deals with family problems, such as physical and sexual abuse, he should understand how it operates and how the court might be supportive of its efforts.

He should discuss with the operators of each program, the process they suggest be followed when a judge wishes to make a referral to them. The judge should be aware of the length of time a healing program might take and the type of report the agency would be able to make to the court. An on-ongoing method of communication should be established so the judge will be aware of changes in the approach of each program, the length of time individual programs are taking, and the ability of the programs to accept additional referrals.

When a person charged with an offence first appears in court, the judge should make certain that he understands the charge. If the arresting officer is present, the judge might ask if the reason for the arrest has been explained to the offender. He might then ask the offender if he accepts responsibility for his alleged actions or wishes to contest the matter. At that point the judge should determine whether a plea should be accepted, if that is the wish of the individual, whether the case should be set for trial, or whether some community service should be asked to look at the situation. He should consider whether the case is one where the victim and the offender might benefit from having the matter referred to a Peacemaker, to a community healing program, to a justice forum, or to a family gathering.

If a referral to a program is proposed and agreed to by the wrongdoer, the judge should make the referral and ask the Local Registrar to make the necessary arrangements. The criminal charge can then be adjourned until an interim report has been received so the judge can see if the person is following through on the program. If there is a limitation period for laying or proceeding with a charge, the judge would likely seek a report in time for a decision to be made as to whether the charge should be proceeded with or not. If the judge thinks the matter should proceed to trial, he should set a date for the hearing.

If the offender has declined a referral and indicates that he wants to enter a plea of guilty right away, that wish should be respected. If the accused is ready to proceed, the judge should hear what the police officer and the accused have to say. He should then stop and consider what disposition would be in the best interests of the victim, the community and the offender. At that stage, rather than imposing a penalty to punish the offender, the judge should consider whether a referral to a support program, a healing circle or some other service, would be more effective. Only if the judge concludes that such a disposition would be unworkable, should he consider imposing a fine, requiring community service, or requiring a period of incarceration.

If the offender wishes to contest a charge, the hearing should be put over for a month to give him time to obtain a lawyer, or another person from the community, to assist or represent him at his trial. The judge would then hear the witnesses for the prosecution and the defence and make a decision on whether the accused is guilty or not. If the verdict is not guilty, that would put an end to the matter, but if there is a conviction, the judge would still have a full range of sentencing and referral options to consider.

The judge's greatest contribution to a successful court system will be his regular presence in each community and his ability to deal with cases in an expeditious manner. Requiring wrongdoers to participate in healing and other programs will add his authority to community efforts. His search for alternatives will indicate his concern for the community and his desire to return it and the parties to a peaceful relationship.

All the judges of an Aboriginal court should be Aboriginal and be fluent in the local language. Some litigants may prefer to proceed in English but there will be many accused people and witnesses who will want to express themselves in their Aboriginal language.

They should not have to have legal training prior to being named as a judge, although they will require some training thereafter. The management committee should develop some standards to follow when looking for a judge. It might want a certain level of education or experience in the justice system. Some experience in administration or in dealing with people and their problems might be looked for, particularly when the court is first established. If many problems in the community deal with young people or with abuse, judges might be selected who have experience working in those areas.

The most important qualification for the office of judge should be the wisdom and fairness of the individual. An understanding of the local people and their traditions and beliefs would be an important qualification. The prospective judge should have demonstrated that he has an understanding of human failings and how people can get into trouble with the law. He should indicate a willingness to apply Aboriginal concepts and practices and to use new and unusual alternatives to incarceration.

The members of the management committee should look for a person who is known to be honest, will not have a built-in bias, will be able to patiently listen to the evidence of all witnesses and render an impartial decision. He should have the strength and independence needed to hear cases involving local politicians or have the wisdom to bring in an outside judge. He should be free of local politics and have no business connections. He should have a concern for victims but be willing to be severe when necessary. He should be a good role model for others in the community.

In Canada, judges are appointed and remain in office until a pre-determined retirement age is reached. While that might be possible when Aboriginal courts become firmly established and a professional body of permanent judges develops, a less permanent appointment process might be appropriate in the interim. My suggestion is that judges be hired on three-year contracts. To guard against the possibility of someone turning out to be inappropriate for the task, there might be a six-month probationary period within which the judge could be let go. If a judge is performing well at the end of his three-year term and wants a more permanent appointment, the management committee should have the authority to make the next term indefinite or for a greater number of years.

I am not a great fan of having judges elected, although that process serves many jurisdictions in the United States quite well. Some judges are appointed by the State government but have to run for office at the time of the next election. The experience seems to be that if they have been doing a good job, they are re-elected for six-year terms. The danger I see with that system is that it appears to be part of a political process and I think that should be avoided in the relatively small

Canadian Aboriginal court systems. It also appears that the Tribal court systems are moving away from electing their judges.

There may be a better argument for electing judges in larger individual courts where the local candidates would be better known, but again I think an appointment process would be safer. Aboriginal judges will be subject to a variety of pressures if they are related to or know people appearing before them, and their performance in those cases should not be a consideration when they have to stand for election. One way to avoid conflicts would be to engage a judge who lives at a distance and who will not have those connections. The other side of the coin is that the judge will be more effective if he knows the community and can speak the local language. This again leads me to recommend that the judges, no matter the type of system they work in, not be elected.

Some very special skills will be required and I believe that careful inquiries and interviews are the best way to find suitable candidates. A former resident who has worked in the broader community might be persuaded to accept an appointment. People who have worked in the regular courts might have the desired skills, as might those who have been involved with community support programs. People who have experience dealing with young offenders or have worked for Child Welfare agencies might have relevant experience. Some of them might even be engaged on a part-time basis to handle special types of cases.

I make no comment on the remuneration to be paid to judges, other than to say that the salary should be more than that paid to other court staff, including the court lawyer and local government personnel. A good rate of remuneration will attract good candidates and will indicate the importance the community attaches to the position.

The removal of federally appointed judges is difficult, requiring investigations and recommendations and finally a joint resolution of the House of Commons and the Senate. The result is that few judges are forcibly removed from office. Some do resign due to the pressure of an investigation and concern about the eventual result, and others resign when they recognize they are no longer able to discharge their responsibilities.

That situation is quite different from one which engages people with little if any background in the law and one that is bound to have significant pressures of its own. In the general court system the judges have been practicing lawyers for many years and those appointing them have a fair basis upon which to assess their abilities. With an

Aboriginal court, the body that appoints the judges will have little if any related experience to examine, and a limited idea of how those selected will perform.

Some other system should therefore be developed to permit the removal of judges who are, for one reason or another, unable to perform their task in an acceptable way. If judges find they are not well suited to the task, or are having a difficult time dealing with the work, they should of course resign, preferably after giving the management committee reasonable notice. The reasons for resignation might relate to the pressure of the job, the difficulty of dealing with high profile cases, or a lack of interest. Judges should not have to reveal their reasons for resigning.

Minor complaints or disagreement with a judge's decisions should not be sufficient grounds to cause a judge to resign or to be removed from office. If however, the committee as a whole is not satisfied with the performance of a judge due to his approach to the system or the way he treats people, there should be a way to terminate his contract. It should not be too easy to fire a judge but there should be a method of removing one from office where the grounds are sufficient.

The members of the management committee should determine, in advance, the type of conduct or lack of performance that would warrant the removal of a judge. These might include a breach of any of the qualifications for office suggested earlier, might include a clear indication of bias, a refusal to follow the law, the mistreatment of litigants or witnesses, a continuing breach of Charter requirements or conduct that demeans the office of judge.

The next question would be to decide whether there has been the severity of conduct that should lead to removal. It should be recognized that some complaints will be frivolous or merely reflect the dissatisfaction of a party who has lost a civil or criminal case. Judges, by virtue of their very task, cannot make everyone happy and complaints should be expected. The question to determine is whether a complaint is widespread and has validity.

In circuit court systems I suggest that the only body that should be able to terminate a judges employment be the management committee. It will contain at least one representative from each community. If a complaint comes from only one community and the member from that community wants the judge fired, that might indicate dissatisfaction with one case but would not necessarily mean the judge is not doing a good job. If other members of the committee are satisfied with his overall work, it is unlikely that they would vote to require his removal. The committee should carefully examine complaints to see whether the action complained of is an aberration or whether there has been a serious or continuing type of unacceptable conduct.

In a single location court the management committee might do the initial screening of complaints. If the majority think the conduct of the judge was appropriate, or that it did not warrant his dismissal, that would end the matter. If however, the committee voted to seek the removal of a judge, an independent review panel, representing a cross-section of the community might be established to hear evidence and argument and decide whether the judge should be removed. If it is difficult to establish an independent ad hoc committee for that purpose, the community laws or court rules could provide for a committee of people who do not live in the community. If there were to be a small committee of that nature I suggest it include an Aboriginal judge and two other Aboriginal people.

In a regional court system the representative management committee would be in a better position to take an independent look at the situation. If the case went to the Aboriginal Court of Appeal and it upheld the decision of a trial judge that would add credibility to the work of the judge. If a decision were reversed that would not necessarily mean that the judge did not act properly. On the other hand, if the Court of Appeal not merely disagreed with the finding of the trial judge, but criticized him in a more personal way, that would be something the committee would want to look at.

The management committee should establish a removal procedure for inclusion in the court rules, and the rules should be incorporated into every contract by which a judge is engaged. To make it fair to a judge who is under attack, the process should require that the judge be given the opportunity to receive the details of any complaint and have an opportunity to respond in writing. If that does not end the investigation, the judge should have the right to attend a meeting where the committee would hear from those supporting the complaint and from the judge. He should be entitled to have a lawyer represent him if he wishes. The rules should have established in advance the percentage of votes necessary to remove a judge from office. I recommend that a two-thirds vote in favour of removal be required.

If a management committee decides to remove a judge from office, the judge should be able to appeal the decision to the system's Court of

Appeal and then to seek judicial review of the manner in which the decision was arrived at.

Judges appointed to Aboriginal courts who do not have any legal education will require instruction in many areas of the law and will need opportunities to meet with one another to discuss matters of common concern. It will be important for them to know how other systems use community justice forums, Peacemakers and other diversion resources. They will need to discuss sentencing criteria and options and exchange opinions and experience with one another.

They should be encouraged to attend programs dealing with family and abuse problems so they can keep abreast of current research on these issues and learn of systems and programs that are dealing effectively with them. Law Schools, Community Legal Education Associations, the Bar Association and Legal Aid would likely be willing to assist in providing instruction, and the court budget should include money for judge and staff training.

As Aboriginal courts become established across Canada, the judges will be able to help one another. Even within the same court, a Chief Judge working with less experienced judges, will be able to assist them as they assume their new responsibilities. He should provide them with reading material and some of his own experience with legal issues and courtroom procedure. I also hope that judges of the regular courts would be willing to discuss the law and legal principles and procedures with Aboriginal judges and help them in the performance of their duties. That might be the best and most practical assistance the new judges could receive.

Where there is more than one judge in an Aboriginal court, one should be designated as the Chief Judge. In the beginning he should sit on cases part of the time and spend the rest of his time getting the court into operation. He should be appointed by the management committee early in the planning stage and well before the court is due to begin sitting. In addition to having the qualities of other judges, the Chief Judge should have proven administrative ability. He should be able to work with Chiefs and Councils, with the police and with the support services in each community. Some experience with the law would be helpful so he can gather legal texts and other material and provide some initial training to staff and other judges. Experience in managing a budget, keeping records and statistics would be of value.

One of his tasks should be to assist the committee organize the court structure and develop the rules of court. With the Administrator and the Legal Assistant, he should identify the services that are already in place in each community and consider how they can work in concert with the court. Possibly his most important task in the planning stage would be to meet with people in each community to discuss the approach the court would like to take, obtain opinions and reactions, and solicit their co-operation and support.

He would need an office close to the Administrator and other staff. He should work closely with the management committee and keep it advised of the needs and activities of the court. A difficult task will be to convert the statistics of the regular courts into the amount of service likely to be required of the Aboriginal court. He would have to estimate the number and length of the sittings that would have to be held in each of the communities and advise the committee of the number of judges and other staff that will likely be required. He should keep it advised of the actual caseload as the court begins to function.

Another preliminary matter the Chief Judge will be concerned about is the appointment of police officers who will accept and support culturally-based restorative measures in as many cases as possible. It would be important for the committee and the judge to know if police applicants are prepared to deal with wrongdoers in a less punitive manner than in the past, and are willing to refer wrongdoers to alternative community systems.

The Chief Judge and the committee should meet with the police service once it is in place, to discuss a common approach. They might discuss the sorts of situations in which wrongdoers might be sent directly to community supports by the police and those where a charge should be laid and the offender brought to court. There should not be any hard and fast rules, but it would be important to know that the judges and the police have the same general approach. Other matters that should be discussed with the police are time limits in bringing cases to trial and the need for Charter warnings to be given. The general approach to bail might also be discussed. The judge would also want to know if police officers would be prepared to organize community justice forums and to act as facilitators.

He would want to urge the committee to establish holding facilities in each community to avoid sending troublemakers to an outside jail, and would want to know when the facilities will be in place. He would also want to be involved in the interviews of prospective judges so he can assist in assessing them.

He should examine the procedures used in other courts and build on their experience. If there are a number of Aboriginal courts being established at about the same time, it would be helpful to initiate provincial or regional meetings to consider various means of getting a court started and how to make it effective.

He should be involved in selecting the Court Administrator if one has not already been engaged. He should help the Administrator establish a system of communicating with and supplying support services to the Local Registrars in each community.

Early in the operation of the court, the Chief Judge should meet with each Chief and Council to explain the court's legal authority and how he expects it to operate. He should listen to their concerns and expectations and indicate how they might be addressed. He should explain the difficult role of a judge, the need for independence in deciding cases, and the need for their support. If a decision has not already been made, the judge should discuss the local services he hopes to have available to handle referrals. He would want to urge the community to establish an office, a holding facility and a place where court can be held.

He would have to become knowledgeable about the services that exist in each community, how they operate, and whether they are willing to work with people the court might refer to them. It may be that a service, such as abuse healing circles, would want to be contacted on each occasion where a referral is contemplated so they could assess the abuser to determine his attitude and willingness to co-operate. An alcohol treatment centre might want to make sure they have room to accommodate another person and want to be contacted before the court makes a referral.

If there are no Peacemakers in a community, the judge might explain what they could do and how they could be selected. Those interested in performing this function should then contact the Local Registrar or the judge to obtain an interview with the management committee. The judge should be part of any interviews that are conducted. He should explain that residents would be sought and appointed by the management committee as the Local Registrar and Court Officer. He should discuss the services the judges will be able to provide to the community.

The Chief Judge, with at least the local representative on the management committee, should hold a public meeting in each community to explain the approach the court plans to take and the various services it will be able to provide. He should indicate how often the court will likely sit in the community, and that it will use either the local language or English, depending upon the wish of a litigant or a witness. He should explain the extent of authority the court will have and what it can and cannot do. He might also indicate that it is the court's intention to keep its work up to date so people will not be involved in a court process for a long period of time. He might also explain how other problems of the past will be avoided.

He will, by the time of the public meeting, have met with the local police, and will be able to report on how they and the court can work in concert. He could solicit peoples' support for community based resources and ask them to become part of them. The concept of family gatherings should be discussed in the hope that residents will be willing to participate if asked to do so. In particular, he might tell the public that the success of the court will depend to a large extent on their support and active involvement in healing wrongdoers and supporting victims.

He should discuss the para-legal services that will be available from the Local Registrar and the assistance he may receive from the court's central office if that becomes necessary. The method of laying complaints or instituting personal and civil proceedings through the court might also be explained. If the Chief and Council have a policy condemning physical and sexual abuse, that should be explained by the representative of the management committee and the judge might indicate how the court can support that approach.

It will be important for the community to learn of and to discuss the objective of applying culturally appropriate practices to deal with people in a compassionate and restorative manner. The intent to support and protect victims, and at the same time restore wrongdoers to their families and a life without crime, should be explained. The intent to make the community a place where residents can live their lives in peace, harmony and mutual respect should be stressed. These principles and the desire to deal with everyone in a positive healing manner are attitudes the people will be pleased to hear.

At the same time, the Chief Judge will benefit from hearing from the community and hearing their expectations of the court. Local people may have suggestions that will enable the court to alter its tentative plans or to try a different approach that will be supported by the community. As I inferred earlier, the approach does not have to be the same in every community.

Each Aboriginal court system, in addition to having a trial court, should have a Court of Appeal. Any convicted person, or anyone who loses a civil case, should be able to ask a Court of Appeal to review the decision. An appeal court can do a number of things. It can change a finding of guilty to one of non-guilty or can convict someone who has been acquitted. It can increase or reduce a sentence that has been imposed, or select a different type of sentence. In a civil case, it can, change a finding of liability, and increase or reduce the amount to be paid.

It can also order a new trial if it thinks that is necessary. In some cases, where a new trial is ordered, the court will instruct the trial judge on how certain legislation is to be interpreted or how a basic principle of law is to be applied. If any evidence was improperly admitted in the first trial, the appeal court can tell the judge how to deal with the issue if it arises again.

Courts of Appeal try not to substitute their own opinion for that of a trial judge. If they find no reason in law to interfere with a decision, and the sentence or award is within reasonable bounds, even if the members of the Court of Appeal might have come to a different conclusion, they usually dismiss the appeal on the basis that there were insufficient grounds to 'interfere with the discretion of the trial judge.'

In the regular system, Courts of Appeal usually limit their hearings to receiving submissions from the parties, or more often from their lawyers. Aboriginal appeals might proceed in a slightly different manner, having in mind the heavy cost of a transcript of evidence and the delay that results while it is being prepared. If the costs are high, many Aboriginal people will be unable to take cases to appeal. One way to keep the costs under control would be for the Court Administrator, when accepting an appeal, to ask the person to indicate the basis of the appeal. If the appeal is against sentence only, or if the ground was that 'the judge didn't believe me,' a transcript would not be required. If the ground of appeal is a single issue discussed during the trial, the Clerk who ran the recording equipment during the trial, could identify it on the tape.

If some issues are still not clear, an Appeal Court should not hesitate to hear some evidence. One or two witnesses might be able to give their evidence on specific issues quite quickly. If significant issues such as Charter warnings are raised, the court should be able to call the arresting officer to testify. The judges would not want to completely retry a case but should have the discretion to hear from any witnesses who might help them arrive at an appropriate decision.

Aboriginal Courts of Appeal should not have to be established on a permanent basis, as appeals tend to be few and far between. An appeal mechanism should nevertheless be available on relatively short notice. The Court Administrator, in consultation with the management committee, might be given the authority to empanel a Court of Appeal from a pre-determined list of possible judges.

In the beginning, when the integrity of Aboriginal courts may be under scrutiny, it might be beneficial to have a Court of Appeal that includes at least one legally trained person. It would be preferable to have mistakes in trial decisions uncovered by a Court of Appeal at the local level, rather than to run the risk of an attack on a decision, or on the whole Aboriginal court procedure, on Judicial Review by an 'outside court.'

There would be some cost attached to bringing a Court of Appeal together and the rules of court should establish a filing fee and rules with respective to court costs. The cost of bringing the court together could be assumed by the court system so individuals would not have to pay anything, or the costs might be left in the discretion of the Court of Appeal. Other possibilities would be to permit the appellant to recover his costs where the case had considerable merit, or have to pay all related costs if the appeal was frivolous.

Where an Aboriginal language is likely to be used during an appeal, only judges who are familiar with that language should be selected. For appeals that deal with difficult issues or principles of law, particularly ones where the jurisdiction of the court itself is in issue, a five-person Court of Appeal might be convened. Aboriginal lawyers from the province or from other parts of Canada, might be asked to be part of the panel. The justice system should name the Chief Judge for the hearing.

If at all possible, appeals should be heard in the community where the trial took place. That would preserve the integrity of the community and would enable community members to observe that part of their justice system in operation.

There should be no further 'appeal' after an Aboriginal Court of Appeal has reviewed a trial decision, but a party to a criminal or civil case that is still not satisfied with the result, should have a further opportunity to have the decision reviewed. He should be able to apply to the regular provincial Superior Court for 'Judicial Review.'

Judicial Review is a well-established process whereby someone affected by a decision of a statutory board or tribunal, may ask a Superior Court to examine the process that was followed. That court will then examine the manner in which the case was handled to see if statutory requirements and principles of fairness and natural justice were followed. It would also look to see if the applicable law was properly interpreted and applied.

An application for Judicial Review should not be entertained until a case has gone through an Aboriginal trial and appeal court. It there was an error at trial it would likely be corrected on appeal, but if it was not, the reviewing court would consider the manner in which both the trial and appeal courts dealt with the case. A review of a case under this procedure is not supposed to decide whether the reviewing court would have arrived at the same decision, but whether the procedure and basic issues were properly dealt with. The reviewing court does not hear any evidence but bases its decision on the record of the proceedings in the lower courts and argument.

The intent of judicial review in an Aboriginal justice system would not be to involve outside courts in Aboriginal cases or decisions, but would be to make sure litigants have been accorded all the rights to which they are entitled and to see that they are treated fairly. If for example, the trial judge refused to allow an accused to give evidence or refused to let his lawyer speak, or the police improperly exerted pressure on an accused to give a statement, the reviewing court could find that those actions were contrary to natural justice or contrary to the Charter of Rights. It could then order a new trial or it could find that the conviction was improper, and enter an acquittal.

The process of Judicial Review is necessary to maintain the integrity of the Aboriginal court system and to assure Aboriginal and non-Aboriginal litigants that they do receive the full protection of the law. It involves outside courts in a limited and less intrusive manner than if the decisions of the Aboriginal courts were subject to direct appeals on matters of fact and law. It avoids the possibility of an appeal court substituting its opinion on the propriety of certain culturally appropriate but unusual sentences applied by an Aboriginal judge, as long as the sentence is not contrary to the principles of natural justice. It enables Aboriginal people to have their own trial and appeal processes, but on procedural issues it gives them access to the superior courts.

For those who are concerned that this process will slow the resolution of cases, I should add that it is not often used. It will nevertheless encourage trial judges to proceed with caution and to make certain that everyone's rights are fully respected. If errors of law are made, the advice of judicial experts should only add to the knowledge of the non-legally trained judges, and be helpful as a new court system becomes established. It provides one of the checks and balances needed in every democracy and in every court system.

16

Trials

Trials are trials some may say. A trial is a search for the truth and a search for justice at the same time. When you get beyond the philosophy and the rhetoric, a trial is a search for a solution to human problems. The problem, or dispute, may be between the Crown and a citizen, between two business associates, two parents or two strangers. It may be a quest for a way to help young children achieve their potential when abandoned by inadequate parents.

There are different methods of trying to achieve these goals. The English, American and Canadian criminal systems involve a prosecuting authority which tries to establish guilt and a defendant who either attempts to establish innocence or at least to show that guilt has not been proven beyond a reasonable doubt. A judge or jury presides and decides which side wins.

In France, and in some other countries, an inquisitory system is used. *Juges d'instruction* are involved at an early stage to unearth and examine the facts, and to see if a crime has been committed. The judge will then decide whether there are sufficient grounds for laying a formal charge and putting the person on trial.

A trial in an Aboriginal court, as I envisage it, would use a combination of these systems and involve traditional dispute resolution approaches as well. The court would be able to offer a variety of solutions and even its approach to wrongdoing will differ from that of the regular courts and the processing of its cases will be unique. The focus will be upon the individuals effected by an improper act, their families and the community. People have to get along with one another in Aboriginal communities and the purpose of the court, and of any trial that is held, will be to correct the harm that has been caused and to heal the relationships that have been damaged.

The regular system's process of investigation, charge, prosecution, trial and punishment would be set aside, or used as a last resort after other approaches have been tried. The Aboriginal court would attempt to accomplish something that has not been achieved in their communities in the past — to improve or alter the attitudes of offenders who have become more and more brazen and think that the legal system can do little to them. It will try to help them change their ways.

The first thing the court should do, even before a trial is contemplated, is to use its authority to discover how the problem or infraction arose. Even if a person has been charged with an offence, that should not deter a judge from inquiring into the nature of the incident to determine its seriousness and effect on others. Possibly the most important thing a judge can do at that point is determine the attitude of the wrongdoer. The judge may be able to exert his influence to have appropriate cases and problems resolved without any trial at all.

If a wrongdoer is prepared to accept responsibility for his actions and for the harm that has been caused, that would enable the court to take a restorative approach and to set aside the thought of proceeding to trial, at least for the time being. A variety of options then become available and I will deal with some of them when discussing 'referral options.' It is only if a person denies his involvement, or believes he has a valid defence, that a trial in the traditional sense needs to be held. In that event, the trial will be a search for the truth and then for solutions that will benefit the offender, the victim and the community.

All trials should be held in the Aboriginal community where the wrongdoing took place or where the civil dispute arose. The main reason for that is to serve the convenience of the parties who have to attend court and other community members as well. It will enable the court to sit where the evidence is available and where the accused, victim, witnesses, family members and other interested people live. Those who have provided services pursuant to a referral from the court will also be available if needed. It is important to avoid the huge expense of travelling to another community to attend court.

It is also important for Aboriginal people to see their own democratic institutions in action. If the court is applying the laws the community has passed and people see their own police and their own judges in action, that should give them a sense of pride. If they see culturally appropriate approaches being applied to wrongdoing and to victims and offenders, that should give them a new sense of satisfaction with the administration of justice. Having court held in the community would enable victims to be accompanied by friends and members of their family that would normally not attend court.

The presence of the court in their own community would hopefully increase the residents' understanding of the law and increase their respect for the legal system. It would permit issues such as physical and sexual abuse to be dealt with without delay. It would let abusers know that the community is aware of what they are doing and that any repetition will not be tolerated. If juries were used, they would enable community members to be active participants in deciding cases.

The residents would, for the first time, see a justice system being administered by Aboriginal people and they would have a place to go for information and advice. The involvement of local people in such an important institution would provide an example of opportunities that might be available in the community and provide good role models for young people.

If the residents can see its police officers and holding facility operators looking after part of the system in a compassionate manner and see the establishment of wilderness camps, they would feel that attention is being paid to their problems. The educational possibilities of having their own judge and lawyer come to the community from time to time, and the permanent presence of a para-legal Registrar, would add to the feeling that progress in the justice area is finally being made. The court, with the people it would employ, would also be a form of economic development and provide encouragement for the development of other local services.

A place to hold court will have to be provided in each community. At the present time there are no standard courtrooms in Aboriginal communities, even though a Provincial Court may sit in some of them every month. At one time, court was held in small or barren poorly heated halls without facilities. Complaints from visiting judges caused many of them to be abandoned in favour of school gymnasiums. The school may be warm and have washrooms for the court party, but I question its use and suggest that it provides a less appropriate venue than the less attractive halls.

Schools are the finest buildings in most Aboriginal communities, while the courts are generally distrusted and disliked. It does not raise the standing of the school to see it used by a court dealing with criminal conduct. Schools are normally seen as providing hope for the future and it seems ironic that the two services should be combined. There is problem enough finding good role models for children, without having people in trouble with the law take over part of the school from time to time. It must also be disturbing for the teachers who are trying to teach high moral standards to the students. During the AJI we heard of a situation where a child in a classroom was aware that his father was appearing before a judge in another part of his school when he was there. One can only imagine what that did to the self-esteem of the child.

Schools are undoubtedly an inexpensive alternative to the run-down halls but they are inadequate. The judge still sits on a collapsible chair at a collapsible table, cheek by jowl with lawyers and police officers. The climbing bars, basketball hoops, and large empty room, hardly present an atmosphere where justice will be done. Nothing indicates the solemnity of the occasion.

The court facilities in a new Aboriginal justice system will need to include a room in which court can be held, an office for the Local Registrar, offices for the Peacemaker and the Court Officer and an office the visiting judge can occupy when he is present. The office of the Local Registrar should be available to the public at least five days a week and it should be easily accessible by the public. It should have a general office and another one where citizens can discuss their problems and seek advice in private.

There should be a room available for the legal assistant where witnesses can be interviewed. Some of the rooms can be used by those who have to be present when court is in session and by others when it is not. The courtroom itself can be used for family group conferences, family gatherings, community justice forums, healing circles and informational meetings when court is not in session.

To maintain the separation and independence the court requires, the facility should definitely not be in the First Nation administration building. It is important for the court to be seen as completely independent and separate from the local government. Each have their own duties and should not be seen as having a connection with one another.

This does not mean that there should not be a respectful relationship between the elected officials and the judges, but it should be an arms-length relationship. The court exists to serve the community, as does the Chief and Council and the court would welcome their interest and support. Chiefs and Elders could add to the importance and the dignity of the court if they attended the opening of a court sitting in their community and wear their regalia to show the community their support for the work of the court. Court proceedings should begin with a prayer seeking guidance from the Great Spirit to see that justice is done, and there might be smudging of the participants to cleanse and prepare them for the tasks ahead.

Some communities may wish to have a standard courtroom with a judge's bench, witness box, jury box, court reporter desk and counsel tables, and there is much to be said for a courtroom that projects an aura of formality. Judges do not sit on a dais to feel important. They are set apart from others to indicate the solemnity of their responsibility and their independence from the police, the lawyers, and others in the courtroom. Their black robes or colourful gowns may look foolish to some, and a remnant of a by-gone age, but they are intended to add to the dignity of the court, its importance to the community, and the importance of the justice process. Aboriginal judges might prefer to wear some traditional regalia appropriate to their office.

Communities which do not want that sort of formality might prefer to have a court or hearing room in which they would feel more comfortable. It might be laid out to accommodate circle trials and more casual proceedings. Judges might dress as others in the community, might wear a buckskin jacket or hold an eagle feather to add dignity to the proceedings and to indicate their solemn responsibilities. The grand oak or marble panels of southern courtrooms might be replaced with pictures of famous Aboriginal leaders like Peguis, Big Bear or Louis Riel, to symbolize wrongs of the past and the need for compassionate justice.

In view of the number of court-related activities that will be required, a separate building might be built and designated as the 'Justice Centre,' or an Aboriginal name that would indicate the type of services available in it. Whatever type of building is provided, it should be organized in a way that recognizes that it will be used by a variety of services on a regular basis.

Judges I appeared before over the years thought they were being complimentary to an Aboriginal witness who had asked for an interpreter, when they said, "Oh, your English is very good, you'll have no trouble." I recall a trial where I presided with a jury where the topic of an interpreter came up. Probably because I was aware of earlier problems with interpreters, I said, "Let's start with English and see how you make out." The question of a translator was never raised again. What I and the other judges really did was deny the witness the right to express himself in his own language. The witness was too polite, or too intimidated, to make the request a second time.

— 258 —

There are problems with the use of interpreters, but they should not interfere with the use of a particular language. Sometimes a seemingly simple question may be asked and it takes an interpreter some time to relay to the witness. Lawyers often object when it is obvious that a straight translation is not given, and want the interpreter instructed to tell the witness to answer 'yes' or 'no.' It was probably not until the AJI that I realized that it often takes some exchanges with a witness for an interpreter to be certain that the full meaning of the question is understood, and more exchanges before the interpreter fully understands what the witness wants to say in response. Part of the problem, I was told, is that there are so many nuances in the conversion of one language to another, that it is difficult for a witness to respond to a question without including an explanation. Straight yes or no answers are seldom appropriate. There are also many English words, like 'guilty' and 'probation,' where there is no corresponding word in an Aboriginal language.

The question should not be — can the person speak English? It should be — in what language can the witness fully express himself to accurately describe what he saw or did? I have taken enough French courses to know how difficult it is for me to carry on a lengthy conversation in that language. I search and hesitate when looking for the words that will convey my meaning and tire as I try to express myself. Often the listener will take pity and switch to English.

If that approach could be taken in our courts that would solve the problem, but a judge in the regular courts can hardly say to an Aboriginal witness, "Use your own language whenever you wish." If they did, the judge wouldn't understand a word. There would however be no problem in an Aboriginal court where the judge speaks and understands the local language. If an interpreter is used, that would be to permit a litigant who does not understand the Aboriginal language to know what an Aboriginal witness has said.

Another problem with the present system is tied to the question of language in a different way. At times it appears that an Aboriginal witness is being evasive or has not understood a question. In reality it may be that because of his limited understanding of English he is not able to give a full explanation of what he wants to say. If questions are asked that he does not fully understand, he may not answer at all. Unfortunately, the situation may be misinterpreted by a judge, who may conclude that the person is unsure of what he saw or heard, or that he is an unreliable witness.

Witnesses should of course be permitted to answer questions in their own way. Those who feel more comfortable expressing themselves in an Aboriginal language should certainly be encouraged to use it in an Aboriginal court. The language of a trial should be the language with which the parties and the witnesses are comfortable and one of the qualifications of the judges should be their ability to understand and speak the language of the communities they serve.

There will undoubtedly be cases where an accused, although Aboriginal, is more comfortable using the English language and, as it is that person whose liberty may be in question, that language should be the dominant one used during his trial. If however witnesses in that trial wish to use their Aboriginal language, that wish should be accommodated without question and if necessary someone should translate what is being said.

In trials with a jury, the jurors should be comfortable with the main language to be used by the anticipated witnesses, and it would be preferable if they did not require a translator. If it is known that a trial will be in an Aboriginal language or involve Aboriginal speaking witnesses, the Local Registrar and Court Officer should put together a jury panel composed of those who will be able to function in that language.

Most trials would likely follow the format used in the regular courts. The prosecution would call witness to give evidence on what they saw or heard and the accused would cross-examine them and the opposite procedure would be followed if the accused calls witnesses or gives evidence himself. Each side would then make a submission to the judge suggesting what the result should be. The judge would follow the practice in the regular courts and find the accused guilty or not guilty.

In that process the judge does not talk to others, but bases his ultimate decision on the evidence that has been presented, the arguments that have been made and the law that applies. There is no communication with the community and the judge remains aloof and independent throughout.

One variation on this type of trial that might be tried in cases where the judge is not very familiar with a community would be to have the assistance of an elder before sentence is handed down. If an elder has been present throughout the trial he might be asked if he wishes to say anything. He might then comment on the accused and his reputation, on the type of sentence he believes would satisfy concerns of the community, or might raise issues that need further exploration. The judge should then have the option of inviting the prosecution and the defence to present further arguments, or might invite them to introduce further evidence.

Rather than having witnesses called to testify and having them questioned and cross-examined, some Aboriginal courts might prefer to use a more traditional form of trial. At one time the Chief and a group of advisors would have met to discuss and deal with a person's conduct. Today an Aboriginal judge, the accused, lawyers or other representatives, those in the category of witnesses and other interested people could be invited to sit in a circle. An inner circle might contain those who wish to speak and an outer circle for those who only want to watch. Those in the inner circle would speak in turn, say what they know of the incident, and make any comments they wish. They could comment upon the prevalence of similar acts in the community, if that is of concern to them.

Following the practice of healing and other circles, everyone, including the judge, counsel and the accused, could sit in the circle. As everyone would have the opportunity to speak after the person next to them has spoken, the judge might, for example, start with the person sitting to his left, and have the accused and his representative sit to his right. That would give everyone the opportunity to comment on what others had said and give the accused the chance to respond to their comments.

If the judge wishes, he might invite everyone to speak twice, the first time on what the accused had done and its effect on others, and the second time on the penalty that should be applied. The wrongdoer would have the opportunity to explain his conduct if he wishes and to comment on the penalty or other solution that has been proposed. He could accept responsibility and apologize, or he could maintain his innocence.

This system might prolong a trial, but it would be akin to a community meeting where all residents are interested in getting to the bottom of a problem and to understand what happened and what should be done about it. If the process is too lengthy for all cases, the court might devise a circle with fewer participants, or limit its use to certain types of cases.

In some cases the judge could make a decision on his own after hearing the comments and suggestions of others. In other cases he might have those in the circle decide the question of guilt or innocence and set the penalty that would apply. In that approach, the judge would have to explain the principles of law the gathering should consider and present a review of the salient facts. If the meeting agrees on what should be done, the judge could formally approve the decision and make it the ruling of the court. If there is a disagreement among the participants the judge would have to make the ultimate decision.

An Aboriginal court might like to use a formal court setting for some cases and a circle method for others. It might want to try something entirely different and should have the flexibility to do so. It should feel free to experiment in the search for a system that will meet the needs of offenders, victims and the community at large. In the long run, two or three systems may become the norm. In any event, it is important that each community be satisfied with the system that is applied.

Rules of evidence have been developed over the centuries and are intended to make certain that witnesses restrict their testimony to what they have actually seen or heard. For example, a person can say, "I saw him running down the street," but cannot say, "they told me he was running down the street." The first is a personal observation while the second is second-hand or hearsay evidence. Even if it is perfectly obvious that the person had to be running, if the witness did not see him doing that, they are not allowed to say he had been running. If the witness says, "I assume he had been running" a lawyer can stop the witness and say, "don't make assumptions."

Rules of this sort are fine for lawyers and judges who are familiar with the process, as they make everyone stick to the real issue before the court. On the other hand, the rules make trials very clinical and precise, and are not well understood by witnesses and accused people. While lawyers argue about whether a witness can say a certain thing or not, even professional witnesses lose their train of thought and forget what they were trying to say.

An Aboriginal court should avoid using rules against hearsay. My experience is that judges and juries can listen to evidence and ignore those parts that fall into the guesswork or assumption category. Aboriginal judges and juries would quite easily be able to do the same.

One of the great principles of British justice is that a person who has been charged with having committed an offence is entitled to be tried by a jury of his peers. The peers of old were those living in the same community. The peers of today, for Aboriginal people, should be other Aboriginal people living in the same community.

As a defence counsel, I liked trials with juries as they provided the opportunity to try to persuade the twelve jurors of the reasonableness of your case. Juries are made up of people with a wide range of life experience and their combined wisdom makes them good judges of character. As they apply their common sense to a case, they seem able to put themselves in the shoes of the offender. They also consider the effect of an incident on a victim but are aware that it is the offender's freedom that is in jeopardy. I particularly liked a fair number of women on juries in rape cases at a time when almost all the judges were men. The women seemed to be able to tell whether a female complainant was telling the truth or not.

As a judge, I invariably thought juries came to the correct conclusion, even if it was obviously hard for them to find some people guilty. There were cases where I thought the jury would come in with a verdict other than the one it did, but I still could never say they were wrong. A Court of Appeal often overturns jury verdicts but seldom because of the decision of the jury. The cause for a new trial is almost always related to something the trial judge has misstated during his instructions to the jury.

Few civil trials are heard by a judge and jury, but the two I sat on were among the most interesting of all my trials. One was a claim of defamation and the other a suit for the allegedly false imprisonment of a person who had been acquitted of theft in the Provincial Court. Juries in civil cases have six, rather than twelve members, and that makes the communication between them and a judge much more personal. I found it necessary to do more explaining to the civil juries as the trial proceeded and to respond to a greater variety of questions than in a criminal trial. I found it a valuable experience as it made me pay attention to matters the jury might not be familiar with.

At the end of each case, after the lawyers had made their submissions, I reviewed the facts and fitted them into principles of law I was asking the jury to consider. The jurors had no trouble considering the facts and weighing the evidence on a balance of probabilities. There was certainly no problem about the jury understanding its responsibilities.

I found that the decision of each jury was accurate in law, although I am not certain I would have been as tough as they were. Each jury found the claim they heard to be without any merit at all. Not only did they dismiss the claim they heard, but when I asked them what damages they would have awarded had they found in favour of the plaintiff, they set damages at zero in one case and one dollar in the other. They were certainly clear in expressing their opinion of the claims.

I mention these experiences to counter any suggestion that juries are incapable of dealing with complicated legal issues and deciding who to believe. The cases helped to convince me of the value to the community of having its members personally involved in the legal process. All juries take their responsibilities very seriously and are a credit not only to themselves but to the legal system as well. After one of the civil trials, the foreman of the jury was so concerned that he wrote the Law Society and complained about the manner in which one of the lawyers had conducted his case.

Juries would be particularly appropriate in close-knit Aboriginal communities. Six local residents would be able to reflect the attitudes of the people. They would understand the effect of a crime on the victim and would be able to understand some of the reasons for the conduct of the accused. They would share the same economic situation as the accused, the victim and the witnesses. Their concern for the residents and the welfare of the community-at-large and the future of their young people would be factors in their assessment of a case.

In my opinion, Aboriginal residents would make excellent jurors. They would be strong when the circumstances demanded, but, at the same time, they would understand the local influences that might have contributed to the improper conduct. They would also be compassionate and be concerned for wrongdoers, as they would be of the plight of the victims of wrongful acts. Local juries would be beneficial to an Aboriginal court. They would ensure that cultural attitudes and values were brought to bear on cases. More importantly, they would guarantee that people from the community were taking ultimate responsibility for maintaining their own law and order.

A jury trial would not have to take much longer than a trial by judge alone. Potential delays could be reduced by quickly putting together a jury panel from the community where the offence occurred. The Local Registrar might be authorized to remove people who are related to the accused or have a personal knowledge of the facts of a case. Eliminating peremptory challenges would shorten the jury selection process. If the use of juries causes a backlog of cases, its use might have to be restricted to those where incarceration would likely result if there were a conviction.

Aboriginal jurors might even be given more jurisdiction than those in the regular system. If a judge could ask jurors for their comments on sentence, that would not only indicate how serious they found the offence to be, but it would allow them to extend their involvement with the case into the realm of solutions. If a judge wants the process to be even more traditional, he could outline the available options and ask the jury to set the sentence themselves. This seems to me to be an appropriate method to apply, particularly if the maximum penalty is not too high and if the judge will have the opportunity to review it later on.

The Canadian Charter of Rights and Freedoms should be recognized and applied in First Nation legislation and in Aboriginal Courts. Adopting the Charter will reinforce rights such as freedom of religion, the right to vote, the equality of the sexes, the requirement of government to hold elections, and the rights of accused persons — rights Aboriginal people want to have.

I am aware that many Aboriginal people do not want the Canadian Charter to apply to them or to their governments. One concern is that the right of an accused person to refrain from incriminating himself and remain silent, is contrary to the Aboriginal tradition which requires a person who has done something wrong to own up to it. Another concern is that it is part of a government and legal process that has failed to protect them. There may be other issues about sovereignty and self-government that raise concerns about using the Charter.

In spite of these concerns, I believe it would be virtually impossible to get government to agree that the protections afforded by the Charter would not apply. Indeed, some Aboriginal women have expressed the need to have the Charter apply to their governments and assist in their protection. It would also be impossible to stop a Superior Court that is examining an Aboriginal Court decision on Judicial Review, from looking to see that the Aboriginal courts had complied with Charter requirements. If they did not, the Superior Court would declare the Aboriginal Court decision to be invalid.

The Superior Courts would consider it part of their duty to all Canadian citizens to see that they are fairly dealt with by any and all tribunals. There are many tribunals in society that might prefer not to have their decisions reviewed, but parties have to have the right to expect legal and administrative procedures that are fair and just, and people require access to the courts to enforce their rights. The reality is that even if the regular courts do not have the right to review Aboriginal Court decisions on appeal, they will have the right to examine them on Judicial Review.

The Charter does not stop a First Nation from identifying other rights. Section 26, which is in the portion of the Charter referring to Aboriginal rights, specifically states that the Charter is not to be construed as denying the existence of other rights or freedoms that exist in Canada. Section 22 permits the use of languages that are not one of the official languages in Canada. In addition to the Charter, I see no reason why the First Nation could not establish its own Charter as well. It could not contradict the Canadian Charter, but it could recite the concepts, principles, and beliefs its members wish to have applied to their personal lives and to their responsibilities to others and to their community.

Finally, there are two basic reasons why I believe the Charter has to be applied and respected by an Aboriginal justice system. The first is that I am sure government would not negotiate the establishment of a parallel court system if the Charter did not apply. The second reason is that, after all the trouble Aboriginal people have had with Canadian courts, they would not want to deprive any of their people of the right to a fair trial. That is basically what the Charter guarantees.

17

Community Participation

Indian and Métis people had well-established ethical principles that defined individual responsibility and the community's expectations of them. They also had ways of dealing with disputes between individuals and with unacceptable or criminal conduct. The objective was always to correct improper conduct and to return the community and its members to a harmonious, or at least a workable relationship.

The Chief had the authority to require troublemakers to follow his directives, and if they did not, he had sanctions he could apply. A troublemaker could be ostracized, shamed, or forced to leave the community. The Métis, when involved in the buffalo hunt, had a recognized code of conduct with penalties that included corporal punishment and the destruction of an offender's property.

Oral histories differ on the exact nature of earlier practices but the basic mores of the society remain. Cultural beliefs remain strong and the responsibility of individuals to one another is clear, at least in principle. As Aboriginal communities attempt to re-take their earlier authority they are also trying to rebuild and revive former practices. They are introducing practices that will enable them to deal with problems in their own way and believe their own way will be successful where the ways of others have failed.

There now exist a variety of community services that apply traditional methods of healing to those who are experiencing problems or have gone astray. They are being applied to youth and adults and deal with issues ranging from criminal conduct, substance abuse, physical and sexual abuse to child protection. Solutions are being developed, but cannot always be enforced because the community lacks the authority to do that.

An Aboriginal court, working in concert with local programs will be able to provide that authority and add the missing factor that will enable the community efforts to succeed. Courts do have substantial authority and it should be used to protect people and to help others correct their behaviour.

An Aboriginal court should support the community services that are in place and encourage the creation of others. Conversely, the programs and services that exist should work with the court to help it apply 'restorative justice.' They should work together where that is possible, to help civil litigants, victims and offenders correct any wrong that has been done and repair any harm that has been caused.

In most situations the programs and the court will function independently but there will be many situations where the programs can help the court with its responsibilities and the court can help them improve their level of service. The programs have the capacity to help individuals if they will accept their services and they can help the courts by offering curative measures the court on its own cannot provide. The courts can use their authority to encourage the people who come before them to utilize local services.

The court can use its authority over adjournments and sentences to require offenders to participate. When an accused first appears in court on a criminal charge, the judge can discuss the situation with the accused and, if he is willing to accept responsibility for his actions, the judge can adjourn the case on the condition that the person attend one of the programs. The judge can obtain a report on the person's progress and if it is satisfactory, can stay (adjourn) the case indefinitely.

If a person pleads guilty or is found guilty following a trial, instead of imposing a sentence immediately, the judge can refer the person to a community resource if he is willing to go. If the person refuses, the judge can still involve a local program by making the person's attendance part of a sentence.

This approach will enable accused persons to deal with their underlying problems. The intent of the programs is to help, cure and reform offenders and others who accept their services voluntarily. This joint approach should be able to correct unacceptable conduct more effectively than merely imposing punishment. If this joint process works, and only time will tell, the result should be better for the individual, the community as a whole and for victims as well. It would enable many offenders to be dealt with without them having to be sent to jail and it should reduce the extent of criminal activity and the amount of recidivism that now exists.

Counsellors, for example, are now in place in most communities to deal with child welfare, personal relationships, substance addiction, crisis counselling and physical and sexual abuse. Some are connected to the schools and the child welfare system while others are connected to alcohol programs and medical services. They provide a wide variety of emotional and practical support. Youth suicide is a problem on many reserves and counsellors are working with community leaders, parents and youth, looking for answers and solutions.

If they do not exist, counselling services for parenting skills, life skills, and personal development should be established. School counsellors should be asked to broaden their services to include adults, particularly parents of school-age children. Anger management programs have produced positive results but few are located in Aboriginal communities. It seems that both youth and adults get into trouble with the law because they temporarily lose control of their emotions. Striking out in anger is understandable, but it is also a reaction that can be reduced or expressed in some other way.

The overuse of alcohol is equally destructive and unfortunately drinking parties often turn into arguments and angry exchanges between friends and family members. The result can destroy the future of the one who lashes out, to say nothing of the one who is killed or injured. These results are avoidable and those that get into these situations are in need of skilled counselling and supportive families. Many need help to improve their self-esteem.

Individual counsellors would hopefully agree to accept referrals from a judge to see if the person with a problem can be helped. Judges will learn, over a period of time, the services counsellors can provide and the effectiveness of referrals to them.

Many communities now have a Native Alcohol and Drug Addiction Program (NADAP) which has councillors in some communities and in the jails. The program works with those who know they are in need of help, and it accepts referrals from others as well. Some communities provide residential programs to help people stop drinking and turn their lives around. In recent years they have expanded their services to deal with drug, gambling and other forms of addiction. The NADAP approach is different from that of Alcoholics Anonymous. It attempts to deal with the addiction in a culturally specific manner. Sweat Lodges and Elder teachings enable people to discuss the extent of their problem and to receive understanding and support in their efforts to overcome them.

NADAP workers would hopefully agree to assist an Aboriginal court by working with people the court believes are having a problem. If the program doesn't wish to divulge anything about its work with respect to a certain individual, it might nevertheless be willing to advise the court if progress is being made. The program workers might also be able to suggest methods a judge might use in doing an initial assessment of people to get an idea of the extent of their problem. If a person is inebriated when he appears in court, the judge might at least ask if the person would be willing to see a NADAP worker. If the person agrees, the Registrar or Court Officer could make the necessary arrangements and ask for a report on the person's progress.

Youth Justice Committees are usually established by the Attorney General of a province pursuant to the Young Offenders Act, and his office assists communities to establish them. Most committees include a local police officer, probation officer and others who have experience working with youth. The Crown Attorney or the police are the referring authorities and Probation Services usually manages the program.

In isolated Aboriginal communities, it would be possible to have a similar committee organized by local volunteers who are interested in working with youth. If the committee receives a referral from an Aboriginal judge or the police, it should meet with the youth to discuss the situation to get an understanding of what happened and his attitude. It could ask the parents to be part of the discussion and ask them to participate in the development of a program the youth should follow. In some cases the victim could be interviewed separately or might participate in a discussion of the incident when the reparation to be made is being discussed.

The committee would endeavour to help the youth understand the effect of his conduct on others and encourage him to refrain from similar conduct in the future. It would attempt to assess his needs and determine the approach that will be most beneficial to him, to the victim and to the community at large. It may offer counselling or may recommend a specialized program of anger management or a substance abuse recovery program. Elders might be asked to provide traditional guidance to help the youth come to grips with his personal problems. They would give support to the offender, help him examine the reason for his inappropriate conduct, help him accept responsibility for his actions, and help him find a way to correct the damage he has caused.

When a consensus is reached an agreement can be drawn and signed. The agreement may require the youth to apologize, to make restitution to the victim, to do some specified community service, or to do other things that are agreed upon. If the offender completes the program, any charge that has been laid could be dropped so the youth would come through the experience without a criminal record. If he does not complete the program, he can be returned to court where he will have to plead guilty or not guilty and be sentenced or have a trial in the usual manner.

An objective of the committee members is to hold youth accountable for their actions without having to prosecute them. Their main focus would be to provide the offender with support and guidance and to help him establish a satisfying and productive life style. They would work with the youth and his family to establish or re-establish an understanding and supportive relationship. They would strive to make things better for the youth, and by doing so, make things better for the family and for the community.

The broader objective of youth justice committees is to reduce the number of youth going through the justice system and to reduce the level of criminal activity in the community. Committees are sometimes involved in establishing programs that will provide recreation and other activities for the youth of the community, whether they have been in trouble with the law or not.

I never understood the significance of the term 'holistic' until my participation in the AJI, but during its hearings the term was continuously used to refer to the type of approach Aboriginal people like to see applied in a variety of situations. Since that time I have found that it is the preferred approach to almost every problem that arises. For example, if a man is involved in a criminal act, the traditional Aboriginal assumption is that he is sick in mind and in spirit. He is seen as acting in a manner that is foreign to his nature and the conclusion is that something has gone wrong. If a family is having internal problems, it too is sick and requires a variety of services and supports.

In a holistic approach, it is necessary to do an analysis to find out how the problem arose, why it is continuing, and the changes that are required to repair the damage that has been caused. In all likelihood, attention will have to be paid to the state of mind of the individual and to the state of mind of others as well. Influences in the community may have to be examined to determine the part they have played in the unusual conduct.

Because the causes of inappropriate conduct are complicated, the search for solutions may be complex as well. Aboriginal people believe that treating the current outburst that has landed a person in trouble with the law is not sufficient. They believe that the totality of the problem should be examined in a comprehensive or holistic way. If a whole family is involved, dealing with issues effecting each member may be necessary.

The holistic healing approach has been applied in residential programs. People with severe family problems are counselled in a comprehensive program to help them overcome their immediate problems. Spouses and children are asked to participate in an attempt to repair family relationships. This approach goes well beyond the particular acts that have occurred. If the family has become dysfunctional, stress is placed on the importance of each family member and their importance to the unit. If a wrongdoer has rejected his family or has treated them badly, the process will show him that the family members still love him and are prepared to try to salvage the family.

Holistic, in these programs, refers to the whole individual as well as to the whole family. Some holistic healing centres have been successful while others have been unable to continue due to a lack of funding and sometimes because of the difficulty in having people remain in the program.

Some Aboriginal justice systems might wish to establish their own holistic healing centre or do so in concert with others. Others might be satisfied to have the same holistic approach applied by their local programs, by their Elders, Peacemakers, counsellors and teachers. Elders are respected teachers and they have a strong influence in their communities. They can teach members of families to love and respect one another. They can impart Aboriginal history and emphasize the culture's traditions. They can speak of the strength of the Aboriginal family in the past, the roles of each member, and how existing relationships can be repaired.

Elders do not go looking for people to help, but are available when called upon. A court can help by asking them to become involved. Their basic approach, as I understand it, is to raise the spirits of the individual and the family through traditional teachings, values and beliefs that will enable them to deal with the past and the future in a positive manner.

Healing Circles are a powerful force in Aboriginal society. I can only speculate on the historical basis for the use of circles. It may have been dictated by the manner in which houses or tepees were constructed, or influenced by sitting around the warmth of a fire. It may have been due to the practicality of the arrangement that permitted everyone to see and to hear everyone else. Whatever the reason, the circle type of gathering is deeply ingrained in Aboriginal culture. Healing circles are traditional forums in which the most deeply felt hurts are explored and dealt with in the context of traditional teachings.

Traditional sweat lodges are round and Aboriginal boardrooms reflect the circle concept. Meetings are often opened and closed with people standing in a circle. The pipe is passed in a ceremonial way around a circle. There are other traditional ceremonies and practices that refer to the points of the circle and to the circle of life.

A circle gathering reflects the importance of each individual. There is no 'head of the table' or 'end of the line'. Everyone speaks in turn, and speaks for as long as they wish. Circles have different purposes and different topics to address. Some are called 'talking circles'. There was recently a talking circle involving Aboriginal urban residents and the Winnipeg Chief of Police. People expressed their concerns about relationships between the police and the community and the Chief responded.

During the AJI, in a community where the numbers in attendance were not too great, we held our hearing in a circle. The comments were taped as usual but the microphone was passed from one person to the next and we all sat and listened while people expressed their concerns or gave examples of their experiences with the justice system. Every person in the circle said something but it was interesting to note the absence of duplication. Those who only wanted to listen and observe, sat in a circle behind the one containing those who wanted to speak.

Everyone in the circle was respectful of the opinions of others. There was little disagreement, although some did add to or qualify what another had said. The presentations were thoughtful and when someone would hesitate as they thought of what they wanted to say, everyone waited patiently until they continued. It appeared to me that the speakers felt protected and supported in this format.

I was impressed with this means of community expression and the presenters seemed satisfied even though there was no second chance to speak and no questioning of any speaker. The quiet emotion and sincerity of feelings made the hearing valuable for us and I think valuable for those who could speak from the relative anonymity of their seats in the circle. It was obviously a less threatening arrangement than the one we usually followed, where people had to come forward to speak directly to us, with the eyes of everyone in the room upon them.

Healing circles are used to help victims recover from the effects of an unpleasant and emotionally disturbing event. Victims are supported as they come to grips with the reality of what happened, are persuaded that the incident was not their fault, and are helped to put the matter behind them and get on with their lives. Other healing circles are designed to have offenders examine their own conduct. They are helped to look at the circumstances that led to their involvement and to consider the damage they have caused. They are asked to consider the feelings of those they have harmed. They are encouraged to accept responsibility for what happened and to consider what can be done to avoid similar conduct in the future.

During a two-day visit to Hollow Water a few years ago I was permitted to be part of three healing circles. Two of the circles contained the accused person, a co-ordinator, two or three local people who worked on cases and participated in healing circles on a regular basis, and about three outsiders. I was the only non-Aboriginal. The third circle must have had 15 or 20 people in it. An interesting and significant thing happened at the beginning of that one. When the offender was brought into the room and saw me in the circle he immediately said, in quite a belligerent tone, "I'm not doing this with a white guy here." Only after others vouched for me and indicated I was there to learn about the process, did he agree to continue. The significance of his comment was that this is an Aboriginal proceeding. It must be run by Aboriginal people and be acceptable to those it is trying to help.

Each circle I participated in involved criminal conduct, where the charges had been put on hold, to provide the community time to see what it could accomplish. The first circle dealt with a young person who had been charged with a serious assault. After an introduction by the circle leader, the wrongdoer was asked to explain what she had done. When she finished, each person sitting in the circle took a turn in expressing their concern for what happened and asking the youth to provide more details about her conduct. The purpose of the first round was to let the circle understand what had happened and, although not stated as a purpose, to require the youth to relive the experience and assume responsibility for her actions.

A second round followed in which each of us took our turn at asking her to explain why she acted the way she did. Each person in the circle either asked questions on that topic or expressed concerns about the situation. A growing understanding developed of what had lead the girl to lash out. The process began to become a healing one as people showed their understanding of the position the young woman was in. At times the exchanges became quite emotional as circle members and the youth shared their pain and their emotions.

Alternative ways in which the youth might have reacted, or assistance she might have sought, were discussed with her. The question of peer influences was discussed and how that might be dealt with in the future. There was no attempt to justify what had happened but the girl found the group supportive and willing to listen to her problems and her point of view. The session ended with promises of support and an agreement to have another circle the following week. In the meantime the youth was to receive personal counselling and remain in a supportive home in the community. The leader of the circle made notes so that when the community efforts were completed, a report could be forwarded to the Provincial Court that had placed her case on hold.

Another session in which I participated involved a young man who had committed an assault causing substantial harm. The question of pressure from older friends and relations arose again. The process was similar to the one in the other circle. The intent was to show understanding and support in exchange for the offender accepting responsibility for his actions and coming to an understanding of how similar conduct could be avoided in the future.

The process was a powerful one and I had never seen anything like it in family conciliation or counselling, or in any court. It brought community members and offenders together to seek answers to mutual problems. The community members were non-judgemental. They were there to fix a problem and not to condemn the person who had made a mistake. At the same time the process supported and protected the victims.

Quite appropriately, I did not sit in on a circle dealing with the sexual abuse of a child, but I was told how they operate. In particular I was told how the position of mothers is strengthened and how children are given the names of several people to whom they are encouraged to speak at the first indication of any inappropriate touching. I was told of the sometimes-difficult task of having offenders admit that what they did was wrong and to accept the fact that they have a severe problem. I was told of the lengthy healing efforts that are often needed to ensure a change in attitude and a safe home environment.

Most offenders know that they are participating with the approval of a court and that they will eventually have to go before the judge again and the support of the court is helpful in having the offenders participate. Healing circles have to involve skilled employees, as it would be virtually impossible to have volunteers organize and operate the program year after year. It has nevertheless proved its value in Hollow Water and should be introduced, in one form or another, into all Aboriginal communities.

The Sweat Lodge is another remarkable example of an Aboriginal approach to the cleansing of the soul. In the darkness and extreme heat of the bent willow and animal hide or blanket-covered roof and door opening, an Elder leads the participants, who are seated in a circle, in prayer and contemplation. The only light is from the occasional flaring-up of the red-hot rocks as water is thrown upon them. Everyone speaks in turn. It would be inappropriate for me to comment on matters that are discussed, but I can say that the ceremony is very moving and very powerful. I do not suggest that a judge order anyone to participate, as I am sure that would be inappropriate, but 'sweats' are conducted by Elders for those who are invited to attend.

Peacemakers have always been a part of Aboriginal tradition and practice, although they have had a variety of names and titles. The Navajo historically had a Naat'aanii (or natani), a headman, to resolve family differences, settle arguments and reform wrongdoers. They were the 'peace leaders' of the Navajo, who have now adopted the title of 'Peacemaker' and established Peacemaker Courts as part of their legal system. The Seneca had a peacemaker system that appears to have been adopted by the State of Pennsylvania in its Peacekeeper Court legislation of 1683.

There should be one or more Peacemakers in each community that is part of an Aboriginal justice system. They could work part-time, either for the court or for individuals if approached by them directly. They could be designated by the court or by the community or merely let it be known they are available to act in that capacity. In some cases of wrongdoing the police might recommend that a suspect see a Peacemaker in lieu of a charge being laid. Whether a charge is ultimately laid might depend on the willingness of the wrongdoer to co-operate in resolving a problem.

Another method of appointment would be to have Peacemakers appointed by the management committee as officers of the court. They would then have extensive authority and important work to do as delegates of the court. Elders and others with experience in helping people should be considered for the task. Diplomacy and persuasiveness would be important qualifications as much of their work will be to encourage people to come up with their own solutions. Their work would not only involve the resolution of specific problems, but would include helping people heal their relationships with one another.

The Peacemaker could meet with an offender to see if they can agree on a plan that would satisfy the victim. That might involve an apology and the payment of restitution or compensation or might involve fixing any damage that was caused. The Peacemaker might choose to involve the families or clan members of both the victim and the offender so broader interests and responsibilities can be dealt with. The same process might be applied to a family dispute or problem, ranging from abuse to the removal of children from their parents. A civil suit for a debt, damage to a vehicle or a home, or any other sort of issue, could also be resolved with the help of a Peacemaker.

A Peacemaker could meet with the accused in an informal manner to see whether he accepts responsibility for what happened. Accepting responsibility is not necessarily the same as admitting guilt, but if the individual shows regret for his actions the Peacemaker has a good basis on which to proceed. He can then speak to the victim to get an understanding of what happened and the extent of any loss or damage that was caused. In a process of shuttle diplomacy the Peacemaker could then explore a variety of options to have the offender make amends for what he did.

If the victim agrees, the Peacemaker might arrange a meeting with the wrongdoer so an apology could be extended. In the process, the victim would hopefully get some understanding about the offender and some assurance that the incident would not be repeated. The Peacemaker might make a written or verbal to the court if the matter is successfully settled. If it is not, he could return the wrongdoer to court for a trial or other disposition.

If a matter is resolved with the help of an independent Peacemaker, both the wrongdoer and the victim would be spared the need for a contentious trial. In some cases a charge might be dropped so the wrongdoer wouldn't have a criminal conviction on his record. The advantage of having matters settled in this way is that both parties would have had their say in discussions with the Peacemaker and with one another and the offender would come to appreciate the harm his actions caused. He would hopefully be less of a threat to the community in the future and the victim would have been able to put the incident behind her.

In family matters, the Peacemaker might be able to help couples resolve their personal and marital disputes. Where children are involved, he could meet with the father and mother separately or together to help them direct their attention to the needs of the children. He could meet with the children as well to understand their reactions to the strife and to see if they have any suggestions for resolving the situation. In some cases, he might recommend a family gathering to involve the extended family or attendance at a community resource if an addiction is at the root of the problem.

The less intrusive approach of a Peacemaker can help people resolve matters out of court rather than having a judge decide for them. The efforts of the Peacemaker should be confidential, so the parties would not be prejudiced if they do end up in court. The court rules should protect the discussions so a judge could not be given any details of what was said during the attempt to settle the case.

With experience, judges would come to know what type of case might benefit from this sort of referral. Unfortunate as it may be, judges would have to be careful not to overload the Peacemakers with more cases than they can handle. Judges may have to deal with the vast majority of cases coming before them but would hopefully refer as many as possible to Peacemakers and other community services. The court should see a reduction in its workload as a result of settlements obtained by Peacemakers.

Variations on the peacemaking role are possible. In cases involving community gaming and fishing laws, disputes over trapline allocation, zoning, the allotment of new housing, and other matters the community might prefer to ask a Peacemaking Board to resolve them.

Such boards could be made up of people who are actively involved in these matters and others who represent the broader community. The process of resolving disputes would be to listen to differing claims and to help the parties reach a solution that would be fair to everyone. The board could be made up of several Peacemakers or potential Peacemakers and its decisions could be subject to appeal to the Aboriginal court.

The process of peacemaking applies the same principles as mediation. An independent person meets with the parties to a dispute, first to get some idea of what the dispute is about and the concerns and feelings of the parties. He would then try to get the parties to discuss their common interest in peacefully resolving the dispute and steer them away from taking hard and fast positions and from making firm demands. Through a process of re-framing and reinterpreting what the parties are saying, the mediator will try to get the parties to abandon their antagonistic positions. As the discussions continue, the people will hopefully become more conciliatory and be prepared to look at the concerns of the other person as well as their own. A successful outcome can be forecast when the parties unite in a search for a solution that will satisfy the interests of each of them and be fair to both.

If a court makes a referral to a Peacemaker, it would likely require a written or oral report on whether the issue was settled or whether the court should proceed with any charge or trial that had been commenced. The Local Registrar should keep track of cases Peacemakers have handled, as the information will be important when evaluating the success of the court's approach to diverting cases away from adversarial proceedings.

18

Family Conferences

There are three other processes with which the court can work that hold great promise for resolving criminal and civil issues. The first two go under the names of "Family Group Conferences" and "Community Justice Forums" and I often use the terms interchangeably as the procedure is the same. The third would also use a similar process but I have chosen to call it a "Family Gathering" to indicate that it applies to family problems.

The process known as Family Group Conferencing was developed in New Zealand from Maori traditional practices. In that country it was intended to involve the family, including extended family members, in the resolution of youth crime and child protection matters. The term Community Justice Forum was adopted by the RCMP in Canada as they were concerned that the term 'conference' was being misunderstood and confused with counselling or with the social workers' 'case conferences.' While the newer term may be clearer to some, it has the unfortunate potential of suggesting it is only appropriate for criminal matters. There is a danger that it may sideline the equally important use of the practice in abuse and child protection matters.

By the time the New Zealand and Australian experience with Family Group Conferences was being considered and applied on an experimental basis in Canada, a fairly standard format had developed. While variations are being tested, the following procedure is the one supported by the RCMP for dealing with conduct that would normally have led to the laying of a criminal charge and the processing of it through the regular courts.

A police officer will first consider whether this method of dealing with a case is worth exploring and will determine whether the wrongdoer is prepared to take responsibility for his actions. If he is willing to participate in a forum, the officer will set a date and ask the wrongdoer to attend and to bring his parents, a brother or sister and anyone else he would like to have with him. The officer will then speak to the victim, explain the process and its purpose (to discuss the offence and to decide what should be done about it) and ask him or her to attend with relatives or other supporters.

The order of speaking to participants that I will refer to has been carefully developed. The forum starts with the chairperson or 'facilitator' having the participants arranged on chairs in a circle with the wrongdoer and his supporters on one side and the victim and her supporters on the other. People who are less directly involved sit at the far side of the circle between the wrongdoer and victim supporters. Nothing is written down until a final agreement is reached and no reporting or recording equipment is used.

The facilitator will briefly describe the incident that has occurred, give the name of the offender and indicate that he is prepared to accept responsibility for his conduct. Even if people are known to one another, he will introduce everyone in the circle and indicate who they are supporting. He will say that the meeting is not to judge the wrongdoer but to understand what happened and to hear how others have been affected. The second objective, he will say, is to see what can be done to repair any damage that has been caused.

The facilitator will call on the wrongdoer to describe what he did. If he is reluctant to say very much, the facilitator will ask questions to help bring out the facts. He will be asked what he was thinking at the time and what he now thinks of the incident. He will be asked who he thinks has been affected, and in what way. If the person does not mention his parents, friends and school authorities the facilitator will ask him if he thinks they have been affected by his conduct.

The victim will then be asked what she thought, heard or experienced at the time of the incident and when she first became aware of it. She will be asked how the incident affected her and what her family and friends thought when they heard about it. The victim's supporters will then be asked what they thought when they heard of it and how they think the incident has affected the victim. The responses usually describe shock, disbelief, and a fear of a recurrence of the incident.

The facilitator will then turn to a parent and indicate that it must be difficult for them to hear what is being said. When the parent has thought about the question and has responded to it, they are asked what they thought when they heard of the event and what has happened since. Parents will often speak of curfews or other penalties they have already imposed. They may say that their child has always been good and that the conduct is out of character, or they may express dismay at his conduct. They may use the occasion to berate their offspring.

The perpetrator can then be asked if there is anything he wants to say to anyone in answer to the comments he has heard. Unless the person is too shy to respond or is feeling the weight of the concerns that have been expressed, he will likely apologize to the victim and to his parents as well.

The discussion will then turn to what should be done to repair any damage that has been caused. The victim and her supporters will comment first and then the parents of the wrongdoer are given the same opportunity and if someone makes a suggestion, others will be asked what they think of it. The discussion continues until a consensus is reached. In the process, the wrongdoer will be asked what he proposes or what he thinks of a plan proposed by others. He will be specifically asked if he thinks the final proposal is fair and acceptable to him. If it is not, the discussion will continue until everyone is in agreement.

The facilitator usually introduces these topics in a particular order. He may deal with each issue separately and go around the circle several times. This is more effective than having each person deal with every issue at the same time. The process carefully separates the wrongdoing from the harm caused and factual matters from the ultimate question of what is to be done to repair the emotional and physical damage.

I have only acted as the facilitator of one forum in a reserve community. A large group of youth between the ages of 10 and 15 had broken into a house, caused some damage, stolen a number of personal possessions and caused extensive damage to a car. The ringleaders each had a parent present and the victim was accompanied by her mother. The investigating RCMP officer sat outside the circle but made a few comments when the circumstances were being described. It was difficult to deal with the large number of youth who were present, but with each person commenting, a picture of what had happened and why it happened finally emerged.

It turned out that there was some longstanding animosity that caused the group, led by one girl in particular, to want to hurt the victim. The victim was particularly upset to hear this, but an agreement was finally reached to have certain goods returned and each parent agreed to share in paying the insurance deductible. The ringleader and the victim agreed to meet to try to iron out their differences.

That forum was held several years ago and I am advised that not one of the youth has re offended. It was obviously difficult for them to have to admit their fault in front of their parents and other members of the community. While I appreciated the opportunity given to me by the RCMP, I am certain the process would have moved more smoothly and would have been more appreciated by the participants if the facilitator had been Aboriginal.

From the standpoint of an Aboriginal community, the most attractive part of the program is that the family and the community, and not some outside agency, has come to the rescue of a wrongdoer and to the support of the victim. A Community Justice Forum is truly a homemade remedy for many problems. The cost to the participants is little or nothing. If the co-ordinator is a police officer who is already in the employ of the justice system, there would be no cost at all, except for the donuts and soft drinks that are served while the facilitator writes out the agreement that has been reached. The break permits the participants to speak to one another and to further the reconciliation begun during the forum.

Forums are held as soon as possible after an incident occurs while it and its effects are fresh in everyone's mind. Moving quickly permits the matter to be resolved before the concerns of the victim escalate and result in further fears and deeper concerns.

In criminal matters a meeting of interested people should be convened to deal with the inappropriate conduct, and it matters little whether it is called a Family Group Conference, a Community Justice Forum or just a meeting. Someone will have to ask people to come and someone will have to chair the meeting. It seems to me that the most logical person to put together a conference or a forum is the police officer who did the investigation and apprehended the apparent wrongdoer, as he would be an influential person in the community and be able to persuade the family members and the victim to attend.

This system differs from the work of a Peacemaker who personally works with the wrongdoer, the victim and their families, and attempts to find a resolution to a criminal act. The Peacemaker may play an active role in getting to the bottom of the matter and in suggesting a solution, but in Family Group Conferencing the facilitator plays a neutral role and leads the wrongdoer, victim and other affected parties through a series of discussions until they arrive at a solution.

If school authorities are present they will explain their concerns but will likely indicate their willingness to have the youth back in school, possibly subject to some conditions. Sometimes the settlement agreement will involve some manual labour to repair damage and in that case the circle will determine who is to supervise the work to make sure it is done.

The procedure personalizes the crime for all the participants and encourages them to find a solution that is acceptable to each of them. It also appears to bring the offender and the victim closer to their own families, as support is shown to the one who is in trouble. A youth might have thought that his parents didn't care what he did. The process can heal attitudes of that kind. By the end of the process, which takes an hour or so, the victim will feel vindicated and the offender will feel that he has done everything he could do at that time to make amends for his earlier actions.

A Community Justice Forum is a restorative justice approach to resolving community problems involving wrongdoers and their victims. It is connected to the exercise of greater discretion by the police and is often an alternative to the laying of a formal charge. The RCMP encourages its members and Aboriginal communities to consider using this approach.

This process deals with the offence in an active way and usually results in a respect for the system that involves only community members. It is hard on the wrongdoer and there is no reason for him to think that he has been treated with kid gloves or has beaten the system.

The Family Group Conference or Community Justice Forum provides benefits to all the participants. The wrongdoer will have been dealt with by the justice system but without a trial and without the stigma of a criminal record. He will hopefully be rehabilitated and will refrain from similar conduct in the future. The parents will have taken some responsibility for the actions of one of their children. They will gain a better understanding of the youth and will hopefully become a stronger and more unified family unit. The victim will have been able to face the person who caused fear and harm and to see him as an individual with problems and feelings of his own. The victim will hopefully have become able to put the incident to rest and to feel more secure than she would have if she had not been able to speak to the wrongdoer face to face.

If the victim can see the wrongdoer in person and hear an explanation for the offence, as silly as the reason often is, the wrongdoer may not appear as inhuman as the victim imagined. Explanations may be as benign as "We just went in to look around," "The door was open," or "The keys were in the ignition." Some will say, "Things just got out of hand," or "We didn't really mean to do any damage." The loss or damage cannot change, but the victim may feel more comfortable when the surrounding circumstances have been disclosed.

It is important that the victim feel that the matter has been satisfactorily completed. Experience to date is that the process is beneficial to victims as it usually permits them, in common terminology, to 'put closure' to the event. A great deal of attention must be paid to the victim to make certain that she has a full opportunity to vent her displeasure with what happened, and care must be taken that any suggested solution is acceptable to her.

The police are enabled to be more pro-active in their work. It permits them to participate actively in finding a satisfactory result without having to rely on the full force of the law or a judge. They come away from a forum with a feeling of accomplishment, and more importantly, feel respected as participants helping the community deal with wrongdoers before their conduct worsens and gets completely out of control.

The court, if a matter is not diverted to a forum by the police, can initiate the forum. The judge can explain how a conference operates and that the accused may withdraw from it at any time and return to court. If the accused agrees, the judge can direct that a community justice forum be established. On being advised that a favourable solution has been reached, the court can enter a permanent stay of proceedings or the charge can be withdrawn. If the judge is advised that no agreement was reached, the case can continue through the usual court process. In either event the court should take comfort in the fact that it has attempted to use community resources to resolve the issue.

The community itself should take comfort in knowing that a reformative approach to justice has been applied. The process should permit members of the community to realize that they are capable of resolving many of their own problems without using the courts at all. It will hopefully benefit from this approach to maintaining law and order, and if recidivism and criminal activity diminishes as a result, the community should be well pleased. Possibly the greatest benefit to the community would be to know that it has a process that can restore social harmony by applying Aboriginal values and traditions.

A Family Gathering would be similar to a Family Group Conference but would concentrate on family problems varying from separation and divorce to child protection. I came across the term 'Family Gathering' when doing some reading on early American Indian tradition and practices. The term was apparently used to describe the coming together of family members to deal with family-related problems, although they may have dealt with other matters as well. It is a term that implies the strength and influence of Aboriginal families and at the same time recognizes that there are family matters to be considered from time to time.

While physical and sexual abuse involving family members may be criminal, they are also serious family issues that deserve special attention. If a family is in danger of disintegrating because of abuse, alcohol consumption or any other cause, its members are clearly in need of help and every effort should be made to try to salvage the family. Some method should be applied to determine the cause of the problem and to consider whether there are resources that can help them resolve their problems.

One of the great strengths of Aboriginal society is the close-knit extended family. Older relatives are revered and are often referred to as grandmother and grandfather, even though there is not the technical lineage required by other cultures. Uncles and aunts often have a special relationship with their nephews and nieces. It is not uncommon for children to be brought up by their grandparents at different stages of their lives.

In spite of this closeness, there is often a reluctance on the part of family members to interfere in the lives of others. The tradition of non-interference is a strong one, but I am aware from dealing with child protection cases that extended family members will agree to help with the care and raising of children, if the parents ask them to do so. The family support is there, even if some parents do not fully appreciate the trouble they are in or are too proud or stubborn to ask for help.

My experience in pre-trial conferences was that Aboriginal parents knew when they were unable to properly care for their children and were delighted to know that someone close to them was willing to care for their children for a while. The problem they often faced was that the Agency would not accept the relatives they proposed and they were afraid of losing their children forever. The Family Gathering would provide an opportunity to discuss the whole issue with extended family members who would be concerned about the husband and wife and about their children.

A Family Gathering is a mechanism that would enable family members to come to the aid of parents having problems and of children who are suffering as a result. It could be convened in the same way as a Family Group Conference, and parents could invite their own parents or other family members to consider their situation and provide moral and actual support. With the help of a facilitator, they could discuss their problems with one another and develop solutions.

The process would be very difficult for the family but if the abuser had agreed to the Gathering and had accepted some responsibility for his actions, he would know that the process was intended to help the family. The facilitator would start by calling on him to explain his conduct. The victim and then others in the circle would comment on it as well. Eventually the discussion would turn to the needs of the children and what should be done to protect them. The discussion would continue until solutions were found.

If it appears that the children should not be left with their parents, the participants, including the parents, would discuss where the children should live and who would be responsible for them. The extent and frequency of visits between the parents and the children should be agreed upon, as should things the parents would have to do if they were ever to regain custody. If some in the circle are prepared to have the children live with them, that should be discussed. If none are able to care for the children, there should be a discussion and agreement on how and where suitable people can be found.

If the family recommends abuse counselling, the facilitator could contact those providing that service. If it is agreed that separate healing circles should be tried, the facilitator or the Local Registrar could make those arrangements as well.

It will take some skill on the part of the facilitator to involve everyone in the discussion and in the solution that emerges. The facilitator should be a neutral person who will keep the discussion going and be able to have all the relevant issues discussed, but in this situation, the facilitator should have some knowledge of the legal system and what might happen if a solution is not found.

There are now Aboriginal trainers who spend much of their time working with Family Group Conferences and Justice Forums and they could easily adapt their teachings and their approach to accommodate family matters. I have spoken to one of them and he would be willing to provide information about the process to community members and to train potential facilitators as well.

British Columbia has taken some steps in this direction. In a 1993 White Paper it gave greater authority to families affected by child protection proceedings and introduced a type of Family Gathering. It recommended that a conference be held with the child, members of the extended family, a person familiar with the case who had authority to enter into an agreement, a person familiar with the child's needs, and anyone else the participants believed should be involved. That group was authorized to come up with a plan for the child which, if accepted by the Agency, would apply.

The process I propose would not leave the final decision up to a child caring agency. A Family Gathering, established with the encouragement of the court, would make the final decision. The process would, I believe, achieve the benefits obtained in New Zealand — a transfer of the authority to deal with family issues from government agencies to families and to the communities where they reside. There would of course be the possibility that if the Conference was not successful, the abuse and its consequences would have to be dealt with in court.

PART VI

The
Feather

19

Sentencing

Sentencing is a difficult task for every judge to deal with. The problem is that every accused, every victim and every set of circumstances is different. The judge will want to see that a victim is protected and compensated if that is possible. He will want to see that the community is safe and that criminal activity is dealt with and reduced. At the same time he has to deal with the individual before him and see if there is anything that can be done to stop him from offending again.

There are official sentencing guidelines but they are very general and often conflict with one another. The Criminal Code, text books and case law discuss principles of sentencing that have been handed down from earlier times. They speak of specific deterrence, general deterrence, punishment, rehabilitation, the protection of society and maintaining respect for the law. These are all valid concerns but they still don't provide much guidance to a judge.

The general public is certainly confused about the reason some sentences are imposed. They wonder how a suspended sentence can be given for the embezzlement of hundreds of thousand of dollars while jail is imposed for shoplifting. (Many women in jail at Portage la Prairie are there for that reason.) Something seems amiss when the penalty for assault causing bodily harm is more severe than the killing of an innocent person as a result of drunk driving.

To make the task of sentencing easier for Aboriginal judges I suggest that the management committees, Chiefs, Councillors and communities at large consider what they want their justice system to achieve when dealing with wrongdoers. Do they want to punish for the sake of punishment, or do they want to repair the damage that has been caused? Do they want to shame and make an example of wrongdoers, or do they want to help them so they will not do the same thing again? Do they want to ignore improper conduct or do they want to do something to correct it and make their communities safer and more pleasant places to live?

The objectives communities decide upon should become the objectives of its judges in the sentencing process. If the communities want to take a healing approach to wrongdoing and to inter-personal strife, the judges should be aware of that so they can apply the type of sentence that will support that objective. If the community wants to see that victims are protected, the judges can try to fashion a sentence that will ensure that result. If it wants abuse to stop, the judges can apply a variety of sentences to assist in that endeavour.

An Aboriginal system, through its management committee and in consultation with the judges, might develop a statement of principles that will record the objectives of the system and indirectly provide guidelines for its judges, police and others to follow. One of the principles might be that offenders should repair any damage they cause. Another might be that victims should be compensated for any loss they have suffered and a third might be that incarceration would only be considered after all other possibilities have been explored.

With principles like these to guide them, judges would still have to take a variety of circumstances into consideration. Some offences will be a serious breach of the law while others will be minor. Some will have been carefully planned and cause a great deal of harm, while others will be more like a mistake and cause little or no harm.

Some offenders will be young and in court for the first time, while others may have repeatedly broken the law and shown a total disregard for it. Some will be a nuisance and others will be a danger to the community. In some situations the judge can be lenient and have a positive chat with the offender, while in others the judge will have to devise a sentence that will either teach the offender a lesson or persuade him to change his attitude. The background of an accused, the way he has been brought up and difficulties he has faced, may make a difference, but the judge will be aware that others with an equally difficult background have never offended at all.

An Aboriginal judge might like to limit his consideration of the record of an offender to what he has done since the Aboriginal justice system was established and pay less attention to his record in the regular courts. I think he should almost give offenders a fresh start in the new system. It would be too difficult to try to reassess the earlier conduct that got the person into trouble with the law if a new approach is being attempted. If the person is willing to co-operate, the judge will want to fashion a sentence that will try to improve him and at the same time deal with any harm that he has caused. Again, I think the attitude of the offender will be crucial.

Before discussing sentencing *per se*, there are ways a court can achieve many objectives without sentencing a person at all. When a wrongdoer first comes to court, the judge can speak to him and get some idea of what happened and some understanding of his attitude. That will enable the judge to determine whether he should try to divert the person away from the court process altogether, proceed to trial, or accept a plea of guilty if that is what the person wants to do.

If he chooses the diversion route, there are several ways in which he can require the offender to make use of services the community has available. One way is to request a person to take part in a program the judge thinks would be appropriate. That can be done after someone has been arrested and brought to court but before any charge has been laid. A second is to do the same thing after a charge has been laid but before a plea is accepted. A third is to do that after a plea of guilty has been entered but before any trial takes place.

In each of these situations, the attendance of the person at a program can be required as a condition of an adjournment. In the last two examples, the person's participation is guaranteed by an order of the court that the police or Court Officer can enforce. The other way in which the participation of the offender can be assured is if the order is a condition of a final sentence. Even that can be a two-stage process. If the person fails to comply, he will be in breach of an order of the court and can be brought back so the judge can impose a different and more severe sentence.

One of the options I include under sentencing is mentioned in the Young Offenders Act and that is to take no further action at all. Instead of accepting a plea of any kind, a judge can withdraw a charge or adjourn a case indefinitely. If nothing happens within six months to cause the police to bring the person back to court, the charge would expire and the accused would not have a conviction on his record. This approach might be used where the judge hopes that being arrested and having to appear before a judge, will be a lesson in itself.

In my early days I acted for a young man who had sneaked into the girls' section at the Sherbrooke Baths. He didn't touch anyone but he was there and was charged and had to appear before Judge Garton at the Rupert Avenue Police Station. When I interviewed him he was crying, shaking all over and was frightened out of his mind. I can't remember whether the charge was stayed or whether a suspended sentence was imposed, but I was convinced (and told the judge) that he would never do anything like that again.

A temporary stay of proceedings might be given when a judge has asked a wrongdoer to participate in a community program and wants to see if he complies. To go a little further, the judge could require the accused to participate in it. When passing sentence the judge could order the accused to take a detox or healing program, participate in a family gathering or work with a Peacemaker. If he does not, he can be brought back to court so the judge can impose another sentence.

If a Peacemaker, Community Justice Forum, Family Gathering or other program has worked with an offender and has reached a satisfactory conclusion to an issue, and the decision is agreed to by the offender, the court could give an order to convert the agreement into an order of the court. This type of 'confirmatory order' would add the court's authority to the agreement and make it enforceable through the court if that becomes necessary.

If the work of a local Peacemaker or program has failed to resolve a problem the judge previously thought it might, the judge would have to proceed to deal with the case. The accused would then have the option of pleading not guilty and having a trial or of pleading guilty. The judge would hear the evidence, or the submissions of the police, to get an understanding of the nature of the offence. The court should develop a method to hear the position of the victim, whether that is by hearing from her personally, receiving a letter or 'victim impact statement,' or having the police or the legal advisor provide the judge with the information.

The judge would then have to assess the seriousness of the offence and impose the sentence he thought appropriate, having in mind the purposes the community had adopted. The sentence might be directed to teaching the offender a lesson, correcting his behaviour or to protecting and compensating the victim.

If during the sentencing process, a judge who is not very familiar with the community should be entitled to seek the advice or assistance of a resident Elder. He should be entitled to ask the Elder to sit with him when submissions on sentence are being made and prior to deciding what sentence to impose. The Elder might mention a situation in the community of which the judge should be aware or might comment on the background of the accused. On the other hand he might just ask a question and leave it to the judge, the accused, or the parties' representatives, to deal with it in their own way.

It is important that the Elder's comments be made in open court so everyone can hear them. If the Elder spoke to the judge privately, that might cause a problem as judges are required to base their decisions on evidence or arguments presented in open court. The accused or his representative should have the right to question the Elder, either to challenge what he has said or to question the basis for his comments. A Court of Appeal reviewing a judge's decision would want to know everything that was brought to his attention and that the accused had an opportunity to answer any and all allegations made against him.

Another method of sentencing would be to have a 'sentencing circle' and there are at least two types of those. The judge, counsel, and interested people from the community could gather to discuss what should be done with the offender. The idea is to give people from the Aboriginal community where an offence has taken place, an opportunity to express their attitude about the incident and to say whatever they wish about the offender. More specifically, they have an opportunity to suggest the punishment, if any, they would like to see the judge impose.

If there has been a healing circle working with an offender, the moderator may have made a written report and wish to participate in the circle to explain the work that was done and how effective it was. He might wish to comment on the effect on the offence upon the victim and the victim's current attitude. Everyone in the circle would then take their turn in giving their reaction to the offence and what should be done to make amends. The victim can speak if she wishes.

The wrongdoer will also have an opportunity to explain his actions and make them appear less severe than they do on the surface. On the other hand, he might admit total responsibility for his wrongdoing and make an apology to the victim, the victim's family and the community. If lawyers are present they would be the last to speak. They would sum up the situation as they see it and suggest to the judge how he should deal with the matter.

The judge may receive a wide variety of reactions to the incident but may receive a fairly unanimous opinion as to what he should do. He will certainly have a sense of how seriously the community views the offence. He would take into account what he has heard during the trial and what he has heard during the sentencing circle. If the circle has made a recommendation as to what the disposition should be, the judge may accept or reject it, but will in any event give it careful consideration. As the final decision is for the judge to make, he will impose the sentence he thinks the circumstances demand.

My guess is that if the community is unanimous in what they think the sentence should be, the judge would likely accept their verdict and sentence accordingly. If however there was a substantial disagreement among those in the sentencing circle, the judge would have to make the final decision.

Another manner in which a sentencing circle might operate would be even more traditional. The judge could ask those in the circle to impose the sentence themselves. In that event the circle would have to keep discussing options until they were unanimous on what should be done. The benefit of proceeding in this way would be that the community itself would take the responsibility for what is to be done with the wrongdoer and what would satisfy the victim's and community needs. It would place the responsibility squarely on the shoulders of the community itself.

Both methods of involving members in a healing circle would probably require some analysis and review before they become engrained in the court's approach to sentencing. The judges and the management committee should moniter the process to see how well it works and how appropriate the results have been. As the process would likely take more of the court's time than a normal sentencing, an assessment of the effect of this approach on the total workload of the court would be appropriate. Consideration might also be given as to whether sentencing circles should be limited to certain types of cases or to ones where the judge is unsure of the sentence he should impose.

Whether a judge does so himself or with the help of others, a practical sentence in many cases would be to require an offender to provide a certain number of hours or days of community service. This should be particularly effective in close-knit communities where the decisions of the court are likely to become known and where the residents would be able to see offenders working.

The judge should determine the details of this type of sentence after discussing them with the offender. The judge would know, or could easily determine, the sort of work that needs to be done that would benefit the community, and it would not be necessary, as it is in the regular courts, to have administrators devise a program of work and supervise it. The Court Officer would do the supervision and bring the person back before the judge if the work was not done.

If a person was ordered to clean the band office, cut the grass and plant flowers, he would be in the public eye. If he was ordered to repair or paint a community hall, he would be on display and benefit the community at the same time. If there were a group of offenders assigned to the same task, the reason for their presence would be obvious. This, I suppose, would be akin to the shaming practices of old.

Sentences can be both moderate and effective. A court could order that there would be no incarceration or fine as long as the wrongdoer does certain things to undo the damage he has caused or the hurt he has inflicted. Restitution and compensation are powerful and positive tools in the sentencing arsenal.

The intent of restitution is to put the victim back in the position that existed prior to the wrongful act. The wrongdoer might be required to return anything he stole or to repair any damage he caused to the victim's home or property. Compensation is slightly different than restitution, but it can also require money to be paid to compensate a victim for a loss. Restitution is inclined to require an offender to 'pay back' or to 'give back' something to the victim, while compensation is to 'pay for' damage that has been caused. A judge can order the offender to pay a sum of money to compensate the victim for damage or loss.

If a victim needs his or her house painted, the grounds cleaned-up or wood cut, the offender might do that. He might also be ordered to keep the person supplied with fish and fowl for a period of time. The work might be embarrassing for the offender to have to do, but that would be part of the penalty. The fact that the personal service has to be performed would be a reminder of the harm he caused and the need to compensate the victim and set matters right.

Care would have to be taken that the victim is content to have the offender working on her property. The Court Officer might have to arrange a meeting between the victim and the offender to make sure there is no apprehension about the offender doing this sort of work. It might be necessary to have the Court Officer closely supervise the offender to make sure that the offender is doing the work and is not upsetting the victim.

If it becomes known in a community that this type of sentence is one the judges will use, the deterrence of others should be effective. Unlike the anonymity of a person appearing in the regular courts, people in the community will become aware of local wrongdoing and what the court is doing about it. I would hope that an Aboriginal court would use this type of sentence for young offenders as well as for adults, and do so in a way that will make the public aware of the sentence.

An order of 'prohibition' should be available as part of a sentence to stop someone from doing something he is doing or that he might do in the future. The order can be issued as part of a judgement after a case has been heard or it can be issued before trial, if it is necessary to protect a spouse or children. If there are allegations of physical or sexual abuse, the alleged offender can be ordered to stay away from the victims and from the family home until the case is heard.

If the abuse is not resolved at trial or through a local program, the order of prohibition can be included in a sentence to protect a victim and others in the community from any danger of improper conduct in the future. The wrongdoer could be prohibited from going to a particular residence or place where he has caused problems in the past. He might be stopped from seeing or phoning the victim, or from having contact with children of a certain age.

The same order could require him to take counselling or participate in a Family Gathering or work with a Peacemaker. He might be required to attend an holistic healing program with his family or attend a substance abuse facility. The order could require the offender to report to the Court Officer on a regular basis to indicate the programs he is attending. If the officer had any concerns as to whether the offender is obeying the order, he could be brought back before the judge.

The judge could order the offender to report to the Court Officer on a regular basis and to indicate the programs he is attending. Instead of leaving it to the offender to report, the judge could ask the Court Officer to personally monitor the performance of the wrongdoer and bring him back to court if he is not abiding by the order.

It might be convenient if Aboriginal communities had a schedule or pre-determined fines for certain offences that a person could pay without having to appear before a judge. On the other hand, sufficient discretion should be left with the judge so he can impose a substantial fine if the circumstances demand it. There would be little sense in fining a bootlegger $500 when he could make that much in a day. If however his stock of illicit liquor is confiscated and a fine of $1,000 or $5,000 is imposed, that would hopefully put a stop to his bootlegging. A fine, or any other sentence, should serve a social purpose and benefit the community by discouraging unacceptable conduct.

The imposition of a fine would require a consideration of the circumstances of the offence and the ability of the person to pay. It would not be effective to fine an unemployed youth $100 if he has no job, no assets and is living at home. He will learn nothing from the sentence if his parents pay the fine for him.

On the other hand a fine can be very effective as it may impose a constant reminder of what can happen if a person breaks the law. If, along with a fine or in place of it, a driver's licence can be suspended for a period of time, that would be another way to deter offenders who commit driving offences. If that doesn't work the court should have the right to have the vehicle that was involved in an offence impounded, whether the vehicle is owned by the offender or not. Offenders who face these types of sentences may act more responsibly in the future. Owners of vehicles would also share the responsibility by making sure the person who is permitted to drive it, does so in a responsible manner.

The removal of a license and a car or a truck can be a severe and effective penalty for someone who likes to drive or needs a vehicle to get around. "Let the punishment fit the crime" is still an apt principle for the courts to apply. Even prisoners in jail accept the validity of this type of sentence. During our visit to the women's jail during the AJI one of the Aboriginal inmates acknowledged that "if you do the crime, you do the time."

Even if a fine can be easily paid, it should not be looked upon as being without consequences. If someone has received a fine for a number of offences on different occasions and then appears before a judge on a charge where imprisonment is an option, the judge may wonder if the person has much respect for the law. If it appears that he doesn't care about the community's laws, and fines have had no effect on his conduct, the judge may decide he needs a serious reminder to stay out of trouble and impose a period of incarceration.

Whatever the fine or other penalty is, it should serve a couple of purposes. It should be stiff enough to let an offender know that they will have to pay for their wrongdoing. It can't be a slap on the wrist or the offender will learn nothing from his court experience. The penalty also has to be severe enough to convince the person not to re-offend.

I suggest that the existing "Fine Option Program" *not* be used in Aboriginal systems. It is cumbersome and unsuited to Aboriginal offenders. The program permits a person who has been ordered to pay a fine, to avoid doing so by performing a number of hours of public service. Supervisors then have to be engaged to establish a work plan and to supervise it to make certain the person does the work. If he does not, he is arrested and sent to jail. During the AJI we found that a great many Aboriginal people were being incarcerated for this reason.

Of even greater significance, we found that many ended up in jail even though the sentencing judge had not wanted that to happen. It is the manner in which the program is established and administered that produces that result. It can be a very harmful program.

If a judge wishes to impose a fine, and he is satisfied it will cause no undue hardship, he should impose the fine. If he wants to require someone to perform a certain number of hours of community or personal service, he should specify the work that is to be done and retain jurisdiction to make certain the work is done and to bring the offender back to court if it is not. There will be no need for him to mix the two types of sentences.

A judge should impose a sentence he believes will be respected in the community. It should have a substantial effect on the wrongdoer and provide the greatest possible benefit to the community. If the penalties I have suggested will not achieve these objectives, the judge will have to consider the imposition of the only other penalty he can impose — incarceration. I will deal with that option under the name of the facility I propose — a Healing Lodge.

20

Healing Lodges

After all other options have been explored and rejected, an Aboriginal judge will be left with the most severe penalty the court can impose. He will have to incarcerate the offender. In the regular system a judge can order that a person be incarcerated but it is then up to the federal or provincial authorities to decide where he will be kept. They can move inmates from one institution to another and determine when they are to be released. There is no communication between the correctional or probation and parole services and the judge.

In an Aboriginal system, the exact place of detention should be determined by the trial judge, and not be left to another authority. The judge will have certain objectives he is trying to achieve in imposing a sentence and should be able to decide on the best place for the person to go and the length of time they should stay there. There should be no other authority that can lessen the term that is imposed.

The judge would of course have to visit places where youth and adults are held and become familiar with their location, the extent of security they provide and the programs and services they offer. When sentencing, he should select the facility that suits the age of the person and the one that will be able to provide the teachings and rehabilitative programs the offender requires. Any review or change in the place of incarceration, or the length or type of sentence, should only be done by the sentencing judge.

A basic expectation of the legal system over the centuries has been that you make criminals better by punishing them and sending them to jail. The Borstal homes in England were supposed to correct wayward youth and prevent juvenile crime. Debtors' prisons of Dicken's era were supposed to teach people to pay their debts. Jails were supposed to stop offenders from continuing their life of crime, but none of these approaches worked when they were tried and they don't work today.

Rather than the justice system changing its approach to unacceptable conduct, the old philosophies and their punitive approach continue to this day. Punishment for its own sake remains in vogue, partly to satisfy the call for vengeance and law and order, and partly because our society has not been able to find a better way of dealing with offenders. There is no consensus on whether resources should be directed to reducing the causes of crime or whether more jails should be built. In spite of the billions of dollars being spent on corrections, the public appears to pay little attention to the monetary and social costs of having people warehoused in our jails.

Boot camps are the current trend in dealing with young offenders, but their devotion to a tough and regimented lifestyle is not going to turn many lives around. It is certainly not going to improve young Aboriginal offenders who are in need of culturally appropriate supports and encouragement to improve their lives and to prepare them for participation in society on their release. I see little in the existing system to indicate that approach is being applied.

Some commentators suggest that going to jail is like going on vacation and that prisoners are pampered and entertained at public expense. Nothing could be farther from the truth. Our jails are horrible places of confinement where individual rights and liberties are suspended and where the months or years of residency are demoralizing and destructive. Association with hardened offenders and career criminals increases the damage to the first offender and bears a direct relationship to what happens on their release. Like the welfare syndrome, the stigma of being in jail is almost impossible to shed. It is difficult to stay out of trouble when former inmates may be the only ones to offer understanding and support, even if the support is of questionable value.

The basic approach of most jails appears to be that they are receiving dangerous people from the courts who have to be locked up and guarded until their time has been served. The fact that many of the inmates are not a danger to anyone is not allowed to divert them from the practices they have followed for generations. Little provision is made for educational and trades-training programs to provide opportunities for employment on release. Although some cultural practices are now occasionally permitted, there are no concentrated Aboriginal-specific programs to deal with the needs of Aboriginal inmates. Even where courses are available, most Aboriginal inmates find them inappropriate to their needs and do not participate in them.

During the AJI we visited all the jails in Manitoba and talked to as many Aboriginal prisoners as we could. Generally, we found them caged like animals, putting in their time lying in their cells, watching TV, or just talking to one another. We saw no productive activities. After years of confinement, many become disillusioned and more and more bitter towards the society they feel has abandoned them. They would like to have productive employment on their release but see that nothing is being done to help them attain that objective. In prison, they learn nothing to help them adjust to the demands of the workplace or of society at large.

The gentler inmates are continuously subjected to the abuse of hardened criminals and to the jail's unsavoury influences. In some of the institutions we visited, the atmosphere was tense and the inmates complained about filthy cells, unpleasant and abusive guards and inmates, and an uncaring administration.

The youth facilities had counselling and other services, but the conscientious efforts of the staff were lost in the manner in which the institutions were organized and administered. The Manitoba Youth Centre contained many Aboriginal youth from rural and northern communities and even more from the cities. Bail having been denied by the courts, many were flown back and forth from the location of the court to Winnipeg until their oft-remanded cases were ready to be heard. The 2000 jail statistics to which I referred earlier showed there were 95 youth on remand in the Manitoba Youth Centre and their time in pre-trial detention varied from two to nine months. Some Aboriginal youth, who have never been to a city in their lives, live in dormitories with others who have had considerable experience with the criminal law.

For some youth, having been in jail may be a status symbol that gains them recognition. Some may initially even think of being there as a holiday. It is quite apparent that the experience hardens youth and makes them contemptuous of the institution, the courts and the law. Any former respect for the law they may have had quickly dissipates. Today, youth facilities are a breeding ground for gangs and for criminal activity. The legal system should avoid sending youth to them at all costs.

The Youth Centre contains male and female youth who are supposed to be in 'open custody,' and still others who have been sentenced to 'secure custody.' I question the legality of having open custody youth in the same building as those on remand, and with those serving time in secure custody. The Young Offenders Act speaks of the need to keep the two types of inmates separate and apart. It provides:

24.2(2) Subject to this section and sections 24.3 and 24.5, a young person who is committed to custody shall be placed in open custody or secure custody, as specified in the order of committal, at such place or facility as the provincial director may specify.

24.1(1) In this section and sections 24.2, 24.3, 28 and 29

"open custody" means custody in a community residential centre, group home, child care institution, or forest or wilderness camp, or any other like place or facility designated by the Lieutenant Governor in Council...

"secure custody" means custody in a place or facility designated by the Lieutenant Governor in Council of a province for the secure containment or restraint of young persons, and includes a place or facility within a class of such places or facilities so designated.

These provisions are being ignored in favour of combining offenders and saving money. The Manitoba Youth Centre is one sprawling building with a central control system that opens and locks doors and controls security. It may be that the different categories of residents are supposed to remain in different parts of the building, but they all feel they are in a maximum-security prison. The recreational activities of each group are limited to one hour a day in the gym and a similar time in the 'campus,' an outdoor field surrounded by the institution's buildings. The interior and exterior doors of the whole facility are securely locked and guarded.

During our visit, youth in open custody complained that their privileges were worse than those in secure custody. The manner in which the facility is organized is badly in need of review. Those on remand should be kept away from those that are serving a sentence. First offenders and those in open custody should be in a totally separate place. Aboriginal youth should be tried quickly or returned to their communities.

The Agassiz youth facility in Portage la Prairie used to be a place where those who had been sentenced, many from the north, lived in dormitories and took part in rehabilitative programs. From time to time they went into the community and did chores for people in need of assistance. Their rehabilitation was an obvious priority, but that approach has been stopped. A massive chain-link fence now surrounds the property and the residents are subjected to a boot-camp life of discipline. The unwritten message is that they are no longer to be trusted and are to be treated like "the bad people they are."

Stony Mountain Penitentiary has about fifty percent Aboriginal inmates, all of whom are treated liked hardened criminals. The worst example of unfair treatment we saw had been applied a year or two before our visit. All the furniture had been removed from the common area of a range containing many Aboriginal inmates. There were no longer chairs or tables where they could gather when not in their calls. As we had been in similar ranges in some of the provincial jails we asked where the furniture and TVs were. The superintendent of the institution told us they had been removed as punishment for a near-riot a year or two earlier. I visited the penitentiary years later and the chairs had still not been returned. During my most recent visit I found the ranges rebuilt. The ranges now have a few small stools with no backs, around a bare table that is also affixed to the floor.

Headingley was the toughest of all the provincial jails we visited. That was understandable to a point, as it houses prisoners who are on remand and awaiting trial, as well as many who have been convicted of violent crimes. It sits in an idyllic location on the banks of the Assiniboine River, surrounded by farmland. In my youth I recall seeing inmates working in the fields planting or bringing in the crop. At one time the inmates used to work on neighbouring farms as well but the practice was halted because (I understand) of complaints from some farmers who had to hire more expensive help. All that has changed and it is now as maximum an institution as the province can devise. It has riots from time to time over the years, each one leading to an inquiry and insignificant changes of one sort or another. Changes seem to benefit the staff more than the inmates.

The jail for women at Portage la Prairie has a large Aboriginal population but has converted most of the cells into pleasant private rooms. Most women are there for minor offences, although many have been there a number of times. Several to whom we spoke were there for shoplifting which they said they had to do as they had no money for diapers and other things their children needed. They didn't care for their lifestyle but found life very difficult as single parents without the skills for productive employment. The problem of racial discrimination in obtaining a job was also mentioned. While the staff tried to be supportive, I saw few programs to help the women turn their lives around.

A major problem, with many repercussions, is that most of the women have children and seldom see them when in jail. Although visiting is permitted, it is almost impossible for friends or relatives to travel the fifty or so miles by bus and bring the children with them. The women live in fear that an agency will apprehend their children before they are released and can return to them. The AJI report recommended that the institution be closed and that the women be cared for in group homes in the city or in their own communities.

The small provincial institutions were better than the large ones. In Dauphin, the individual cells and bars had been replaced with dormitory living. Many of the inmates were allowed to leave the jail every day to work in local businesses and some turned out to be such good workers that their employers kept them on after their release. They had a head start on the vast majority of jail inmates who, after two years of incarceration, had not improved their skills or work ethic at all.

The facility at Egg Lake, a satellite operation of the provincial jail at The Pas, is another successful example of a work-related institution. It is an isolated work camp and houses only Aboriginal prisoners. With the exception of a few rooms, there are no bars on the windows and no locks on the doors and the inmates are trusted not to escape. They work along the highways cutting brush or building and maintaining parks and campsites. Its program is good but it suffers from the lack of Aboriginal staff and culturally appropriate programs and training.

There are few escapes although an inmate occasionally walks away and goes home when his sense of family responsibility requires his presence. He is prepared to take the consequences, but it seems unfortunate that the residents do not feel comfortable expressing their concerns to the administrators so a leave of absence can be arranged. The penalty suffered by those who do escape, is that they are transferred to Headingley and under normal circumstances that is a substantial deterrent.

The work camp at Milner Ridge was an excellent concept, but was not as well administered as Egg Lake. It had a mixed population of Aboriginal and non-Aboriginal residents and guards. Instead of a positive rehabilitative program the place had the atmosphere of a regular jail. Part of the problem was that many of the guards came from Headingley on a seniority basis and brought with them their old ways of doing things. We heard stories of mistrust and friction between the staff and the inmates.

It seems to me that the helping and supportive attitude of the staff at Egg Lake should have been applied at Milner Ridge. The Superintendent at Milner Ridge had an excellent rehabilitative approach and was trying to do a good job, but seemed to be hampered by senior departmental decisions and seniority demands. He should have had the authority to screen and select both the inmates and the guards, at least some of whom should have been Aboriginal. If that authority had been permitted, the camp would have been as successful as the one at Egg Lake. With rehabilitative programs it would have been even better.

I mention the horrors of existing jails, and the inappropriateness of their programs for Aboriginal inmates in some detail, for the express purpose of indicating the types of institutions that must be avoided in an Aboriginal justice system. There are better and more effective ways of dealing with those who have to be incarcerated.

Each Aboriginal justice system must have places to which its judges can send wrongdoers who have to be removed from their communities for a period of time. I suggest those places not be called 'jails' but have a name that indicates to Aboriginal people what their purpose and approach will be. Although Aboriginal people may find a better name, I will call them Healing Lodges as that term seems to exemplify the desire of Aboriginal people to have places where those who are having trouble meeting the expectations of their community can be helped to improve in mind and in spirit. It is a term that is beginning to be used in custodial institutions in Alberta, Saskatchewan and Manitoba, and presupposes an emphasis on healing and implies the use of traditional beliefs and practices.

Each Aboriginal justice system should establish its own Healing Lodge or start one in conjunction with neighbouring systems. It will take a while after regional court systems are established to determine how large a facility and how many of them will be needed, but I would hope they would not be too large and would be fairly close to the communities from which their residents will come. There must be separate facilities for men and for women in different locations, and certainly for male and female youth as well.

All Healing Lodges should contain only Aboriginal residents and the staff and administration should also be Aboriginal. This is important because of the need to have a free and easy and open communication between the residents and the staff. Aboriginal staff would understand the pressures facing the offenders and be trained to explore appropriate solutions with them. They should be fluent in the local language and be trained in providing advice and guidance.

Programs should be directed towards building or re-building the self-esteem of the residents, and providing them with information and skills to help them adapt on their return to their families and communities. Elders and teachers should play a significant part in the design of the sort of programs the inmates need. A wilderness setting would provide privacy and a peaceful opportunity to consider future plans and aspirations. Hunting and fishing, cutting wood, repairing or building facilities would provide much needed personal satisfaction.

Aboriginal history and tradition should be taught and traditional ceremonies should be conducted on a regular basis. There should be sweat lodges, healing circles and other programs geared to helping the residents and preparing them for their release as better citizens. Work-related education and skills training should also be provided.

To accommodate the more difficult offenders, a province-wide Healing Lodge might be established. It might have to be more secure than the others, but could nevertheless take a healing approach to the offenders who will likely never have had that sort of opportunity in the past. It should still only accommodate people sent there by an Aboriginal court and should be run and managed by Aboriginal staff. It should offer the same approach as the other lodges and provide the same sort of encouragement and support the residents require.

The staff or leaders of each lodge would have to be carefully selected and trained. They should receive training and education in Aboriginal history and tradition and in the ceremonies to be used. They should be tested on how they would approach residents, and those with aggressive or old-line custodial thinking should be rejected. Their ability to assist in dealing with personal problems and in providing hope and encouragement should be a precondition to employment.

The residents should build the Healing Lodges and some of the early staff should have experience in the building trades and be able to teach the residents as they assist in the construction. Working on construction would be a positive learning opportunity.

The Aboriginal staff should play a different role than the 'guard' of the regular system. They might be called leaders or be given a name that would describe their function to Aboriginal people. Some should teach an Aboriginal language and cultural and historic practices. Others could help with upgrading education and the provision of skills in a variety of areas. All the teachings and all the programs should be geared to enhancing the self-image of the residents. These are among the objectives of the Ochichakkosipi Healing Lodge in Manitoba that I mentioned earlier.

Some leaders might spend time talking to the residents to help them decide what they would like to do when they go back to their families and their communities. If a person would like to find employment in a certain field, the leader should contact employers or employment agencies to see if work can be obtained for the person when they leave.

While I suggest that the Healing Lodges be part of Aboriginal justice systems and serve only offenders sentenced by an Aboriginal court, it would be possible for the province or federal government to establish other healing lodges for Aboriginal offenders sentenced by the regular courts. That would be a positive step but its success would turn on the staff and management being Aboriginal, and the provision of the type of programs and approaches I have described.

Aboriginal judges should retain authority over the residents of the Healing Lodges. They should start by designating the particular institution the offender is to attend and should receive reports on his progress from time to time. That would not be to spy on the residents but to let the judge know how well the sentence he has devised is working. If there are problems, the judge should know that as well. If an offender has a problem with a lodge, he should be able to apply to the judge to vary the sentence or the place of incarceration.

In the regular justice system, when a judge sentences a person to jail, the length of actual time in custody is automatically reduced by the National Parole Board by virtue of the Conditional Release Act under which it operates. Most inmates become entitled to full parole after serving one-third of their sentence, and to day parole six months earlier. In 1996-97 about half the applications for day parole and about two-thirds of the applications for full parole were granted. Even if early parole is denied, offenders are entitled to statutory release on full parole after serving two-thirds of their sentence. The parole system is based on the belief that it is better to have people returned to the community in a gradual, controlled and supported manner, rather than turning them loose without any support. I take no objection to that philosophy, as far as it goes.

This automatic reduction in a sentence doesn't make any sense to Aboriginal people, nor does the fact that so much authority rests with the Parole Board. Part of the concern is based on the fact that fewer Aboriginal people receive parole and are more often returned to prison for the breach of what are often inappropriate parole conditions. Others within the justice system are also concerned that this interference with a judge's determination of an appropriate sentence, demeans the role of judges and reduces the integrity of the courts.

When offenders are released on parole, conditions are always set. These may include a requirement to find work and stay employed, refrain from the use of alcohol or drugs, stay out of their home community, have no contact with a victim and be of good behaviour. Unfortunately many Aboriginal parolees either misunderstand the conditions or find them impossible to meet. Forcing a person to stay away from their home and their families is an impossible condition if the person's only home is on a reserve.

An Aboriginal justice system should not contain any parole provisions at all; rather the offender should serve the full sentence set by the judge. There might however be an exception to enable unusual situations to be reviewed. A person who has been incarcerated should be able to apply to the judge that imposed his sentence, after one-half or three-quarters of it has been served, to either alter the sentence or to seek release on probation. After hearing from the offender and receiving a report on his conduct and progress in the facility, the judge should be able to reduce the length of incarceration, release the person on probation, or require him to complete the term originally set.

The judge would have to assess the sincerity of the individual and the likelihood that he would stay away from future criminal activity. More importantly, he would want to assess the benefits being provided by the institution and decide whether continued residence would be more beneficial to the individual. He would want to know how the inmate is doing and whether the benefits he anticipated at the time of sentencing have been realized. In addition to considering the progress of the offender, this practice would enable the judge to review the appropriateness of the original sentence and that might cause him to try a different approach with others. In the regular system, judges receive no reports and have no idea whether the sentences they have imposed have achieved their intended purpose.

This sentence-review authority would not only leave the control of the individual in the hands of the court; it would place an added responsibility on the court to devise punishments and other solutions that will benefit the community and the wrongdoer at the same time. It would be another new approach to the administration of justice that would be possible in a system where those administering the law are close to the people and the communities they serve.

If the Aboriginal court retains control over its sentencing, it should also be directly involved in the release of a person on probation. If a judge decides to release a person on probation he should impose whatever conditions he thinks appropriate. Conditions might require the person to participate in a local program or to do work for the community. They might require the person to participate in a Community Justice Forum or a Family Gathering if that has never been tried. Probation would then not be seen as the end of the court's involvement but as another opportunity to help the wrongdoer, victim, and the community.

Probation should not be an automatic right. As with the review of a sentence, it should be something a judge could consider but it should not become the norm. If a person has secured employment, that might justify his release, as might the desire to participate in a Family Gathering, but the mere passage of time should not cause a judge to change his sentence. If there is to be early release in a certain case, the Court Officer should monitor the person's performance and report any problems to the judge. The judge should be able to send the person back to a Healing Lodge or to vary the conditions of release if the person has been brought back to court for failing to live up to the conditions previously set.

The Court Officer should not be classed as a probation officer but might be named as a Parole Officer by the federal authorities if they want someone to supervise federal offenders who have been released on parole. The National Parole Board in its Corporate Policy on Aboriginal Offenders of April 1996, supported culturally appropriate procedures. Several sections of the Corrections and Conditional Release Act provide a basis for co-operation with Aboriginal communities.

Parts of Section 81 provide:

(1) The Minister, or a person authorized by the Minister, may enter into an agreement with an aboriginal community for the provision of correctional services to aboriginal offenders and for payment by the Minister, or by a person authorized by the Minister, in respect of the provision of those services.

(3) In accordance with any agreement entered into under subsection (1), the Commissioner may transfer an offender to the care and custody of an aboriginal community, with the consent of the offender and of the aboriginal community.

The ability of an Aboriginal system to have its own jails or Healing Lodges is essential to its success. It completes the justice system that will have the capacity to deal with offenders in a culturally appropriate and positive manner. With the jurisdiction I have defined, it should be successful in keeping large numbers of Aboriginal people out of the regular courts and keeping even more out of jail.

Final Thoughts

"Are you going to upset the judiciary again?" asked one of my less critical associates.

"I certainly hope not," I said. "I'm not criticising judges or lawyers. If there is discrimination or other problems with the way the system operates, they are systemic. The solution is in the hands of government. The federal government can amend the Criminal Code to cure a number of problems and can get moving on new Treaties and self-government; provincial governments can create Aboriginal courts to provide the services that are lacking."

My grandchildren, for whom I initially started writing, will hopefully see some positive changes during their lives, but at the moment I'm not too optimistic. Having in mind the length of time it took Canada to destroy Aboriginal people, the problems are not going to be cured overnight. Ten years ago I used to say it would take 25 years to turn things around. Now when people ask "how long will it take?" I say it will take 100 years. If that's true, I should be writing for my great-great grandchildren, but surely it won't take that long.

I still find it hard to understand why so little has happened when dozens of reports have recommended change. It seems irrational for government to spend billions of dollars erecting and operating jails, while turning a blind eye to methods that would make those expenditures unnecessary.

Jurisdictional disputes between the federal and provincial governments don't help. The federal government accepts most of the responsibility for Indians living on reserves, but accepts no responsibility for them when they move to the city. The provincial governments have jurisdiction over the administration of justice but are reluctant to make improvements for Aboriginal people unless the federal government will provide equal or greater financial support.

Aboriginal people are caught in the middle. It may be that the only way to resolve the impasse is to have another constitutional round, like

Meech Lake or Charlottetown, where Aboriginal people are at the table and where their constitutional authority, and that of the federal and provincial governments is re-examined in light of existing needs. If changes are not made, Aboriginal people will remain neglected and forgotten and Canada will continue to be criticized by the United Nations and other countries for abandoning its indigenous people.

I have made no attempt to suggest that an Aboriginal court be established in an urban setting. One should be easier to establish in all-Aboriginal communities and they will likely have to be the testing-ground to show what improvements are possible. The regular courts might nevertheless make use of some of the referral options I have mentioned.

A number of Aboriginal programs now exist in cities although they are not organized to work with the courts and may not be widely known or easily identified. For example, there are Aboriginal people living in Winnipeg who were intimately involved with the management and operation of the Hollow Water healing program. There are gang and addiction services that work with offenders and potential offenders and there are hundreds of Aboriginal people who have worked with Ma Mawi Chi Itata Centre and Child and Family Service agencies. There are sexual abuse services and youth justice committees. Many Elders who could be trained as Peacemakers live in the cities as well.

Community Justice Forums are being used by the RCMP and the Manitoba Department of Justice is interested in expanding their use and assists in the training of facilitators. Trainers with the RCMP and Probation Services are available to describe the process, to indicate how it may be applied and to do training.

The problem is there is no organization to draw these resources together and there is no connection between them and the regular courts. It would be worthwhile if the Minister of Justice would establish a working group made up of administrators, judges and representatives of Aboriginal agencies. Such a group could consider whether the harnessing of these resources would be of value to the courts. It might consider how the courts could convey their needs to a particular service and how it might make use of their expertise in a specific case. An Aboriginal organization might be identified to keep and to circulate an inventory of services that exist and to act as a clearinghouse. It might receive requests from the court and locate those who might be able to help. If some training is required to accommodate people to the rules of the courts, the committee might consider how that could be done.

These services might allow an urban court to enjoy some of the benefits of an Aboriginal court system. If benefits result, another look might be taken at what if any additional services could be added. Some day it might even be feasible to have legally or non-legally trained Aboriginal judges attached to the regular courts to deal with certain types of cases involving Aboriginal people. Ten percent of the residents of Winnipeg are now Aboriginal and they are overly represented in the courts and in the child welfare system.

The Supreme Court of Canada and the British Columbia Court of Appeal, in the Delgamuukw case, both recommended that negotiation, rather than the court process, be used to resolve Aboriginal issues. They did not impose any limitations on what could be negotiated or what the outcome should be. In spite of that, government negotiators continue to argue that their hands are tied, as if the initial trial decision had not been overturned.

In the spring of 2000 I sat in on a treaty negotiation session in Victoria, B.C. where the federal and provincial lawyer-negotiators were playing hard ball. They came up with all sorts of reasons why they couldn't agree to the proposals being made by the First Nations. At the end of the session the chairman asked if I had any comments or reactions to what I had heard. I directed my comments to the lawyers for the Crown and said "I suggest you go away, put on your fiduciary hats, and come back with proposals you think are in the best interests of the Aboriginal people."

I am saddened to see that there is no greater recognition of the Crown's fiduciary duty to Aboriginal people today than there was ten, 100, or 250 years ago. I hate to suggest that lawyers be kept out of treaty negotiations, but I think it realistic to at least suggest that they come to the table with a mediative approach, so the process can be a joint search for solutions. With that approach, they can be of real service to the country and to Aboriginal people in finding a reasonable accommodation between the rights of Aboriginal people and the interests of other Canadians.

Another example of how things remain the same, in spite of the rulings of the Supreme Court of Canada, is the standoff at Burnt Church, New Brunswick. It was terrifying to watch television depict the hauling of lobster traps from the water and government craft ramming and destroying Aboriginal boats. I asked myself, "Where is the rule of law? Are we living in a police state? Have any criminal charges been laid, or is the Federal Department of Fisheries and Oceans just acting on its own interpretation of the Supreme Court ruling and taking the law into its own hands?"

No matter who is right or wrong in the interpretation of the Marshall decisions, this sort of confrontational attitude on the part of government invites the same approach from those who feel they are being oppressed. I am surprised and relieved that blood wasn't shed, but the dispute is still not settled and if it is not resolved by the time the lobster are ready to be harvested again, we may be in for another dangerous confrontation.

Perhaps a public outcry will induce some activity. Even crass selfishness should encourage government to change its approach to Aboriginal needs. If it would insist on the employment of Aboriginal people, billions of public dollars would be saved. If it permits the establishment of Aboriginal justice systems, many lives will be reclaimed. If it does not, Aboriginal people will continue to clog the courts and the prisons. If federal and provincial governments do nothing, court and other battles will continue and the relationship between Aboriginal people and Canadian governments will continue to be poisoned.

The late Chief Justice Brian Dickson of the Supreme Court of Canada gave me only one piece of advice as a trial judge. He said: "Make sure you get your facts right." I assume he meant that he and his fellow judges could deal with the legal issues, but they needed a solid base of fact on which to consider a solution.

Most of what I have written falls into the category of personal observation and opinion. Much of it deals with what I believe will result if governments permit Aboriginal Courts to be created. There are only two things I can say as matters of fact:

1. There is a massive problem with the manner in which justice services are now being delivered to Aboriginal people.

2. Something has to be done about it.

I am not saying it will be an easy task to establish an Aboriginal justice system. It will not be easy. It will require substantial changes in approach by many people. It will need Aboriginal people with no experience with a court system to devise one and to make it acceptable to their communities. It will require those with a desire to serve, to become judges, court officers and healers. It will require a change of approach by provincial and federal governments. Above all, it will require a spirit of co-operation and the determination to make it work.

It will work if it is established and run by Aboriginal people for Aboriginal people. The reason it will work will be because it will be their own creation and their own system. It will return some of their long-lost authority over their lives and it will reflect traditional beliefs and practices. They will take pride in it and Aboriginal people will respond to the influence of a feather, not a gavel.

Index